Graham Ward is Regius Professor of Divinity at the University of Oxford. His books include *Barth, Derrida and the Language of Theology*, *Radical Orthodoxy: A New Theology* (edited with John Milbank and Catherine Pickstock), *Cities of God*, *The Certeau Reader*, *Cultural Transformation and Religious Practice*, *True Religion*, *Christ and Culture* and *Religion and Political Thought* (edited with Michael Hoelzl).

'When we think of beliefs we think of views and ideas, while (a bit more technically) philosophers speak of "propositional attitudes" or "judgments". In his extremely original new book Graham Ward explores operations of belief that go much deeper: dispositions (some of which act at the physiological as well as cultural level) prior to conscious attentiveness, and thus informing perception, interpretation and action prior to rationalization. This is a bold and brilliant thesis, cogently worked out by the author, with ramifications well beyond Christian theology.'

FERGUS KERR, OP, Honorary Fellow, University of Edinburgh, author of *Immortal Longings: Versions of Transcending Humanity* and of *Theology after Wittgenstein*

'From ghosts in Cambridge to angels in Ely, from the Lascaux caves to the Brighton of Graham Greene, and from the neurons in our brains to the dust between galaxies, Graham Ward's astonishing ability to command both sciences and humanities is here brought to bear on the mystery of belief. We may think ours a sceptical age, but in fact we are all too gullible; enjoined from all sides to believe in this or that – from the supplements that will give us longer life, to the governments that will cut our taxes – we willingly succumb to such blandishments. For our ability to believe is what makes us truly human, and our ability to believe in believing – to have faith in what we cannot see – is what opens to us the mystery of a believable world; the strange congruence of imagination and reality. In this remarkable book – which is not a work of theology, though written by one of today's most astute and cultured theologians – we are led to see the mystery that we are to ourselves, and so too the possibility of the transcendent from which our world may come.'

GERARD LOUGHLIN, Professor of Theology, Durham University, author of *Alien Sex: The Body and Desire in Cinema and Theology*

GRAHAM WARD

Unbelievable

Why We Believe and Why We Don't

I.B. TAURIS

LONDON · NEW YORK

Published in 2014 by I.B. Tauris & Co Ltd
6 Salem Road, London W2 4BU
175 Fifth Avenue, New York NY 10010
www.ibtauris.com

Distributed in the United States and Canada Exclusively by Palgrave Macmillan
175 Fifth Avenue, New York NY 10010

ISBN: 978 1 78076 735 2
eISBN: 978 0 85773 483 9

A full CIP record for this book is available from the British Library
A full CIP record is available from the Library of Congress
Library of Congress Catalog Card Number: available

Typeset in Sabon Monotype by Tetragon, London

Printed and bound in Sweden by ScandBook AB

CONTENTS

For David Moss
in friendship

ACKNOWLEDGEMENTS

This book has been in the making for many years. I was working on an edited selection and translation of Michel de Certeau's essays when the first volume of the Radical Orthodoxy series, *Radical Orthodoxy: A New Theology*, appeared. De Certeau was himself interested in the association between belief and making-believe, and within a matter of months I was being emailed about subscription fees to the new 'movement' and where the local branches of Radical Orthodoxy could be found. Evidently, what John Milbank, Catherine Pickstock and myself conceived as a series of theological books chimed with a certain theological desire at that time. Michel de Certeau's interest in belief and making-believe took on a new and profound relevance.

The idea for a book exploring the nature of belief simmered away, finding occasional expression in a couple of essays published in Britain and Germany. Then one winter's evening, after a severe snowfall, Alex Wright from I.B.Tauris and I met for a drink in a hotel in Cambridge, and I found myself describing the interdisciplinary project on belief that I was beginning to conceive. He was excited and encouraging, and before the evening was over I promised the book for some unimaginable point in the future. Then that point grew closer and closer and the work began.

This book would have been impossible were it not for the many years of conversation about these ideas with Dr Michael Hoelzl at the University of Manchester and my arriving at Christ Church, Oxford. One of the amazing discoveries I made at the College was a group of young Junior Research

Fellows (JRFs) and senior students eager and curious to talk about ideas – even when those ideas had affinities with religion. The discussions I have had on microbiology, on the relationship between physics and biology, evolutionary development biology, evolutionary anthropology – all fields I have entered with enormous trepidation – have given me the confidence to write about them in relation to belief. The views are my own and the arguments I had were very frequently trying to set me right, but the quality of the debates and the energy with which they were conducted fired me to go on with my explorations. I have also been fortunate to have a number of bright and intellectually curious postgraduate students who are interested in and who have worked upon theology in relation to affect and experience. I have a debt of gratitude also to these people and the conversations we have had. Finally, I have to thank Alex – without whom, as they say, this book would not have appeared. I dedicate it to my long-time friend working in the depths of Devon, David Moss.

INTRODUCTION

A Winter's Tale

t would be recorded by the BBC for part of its Christmas broadcasting. It is a mid-November evening at the oldest college in Cambridge, Peterhouse, which dates back to the thirteenth century. A thin mist rises from the river Cam, curling around the lantern lights of Chapel Court. It is a Wednesday, a College guest night, and the ancient dining hall, with its Burne-Jones windows, throws shadows across the meticulously kept lawn. Inside, the Master is presiding, a difficult and sometimes tempestuous man. The High Table is full, the Fellows in their gowns with their guests. They are being attended by a team of College servants dressed in black jackets and striped waistcoats. They are serving them from silver platters with silver spoons. The first course delivered, the company eating and the white wine being quaffed, the butler approaches me discreetly from behind. I am seated three down from the Master, with whom my history to date has not been easy. 'You're needed in the Combination Room, sir,' he says, very quietly. I turn my head towards him, gradually, subtly. It is not regarded as polite to leave the Hall before the Master; in fact it is downright discourteous. The butler bends, almost squatting so he can speak into my ear. 'It's urgent, sir.' I cannot turn to face him, but look towards the Master, who is speaking loudly and emphatically to a well-dressed man on his left – his own guest. Briefly I catch his eye and mouth an apology, which I am not sure he receives, before standing and leaving the High Table to follow the butler. Those who know that protocol has been breached exchange glances, unspoken questions and silent concerns. The guests remain ignorant.

The Combination Room is next door, through a short stone passage housing a spiral staircase that winds up to a stone turret where a bell hangs. The thick, heavy bell rope, pulled to summon students and Fellows to dinner, has been tied back. Along with the dining hall, the Combination Room is one of the oldest parts of the College. It is lined with dark oak panels and has two fireplaces, one along the wall to my right, the other immediately on my left. An old grandfather clock strikes the hour: eight. Earlier in the evening the guests gathered here for sherry before lining up alongside the Fellows who had invited them, ready to enter the Hall. Between courses plates are warmed here in a large, movable cabinet. The butler's staff then place the plates before those at the High Table as the food is brought in from the kitchen at the far end of the Hall, on the other side of the minstrels' gallery.

My initial observation on moving from the heightened tensions of the Hall and the heaving jollity of undergraduates: hundreds of fragments of broken china, white and monogrammed, some large, some only tiny shards, scattered on the oak floor by the plate-warmer. The butler points left towards two of his staff, familiar faces, sitting on chairs on the other side of the warmer in front of the fireplace. There is no fire lit; the evening outside is mild, with rain threatening. In the Combination Room the air is considerably colder, but not so much that my breath freezes. The other fire along the right wall, on the far side of a large bay window that overlooks the Fellows' Garden, had been lit for the sherry pre-prandial. I notice that the log ashes are still glowing, but only give it a glance because of the damp chill elsewhere. My attention is on the two men: one dark, slender and small, the other much more solid, with a young round face that is usually ruddy and jovial.

'Tell the Dean what you saw,' the butler instructs them.

But both men are white and shaking. They look up and just stare at me as if beseeching *me* to articulate what they had experienced and can't comprehend. I stand before them in my dark suit and my black gown, taking in the depth of their shock. They continue to say nothing. Their heads gradually sink as they stare once more at the floor. They are trembling, and I turn to the butler, feeling confused and ashamed without really knowing why. I can't piece together a scenario to account for what I see and feel.

'It was a figure, sir. A man. They said he walked from over by the door there,' the butler explains. And he points to the far left corner of the Combination Room, where double doors are opened on Wednesday and Sunday evenings during term to receive the Fellows and their invited guests. They are closed now, as they should be, the Fellows and their guests being at dinner. We can hear laughter and ululations of a hundred different conversations even through the thick wall of stone that separates the Hall from the Combination Room. 'He crossed the room,' the butler continues, turning abruptly to his right, 'and disappeared in front of the bay window.'

'It didn't walk,' the dark-haired man adds, his hands clasped together and his head still hung. 'It moved. And it wasn't a man.'

'It was like a man,' the other corrects, lifting his head, his wide eyes seeking mine as if not wishing to focus on anything else in the room. 'But it was blurred.'

'It had a face. It floated,' the first man adds.

'And there was a knocking.'

'Was the knocking loud, Ray?' I ask, not because the question seems relevant but because I'm trying to re-engage them both.

The smaller, darker man just shrugs his shoulders and the other doesn't reply. He continues to stare at me.

'We need to start serving the main course, sir,' the butler says.

'Ray and Mark need to sit this out somewhere.'

'Not with the other kitchen staff, sir. We should serve and get this mess cleared up before telling them anything.'

There is a small room at the back of the Porter's Lodge, sometimes used as a medical bay if a tourist visiting the College suddenly becomes ill. They would wait for the paramedics there. 'I'll take them to the Porter's,' I say. 'Then I'll go back in.'

'I should inform the Master, sir. What should I tell him?'

'The truth. They believe they saw a ghost.'

By the time I arrived back at High Table the story had been somewhat changed. The low-voiced chatter was all about the 'sighting', and the Master was looking both angry and contemptuous. The Fellowship was composed of senior scientists, some working on projects that would come before the Nobel Prize Committee, and eminent figures in the disciplines of history, international relations, theology, economics, architecture and linguistics. There was also a scattering of post-doc Fellows working in the social sciences, humanities and medicine. The Senior Fellow was an engineer of international repute. The Bursar (who was also in charge of the Development Office) was flushed with amused excitement.

It was the Bursar who ensured the newspapers had the story by the following morning, and by the end of the week Reuters were sending it around the world. I was contacted by journalists wanting more details, was given a slot on the *Today* programme and interviewed live on the radio. For more than a fortnight, until the term ended, the Peterhouse ghost was the theme of animated debate and the butt of jokes around any number of Oxbridge Common Rooms, London clubs, the Royal Society and the British Academy. The Bursar even claimed to have sat all night alone in the Combination Room and spoken personally to the phantom.

What remained remarkable throughout was the division of opinion in the Fellowship itself. Some Fellows who lived in swore they could not pass by the Combination Room at night because they were fearful; several Fellows, and not all scientists, combed the room and pored over architects' drawings that labelled where the water pipes and electricity cables were. I had a stand-up row with the Master, who was convinced I had disgraced the College by submitting it to the ridicule of the scientific world and the media. In fact, though an Anglican priest, I was myself sceptical of any belief in ghosts: they didn't fit easily with a Christian understanding of the resurrection of the dead, life after death and the indissoluble union of body and soul. The College archivist and librarian dug up the story of a bursar in the eighteenth century who had hanged himself from the bell rope, jumping from the stone spiral staircase lodged between the Hall and the Combination Room. Older plans of the College revealed that the Victorians had added the bay window to replace a door out into the Fellows' Garden that had once been at exactly the point where the figure had disappeared. No one disbelieved that the two College servants had witnessed something; everyone disagreed about what it was that they had witnessed.

The Fellows' Garden, overshadowed by tall, black trees, leafless in the approaching winter, remained empty and forlorn. A white wizard offered to exorcise the room; I had a long conversation with the Bishop of Ely, whose thirteenth-century predecessor had founded the College, and was advised to wait to see if there were any further 'occurrences' before calling in the diocesan exorcist. 'I don't know whether I believe in ghosts,' I said confidentially to an older theologian friend who was a prominent Dominican prior. 'Yes,' he murmured, with quiet concern. 'We had a room on the top floor of one of our priories that no one would go into and no one would be put up in for the night because there was a dark, malevolent presence in there that everyone sensed. Things happen that cannot be easily explained away.'

The two College kitchen staff came under repeated pressure – from their families, friends, other members of College staff, members of the common room and undergraduate and postgraduate students – to elaborate more on the events of that evening. Had they had a drink? What were they talking about before they entered the room? Did they believe in ghosts? Had either of them experienced anything like that before? Did they have their backs to the rest of the Combination Room as they stooped to reach the plates from the plate-warmer? Did one of them see it first? Did they both see exactly the same thing? Was the knocking prior to the appearance? Is that what made them turn around, or was there knocking throughout? Was the knocking coming from the door or nearby? Had they perhaps associated the knocking with the door? The questions circulated copiously like the black cloud of bats in the Malabar caves in E. M. Forster's *A Passage to India* that so traumatised and then illuminated Mrs Moore. The College servants said less and less. Even when the men answered the questions, this could not resolve what had happened; the enquiries were symptoms of an emotional and mental disturbance that took hold of the whole college, and the servants happened to be at the centre of it. The disturbance spiralled centrifugally to enfold as many others as would stop and listen, petering out finally with distance that was both temporal and spatial.

What was curious to me about the ghost story was not whether it was true or not. Damp chills in rooms, I was informed by a psychology don, can be explained by the close relation between emotional affect and the environment. Our emotional intelligence continually registers such changes when something of significance has occurred in a place.

What remained curious to me was the way any number of belief systems were brought to the surface by whatever happened and its labelling as the appearance of a ghost. Perhaps 'systems' is a little too precise; it was more about the ways people saw and interpreted the world, and made sense of their experience. For some the possibility that it was a ghost seemed as acceptable as kippers for breakfast: unusual, but not without precedent or outside the realms of possibility. They spoke to each other of similar occurrences and other 'sightings' in the history of the College. For some any notion of the supernatural was pre-scientific and unenlightened superstition. A haunting was not something that they could even spend much time on; their world views just didn't entertain such phenomena. Such stories were unbelievable. Explanations could be offered for a floating pale blur that seemed to have the appearance of a man: psychological, neurological, physical, chemical (was there a gas leak, perhaps?). They debated the possibilities without conclusion. Not all whom I would identify with this group were scientists, and indeed not a few scientists did talk of phenomena that resisted explanation or, at least, the explanations currently available. One even lamented that we needed more complex models of materiality. For others (the majority, I suspect) it was impossible to achieve the certainty of either believing in the possibility of ghosts or that no such phenomena were possible. In their wavering they were probably the most disturbed by what had occurred in the Combination Room, because personal experience of the two people involved in the incident convinced them that the servants had in fact witnessed what they said they had. After all, there were two of them. The butler also believed the two men, and these 'waverers' trusted the butler's judgement. But nevertheless such occurrences were outside their own experience and what they believed possible in the practices of everyday life. They were unbelievable; Hallowe'en was a purely commercial venture, along with zombies, vampires, Merlin and angels: new opiates for the masses. But what is believable? And what is unbelievable? And what makes something either one or the other? These are the questions I want to get some insight into in the book that follows. After all, those who believed that what the two men saw was a ghost were among some of the most educated and intellectually able people in the country.

INTERPRETATION AND BELIEF

In the closing years of the 1960s, the French philosopher Paul Ricoeur produced *The Conflict of Interpretations*, an important and groundbreaking collection of essays in the science of interpretation, hermeneutics. The essays cover a wide range of interests and interpretations of world views: structuralism, existentialism, psychoanalysis, anthropology and religion. If the metaphysical dream of thinkers like G. W. F. Hegel was to articulate a universal ontological condition and a dialectical process of history whereby all conflicts would be synthesised; if the liberal dream of social theorists like Jürgen Habermas and John Rawls was to define a set of norms for public reasoning that would allow conflicts to be discussed and a consensus arrived at; then Ricoeur's project almost seemed to be a celebration of pluralism. I say 'seemed' because the pluralist interpretation of signs, symbols and texts, which Ricoeur recognised as endemic to what he called the 'over-determination' or rich surplus of meaning in discourse, all related back, for him, to a universal ontological condition.

To explain (and to clarify why this 'hermeneutical turn' was groundbreaking): like Heidegger before him, Ricoeur affirmed that being human is also to be immersed in language. Meaning and understanding are, for human beings, existential; they concern our very living and ability to live. Life is 'the bearer of meaning', Ricoeur tells us. We dwell in life-worlds that our use of language generates. Now Heidegger's analysis of 'being there', or *Dasein*, was a project orientated towards a phenomenological investigation into the relationship between understanding and being; that is, understanding not simply as a cognitive act in our coming to know something, but as a mode of being in itself. As a mode of being, understanding enables us to relate to the world, make sense of the world and our exchanges with it, and give shape to that world. It is in this way that understanding is existential. So when that understanding starts to wobble, weaken and fold, then – as Sartre describes in his novel of 1938 – human beings experience a highly physical and psychological nausea. But if Heidegger enabled us to recognise our openness to being through the way understanding forces us to engage with our life-world, he did not pay enough attention to the way understanding as a mode of knowing passes into understanding as a mode of being. And it is at this juncture that Ricoeur breaks new ground, because the transition from knowing to being that understanding goes through requires that attention is paid to language, its meaning and its interpretation. And so hermeneutics has to be 'grafted on to' (Ricoeur's metaphor) phenomenology. The subject

> that interprets himself [*sic*] while interpreting signs is no longer the *cogito*: rather, he is a being who discovers, by the exegesis of his own life, that he is placed in being before he places and possesses himself. In this way, hermeneutics would discover a manner of existing which should remain from start to finish a '*being-interpreted*' [...] It is first of all and always in language that all ontic or ontological understanding arrives at expression.

Of course, anyone working in the liberal arts is all too familiar with the surplus of meaning and the conflict of interpretations. Poems, novels, films, music, artworks and dance all generate a multitude of interpretations of their meaning. And the author is not necessarily the best judge here. The time at which Ricoeur was writing – as Ricoeur himself was aware – saw the exponential explosion of any number of interpretative methods: Marxist, Freudian, Lacanian, structuralist, poststructuralist, feminist, womanist, deconstructive, queer and postcolonial readings (to name only the most prominent). But in response to the opening of an endless semiosis, where signs could be read in any number of arbitrary, subjective ways, and world views became just constructions of some Heraclitan flux, interpretation can be reined in. It can be delimited in ways that point to an evaluation of interpretations. And Ricoeur spent most of his career trying to define more closely an architecture of meaning in the face of other philosophers (predominantly also French) who extolled the infinite deferral of signification and drew attention to the subsequent politics of meaning.

An architecture of meaning may be too ambitious, but, more pragmatically, there are bad, good and better readings. Texts, images, symbols, signs all have contexts. We can tabulate three of them: a) the contextual web of immediately related signs (since no sign can mean anything on its own); b) the context in which the chain of related signs or discourse emerges; and c) the context in which both a) and b) are being interpreted.

Their immediate contexts are other signs – the rest of the poem or the novel; the other works created by the same author, film-maker or architect; the other behavioural aspects and objects composing the details of any event, for example. Their secondary (though not in any simple hierarchical sense) contexts are the material histories, cultures, politics, sociologies and economies in which they are situated. Their third context is the community in which the readers of the signs are themselves situated. On this third context, witness the struggle among literary critics and students of literature in interpreting and appreciating the early-nineteenth-century manners of Fanny Price in Jane Austen's *Mansfield Park*: virtuous heroine or stuck-up prig? Nevertheless, through the evaluation of the interplay between these three contexts, bad, good and better readings can be calibrated (and examined) according to their depth or what the American anthropologist Clifford Geertz called 'thick descriptions' of meaning in terms of contexts.

And it is not only the 'soft' sciences in the humanities that have to deal with these interpretative contexts. At the time Ricoeur was writing, the 'hard' social and natural sciences had to recognise the histories, sociologies and prejudices that constituted their 'objective facts'. At Peterhouse there was a Junior Research Fellow whose project, in cosmology, was to comb through past hypotheses in this field, examine why the historical conditions and scientific establishment had found them objectionable at the time, and assess the potential for a re-examination of their claims.

In a sense the frenetic search for explanations that followed the sighting of what the media called the 'Peterhouse ghost' could be seen as a conflict of interpretations. The event was immediately composed of a set of overlapping and complex 'signs': the temperature of the room, the pallor of the faces of the two College servants, their own accounts of what had happened, the mediated accounts of the butler as the first witness on the scene. And that was just for starters. Ricoeur wrote: 'it is only in a conflict of rival hermeneutics that we perceive something of the being [the subsisting ontology] to be interpreted [...] each hermeneutics discovers the aspect of existence which founds it as method.' So, for a couple of historians, the meaning of the 'event' had to be supplemented by other signs: records of the suicide of a former bursar and plans showing the previous design of the room. For a couple of the psychologists, other sets of signs needed to be brought in: statements about the personal backgrounds, interests, even pathologies of those who had witnessed the phenomenon first-hand. And a couple of the scientists also produced, or had produced for them, further sets of signs (data): descriptions of the electrical wiring, gas and water pipes in the room, the angles on polished surfaces that might reflect or refract the headlights of a passing car.

But this was only 'in a sense' a conflict of interpretations or interpretative methods. Interpretation, as Ricoeur saw more than others, was orientated towards semantics. And semantics are the province of what cognitive scientists like John F. Kihlstrom label 'procedural' and 'declarative' knowledge – knowing and the process of coming to know governed by consciousness and formulated in propositions. For all its originality and concern for appreciating and examining the life-worlds in which human beings dwell and make sense, Ricoeur's 'conflict of interpretations', rather like most academic seminars on subjects as diverse as aliens and alienation in the films of Ridley Scott or the influence of climate change on human evolution, remains all too cerebral, too governed by self-conscious agents. But then Ricoeur was a philosopher. The intensity, energy and emotional investment of the questioning surrounding the 'Peterhouse ghost' indicated deeper levels of embodied engagement and reaction: people were excited, frightened, shocked, curious and angry. They were touched imaginatively, affectively and existentially. Their views of the way the world worked, their appreciations of its order and meaning, were threatened. A gap opened that was as much intellectual as corporeal; a more primal 'nausea' was felt that gave rise to and even necessitated the intellectual endeavours that constituted the conflict of interpretations. Of course, in time, the fervour diminished; the urgency for explanation cooled. The Christmas vacation came, the College closed, media attention turned elsewhere and, with the return of the students for Lent term, the routine of teaching and research continued. The 'sighting' was not forgotten. It is still not forgotten. But what took place in the Combination Room on that damp November evening was folded back into business as usual. There have been no further occurrences. To date.

WHAT LIES BENEATH

This book is concerned with what is prior to interpretation and the impact it has on the way we think and behave. It wishes to examine, through various intellectual disciplines, 'what lies beneath'. Kihlstrom, in a classic article titled 'The Cognitive Unconscious', set out to provide a provisional taxonomy of nonconscious mental structures and processes. And although this study will move beyond mere examination of the 'mental' (exploring the terrains of the affective and physiological), Kihlstrom recognises several indices for 'what lies beneath'. He treats three forms of nonconscious activity: automatic responses, where we have learnt something by practice such that it requires little conscious attention to engage with that practice; subliminal perception, where stimuli too weak to be consciously detected (exposed to us for between one and five milliseconds) impact on our impressions, judgements and actions and engage 'preattentive processes'; and implicit memory, where events that cannot be consciously remembered have a palpable effect upon our experience, thought and action. He lists, albeit tentatively, a fourth form of nonconscious processing related to hypnosis and amnesia, suggesting that 'posthypnotic' suggestion and 'hypnotic amnesia' both expand the domain of nonconscious activity and give some insight into nonconscious structures; but for our purposes we can leave that investigative probing to one side. One concluding point is salient: Freud's 'unconscious' is not nearly as amorphous as he supposed, but it nevertheless subtends all our conscious processes such that 'consciousness is not to be identified with any particular perceptual-cognitive functions such as discriminative response to stimulation, perception, memory, or the higher mental processes involved in judgement and problem-solving. All these functions can take place outside of phenomenal awareness' (Kihlstrom).

Kihlstrom published his article back in 1987, and considerable work has since been done on every aspect of the forms of 'cognitive unconscious' he exposed. For example, more recently, neuroscientists explored that important 'time lag' in the way human beings respond to the circumstances in which they find themselves. In his book *Emotional Intelligence: Why It Can Matter More than IQ*, Daniel Goleman, a writer of popular science (we will get to the scientists themselves in Chapter II), re-narrates a story told to him by a friend. The friend is eating a late lunch at a café beside a canal in England. He becomes aware of a girl at the side of the canal staring, frozen-faced, into the water. Immediately he jumps into the water, still fully dressed. Only then does he realise the girl is staring at a toddler who has fallen into the water; a toddler he is able to rescue. The point of the story is to demonstrate, and add further evidence to, a neurological phenomenon. In Goleman's words:

> in the first few milliseconds of our perceiving something we not only unconsciously comprehend what it is, but decide whether we like it or not; the 'cognitive unconscious' presents our awareness with not just the identity of what we see, but an opinion about it.

There is a mode of liminal processing, related to embodiment and affectivity, which 'thinks' more quickly and reacts more instinctively than our conscious rational deliberation. Beneath and prior to interpretation, and the conflicts of meaning, lie sets of remembered associations and assumptions woven tightly into the processes of how we *make* sense. These associations and assumptions have been taught and arrived at; they are not innate, they are not genetic – but they are not always articulated. These assumptions constitute what some social anthropologists (Pierre Bourdieu, for example) have called 'habitus' – encultured dispositions, socialised mindsets and biases.

It is to these dispositions and biases (some of which act at the physiological as well as cultural level, as we will see in Chapter II) that I am pointing when I speak of 'beliefs'. Philosophers often wish to speak of belief as 'propositional attitudes' and, as such, speak about 'judgements'. But I wish to begin by describing the operations of belief that come before judgements. They are 'dispositions towards judgements' or even 'dispositional attitudes' – where 'attitudes' picks up something of the affective as it pertains to believing. Just as Kihlstrom (among others) shows that our 'cognitive unconscious' arrives at judgements and impressions prior to conscious attentiveness, so we can infer that beliefs inform perception, interpretation and action prior to rationalisation. Furthermore, there is no linear route from perception, belief and thought to interpretation and action, as our canal-side story exemplifies. If actions can precede consciousness and interpretation, then we are examining not a linear process but a complex set of feedback and feedforward loops in which believing is deeply implicated.

THE QUESTIONS: WHAT MAKES A BELIEF?

So three sets of questions emerge, each nested within a single interrogative: what makes a belief believable? The first set of questions unfolds from 'what makes a belief'? What is involved in the nature of believing; what constitutes it as an act? How does believing relate to other 'aspects' of being human? Having to put inverted commas around 'aspects' points to belief's inchoate and subtle character. It is difficult to name what it is. Of course, beliefs can be cognitive, as the very ability to affirm 'I believe' demonstrates. Beliefs can have explanatory value, as the developmental biologist Lewis Wolpert has recently claimed in his examination of 'causal beliefs' that arise from clarifying the nature of cause and effect. 'Causal beliefs', which Wolpert argues are at the very root of believing itself, are 'ideas about how' disciplines such as science, say, win out over religion because of their commitment to efficient causation. But if belief impacts on perception, cognition, judgement and evaluation – even precipitating action prior to these cognitive activities – then it is not simply cognitive, and can indeed *inform* why we explain things in the ways we do. The origin of belief does not lie in the early scientific imagination, seeking out 'reasons for'. Such a view already assumes reasoning is instrumental – and it's only partly so. Beliefs are deeper, earlier, and more primitive than 'reasons for'.

Similarly, although experimental psychologists and neuropsychologists can demonstrate a connection between belief and emotion, belief and wellbeing, belief and unhappiness – such that we can find ourselves disposed towards certain states of mind, certain moods, and even act upon these states and moods without fully understanding why we have acted – belief is not an emotion. Nevertheless, it is a mental behaviour: it is involved in certain neural and somatic processes, with effects on both cognitive and emotional life; both intellectual and corporeal activities.

And I do not wish to establish any Cartesian dualisms here. In fact, believing queers any dualist possibilities between mind and body – as most thinking does, according to contemporary neuroscientists. But how does it relate to other dispositions that appear to inform both the cognitive unconscious and consciousness – dispositions like desire, yearning and hope? Etymologically, the English word 'belief' is related to the Anglo-Saxon root '*laub*', from where we get 'love', and also 'worship', or 'praise'. The German *Glauben* ('faith' or 'belief') still retains some of these echoes. How does belief relate to these other fundamental aspects of being human?

We will explore this first set of questions by examining what archaeologists, anthropologists and evolutionary biologists can tell us about the origin of belief, its relation to human evolution and the early signs that indicate the processes and operations in which belief is necessary. We are constructing in this first set of questions both an archaeology and an architecture of belief. Although this primitive and primordial believing leads to specific forms of prehistoric ritual, symbolism and religion, these specific forms and their historical development are not the focus of my interest or examination. In answering this first set of questions (in Chapters I to II), my focus is on demonstrating the universal nature of believing itself; believing as an anthropological condition.

Tackling this first set of questions, and indeed the work of current archaeologists and anthropologists with respect to genetics, the making of the human mind, the appearance of 'intentional' acts and the development of language and symbolic actions will lead us into an enquiry into what might broadly be termed the biology and neuropsychology of believing: what is involved physically and mentally in coming to believe and disbelieve. In Chapters III and IV we will explore the physiological and psychological architecture of believing: its relations to the left and right hemisphere activities in the brain and its relation to the debates about consciousness. If I have little to say at this point about what have variously been called 'memes' (Dawkins) or 'psychogenes' (Giovannoli), it is because they are alarmingly imprecise terms. Dawkins himself, having invented 'memes', dropped the term, only recently taking it up again in his polemic against theism, where the term became useful as a description of religion as a cerebral virus. But I will have more to say about language and its development of optative and subjunctive moods in verbs, and, therefore, its relation to social context. For language is both a shared means of communication and a mode of symbolic storing which enables knowledge to be disseminated, passed on and learnt.

WHAT MAKES A BELIEF *BELIEVABLE*?

The archaeology and architecture of belief provide us with the beginnings of a structure of believing; a structure which, with the help of analytical philosophers of consciousness (in Chapter V), we will begin to map out. There are certain normative conditions for the possibility of belief, associating it with mental imaging, intention, perception, judgement, image-making, knowledge, senses of the self and others as agents, and relations of trust or distrust with respect to agency. As such it is not only an integral part of numerous forms of symbolic action, but also the production and dissemination of ideology. It is only once we understand this structure that we can tackle a second set of questions about what *makes* a belief believable; that is, the politics of belief.

To engage with this second set of questions, and to develop a structure of belief, we need to recognise how the structure is modified in different cultures and histories. It has recently been argued, by archaeologists and anthropologists, for example, that the difference between Neanderthals and *Homo sapiens* with respect to the tool manufacturing and technological advances that made *Homo sapiens* triumph over their hominid cousins lay not in their brain size (Neanderthals had larger brains), genetic evolution or the ability to communicate. The difference between what is called the Mousterian tool use of Middle Palaeolithic Neanderthals and the Aurignacian tool use by Upper Palaeolithic *Homo sapiens*, migrating from northern India through the Fertile Crescent from around 50,000 years ago, was not the result of anatomical, genetic or intellectual variances. The difference was cultural – even though cultural difference can further biological adaption and so biological evolution. It was the cultural isolation of the Neanderthals from these technological developments and their subsequent incredulity about their value that led to the differences between these hominids and what archaeologists call Anatomically Modern

Humans. It was not that the Neanderthals were thick country bumpkins compared to city-savvy *Homo sapiens* (Oppenheimer). There is further evidence that these 'cousins' were also beginning to accept and learn the new Upper Palaeolithic technologies before their extinction around 25,000 years ago.

Similarly, the French historian Michel de Certeau, in his examination of the outbreak of demonic possessions in the seventeenth century in the town of Loudun, exposes a cusp in the changing structure of believing. Loudun became a theatre in which old assumptions about spirituality, body and soul, the satanic and the divine (held by the local people and various doctors of the Church) were being displaced by more recent attention by medical practitioners to symptoms, their somatic aetiology and prognosis. The status of perception and the definition of the natural were changing in ways that challenged the credibility of the old beliefs. The physician takes over the role of expert from the theologian 'as the witness of lay knowledge [...] takes up where clerical knowledge leaves off.'

The structures of believing are bound to historical transformation and cultural context, so to pursue our study further we will then sketch what I will call the synchronic and diachronic axes of belief in Chapter V, charting the changing status of 'belief' and the changing structure within which belief operates, or is allowed to operate. This will foreground the politics of credulity and the complex relations between believing, making believable and making people believe. It will also point to a shift in modernity with respect to the hierarchical distinction between knowledge and belief.

That hierarchy is becoming threatened in contemporary cultures that celebrate and promulgate so-called 'virtual realities'. If, as de Certeau's study of the conflict of interpretations that arose from the multiple events of demonic possession in Loudun shows, modernity invested great value in the immediate apprehension of a perceived reality as true knowledge, then our current and profound engagement with a variety of virtual realities has given rise to a cultural and historical transformation. Consider the following advertising slogans: Sky TV's 'Believe in better', Sony's commercial 'make.believe' or Nintendo Games' 3DS promotion, 'Believe your Eyes'. Team GB adopted the motto 'Genuine Belief' for London 2012 and Justin Bieber chose 'Believe' as the title of his acclaimed album, as did

Britney Spears for her own brand of perfume. Consider Apple's TV commercial for the iPad 2, opening with the phrase 'This is what we believe'. Consider also this comment on Obama's first term in office by a leading political scientist: 'The belief Obama stirred was not belief in particular projects, possibilities, or trajectories. Rather his gift to progressives was belief itself – belief in belief' (Wendy Brown).

It is evident that the status accorded to believing has changed in the West. It has changed in line with recognition by historians, philosophers and sociologists of science that evidence is not the foundation of truth. Evidence can be contested. Evidence is manufactured (in laboratories, for example). Evidence always has to be interpreted. The facts of a case have to be assembled, and someone, or a collection of someones, has to make that assembly for some reason. The levels of intention and purpose behind this assembly indicate biases and prejudgements through which what is perceived is perceived *as* something. It is never just simply perceived as such. For the German philosopher Immanuel Kant this was fundamental for his critical philosophy: we have no apprehension of things in themselves, things as they are. 'Perception is empirical consciousness, that is to say, a consciousness of sensation. Phenomena as objects of perception are not pure, that is, merely formal intuitions [...] they contain the real of sensation, as a representation merely subjective.' There is then a sensory adaptation and the notion of that adaptation will receive considerable development from Darwin through to contemporary evolutionary biologists, but it points towards a general learning process (by trial and error) where we approach knowledge, but where *approach* is not *having* knowledge as such. There is a fundamental incompleteness. So, in the decision about what counts as a fact there needs to be some appreciation of who is counting, what is discounted, and why. There is then a politics (explicit or implicit) involved in all believing and making believable. And even disbelief is a form of belief.

At this point I will also explore the light that can be shed on the question of believability and belief through the examination of 'poetic faith' in literature. The aesthetic appreciation of the act of believing introduces aspects of the structure of belief hitherto concealed: most explicitly, the work of the imagination. As far as I am aware, no discussions of belief by biologists such as Terrence Deacon, philosophers like Daniel Dennett or neuroscientists such as Antonio Damasio relate belief to imagination and our aesthetic engagement in literature (or film), in which disbelief is suspended. The evolutionary psychologist Merlin Donald is an exception here, reminding all those concerned with cognitive science that literature 'is perhaps the most articulate source we have on the phenomenon of human experience.' My literary exploration reveals implicit relations between belief, imagination, the ethics of freedom and the practices of hope. These relations will become important in the analyses that follow of the politics of belief and the nature of transcendence.

WHAT *MAKES* A BELIEF BELIEVABLE?

We open here our third and final set of questions focusing on what *makes* a belief believable; that is, we begin to think through the conscious social production of belief. Here we will have to talk about myth, its production, its impact and its ability to manipulate. Beyond the conflict of interpretations of experience, as Michel de Certeau saw in the events at Loudun, is a complex politics: a cultural politics as one dominant view of understanding the world (the spiritual) gives way to another (the medical); but also a state politics concerning sovereignty (the Church's, the King's). Because knowledge is founded upon the structures of believing, whatever the Enlightenment concern with its neutrality and objectivity, it is always the high ground to be attained, to be won, by someone, by some party, at the cost of someone else, at the cost of another party or multiple parties – each contending for the same elevated perspective.

Both cultural and state politics, as deployments of power, are related to social organisation and the establishment of a hierarchy of functions – the development of a social imaginary. Religion has been viewed here as important in this evolution of functions. But power comes in different forms: physical power (to hunt, provide food, ensure a distribution of that food and to reproduce), intellectual power (to teach, to conceive new and more efficient ways of accomplishing daily tasks, the ability to make better tools, to communicate in persuasive ways, to problem-solve), economic power (to have wealth or to own those items understood as socially valuable), symbolic power (to be the son or daughter of a 'leader', to belong to a caste elevated above others, to have access to limited resources such as magical or supernatural forces), and cultural power (access to knowledge and tradition and the possession of abilities that are not widely available to all but are socially esteemed, like the ability to heal, to paint, to play a musical instrument, to cook).

No doubt there are also other forms of social power, and politics concerns not simply the ordered governance of such powers but also inner jostling among these powers for their importance in that governance. The social imaginary and the cultural competition for value are both founded upon making what might be believed believable by any number of other people. To make any set of ideas about the world believable means winning support, and therefore the social and cultural resources accorded such support. This politicking demands strategic thinking, the mapping and grading of alliances and hostilities, the command of organs for disseminating influence, countering other influences and forums for such dissemination and countering. It may require deception, selection and interpretation of available material in the battle to win hearts and minds. All this is the terrain of belief and making that belief believable. The tactics employed may require deception, the utilisation of fear or bribery, and appeals to and the solicitation of acknowledged social and cultural authorities.

All that can be learnt about the nature of believing, what *makes* a belief, and all that can be learnt about what makes a belief *believable*, are employed in the *making* of a belief believable. There is a reaching down into levels of being human that are profound, rooted in evolutionary development, neurological substrates, and somatic and affected conditions. It is little wonder then that the real struggles (for survival, for health, for wealth, for well-being) take place in this domain. Believing concerns our hopes, dreams and desires – present and future. It concerns also our fears and suspicions. It is within the context of this struggle for our minds that we must examine the role of religion, ideology, utopia and truth in the production of belief, myth and the wars of ideas promulgated by different systems of belief.

What began as a ghost story, a tale told in winter around the dying embers of a fire, will culminate in a universal competition with the very future of humankind at stake. The seventeenth-century political thinker Thomas Hobbes conceived the possibility that human beings are a pack of wolves ready and prepared to devour each other – *homo homini lupus est*. But attention to our capacity to believe refines that description: we are intelligent, conceptualising, imaginative, duplicitous, truth-hungry, hope-driven wolves fighting to understand what it is we are pursuing. We have to remember, over the millions of years of our co-evolution, many species of *Homo* have lived, all of whom, except ourselves, became extinct. Are *Homo sapiens sapiens* also to be superseded? Will our hard drives and USB sticks also be found fossilised in the deserts and tundra to come? Will we too go the way of Ozymandias?

> Two vast and trunkless legs of stone
> Stand in the desert... Near them, on the sand,
> Half sunk, a shattered visage lies, whose frown,
> And wrinkled lip, and sneer of cold command,
> Tell that its sculptor well those passions read
> Which yet survive, stamped on these lifeless things,
> The hand that mocked them and the heart that fed:
> And on the pedestal these words appear:
> 'My name is Ozymandias, king of kings:
> Look on my works, ye Mighty, and despair!'
> Nothing beside remains. Round the decay
> Of that colossal wreck, boundless and bare
> The lone and level sands stretch far away.

PART ONE

Belief in the Making

I

Into the Cave: The Archaeology of Believing [1]

Did Plato get it wrong? Or are we reading him through post-Cartesian lenses in ways that cannot appreciate the shades and shadows of meaning? Three tropes have become a major focus for critical attention in Plato's *Republic*: the simile of the sun, the analogy of the line and the allegory of the cave. We are not ready yet to enter the cave. So it is with the analogy of the line, and the account of belief that it offers, that we must start.

As philosophy students we would draw the vertical line and learn its various cuts and its overall hierarchy from the bottom to the top. The analogy is an extension of the previous simile of the sun in which Socrates explains to Glaucon how it is we come to know things. The sun is in the visible world what the Good is in the intelligible world. In the visible world it is the sun that nurtures vegetation and gives light. The light makes things visible and (in ancient Greek optometry revisited by recent scientists) enables the eyes to see by empowering the faculty of sight. In the same way, the Good is the source of truth and reality that enables us to understand concepts, illuminating the mind and empowering the faculty of knowledge.

The line analogy adds further detail to Socrates' depiction of the degrees of knowledge. The line is divided 'into two unequal parts', the bottom part representing the visible world and the top part representing the intelligible world. The two parts are then subdivided 'in the same ratio'. So we have four domains, two in the visible world and two in the intelligible world, organised hierarchically. At the very bottom of the visible world Socrates places '"images", I mean first shadows, then reflections [...] and all that sort of thing.' The Greek word for 'images', which will become relevant, is *eikasia* (likeness, representation, an estimation of something). Then there follow 'objects which are the originals of the images – the animals around us, and every kind of plant and manufactured object' – the furniture of the world, one might say. Socrates describes this as the realm of 'opinion', and 'opinion' is the concrete manifestation of that which was imaged. The Greek for opinion here is *pistis* – 'belief' – but it also has the suggestion of that which gives confidence, that which one can trust, that which confirms. As such our living with and among the material objects of the visible world will always mean that we live in the realm of belief.

This realm gives way to a higher form of knowledge in which 'the mind uses the originals of the visible order in their turn as images'. Here the seeming passivity of perceiving objects in the world (seemingly passive because the sun simile has informed us that seeing is *actively* engaged with light from the sun and what the sun illuminates) becomes an active process, reasoning – and reasoning seeks conclusions 'through a series of consistent steps' based on assumption or hypothesis (*pistis* or belief). Socrates illustrates this realm with an example from geometry and calculation. Reasoning has a mathematical character and is defined in Greek as *dianoia*. *Dianoia* is an interesting word. It means 'intentional thought', 'thinking process', 'thinking faculty' and 'understanding'. What is interesting about it is the prefix *dia*, which denotes movement or passage through something and towards something else. *Dianoia* is thought that is still in process and is incomplete. It is thought that is directed somewhere – and so 'intentional'. It is 'about' something.

Why is this significant? It is significant because the fourth and upper realm of Plato's line is given over to a final and completing intellectual process that takes the conclusions arrived at through *dianoia* and delivers for them 'a first principle which involves no assumption [and is] without the images used in the other subsections.' The highest form of intellectual endeavour is then to recognise first principles that, like the sun in the first simile, are the condition for the possibility of knowledge. This intellectual endeavour is named the science (*epistēmē*) of dialectic, and through its exercise we arrive at intelligence (*noēsis*).

Now we may feel close to how Glaucon felt after this Socratic description of knowledge and knowing. 'I don't quite understand,' he confesses to Socrates. So, on the epistemological line, Glaucon is evidently falling somewhere between believing and intentional thought. Socrates, with infinite patience, attempts a further elaboration. But before we are to embark on that elaboration, we need to note here the place of belief (*pistis*) in the end-directed or teleological scheme of coming to know. Is belief a form of inferior knowledge, and so not really knowledge at all? Is it the kind of knowledge that we must discard in and through reasoning in order to come to a true intelligence of what is? Does belief like the morning mist evaporate as the sun of certainty arises? Is belief the stuff of infantile fantasies that enlightened maturity returns to the toy cupboard? In Chapter IV we will see how philosophically this came to be the view of 'belief' in the Enlightenment and how the difference between belief as opinion and knowledge as 'a thing to be true' (Kant) was mapped onto two other hierarchies: objective judgement over subjective judgement and public conviction over private persuasion. This line of thinking, when it enters the force fields of secularisation, bends towards a further hierarchy: science over religion, religion being superstitious illusion that we will be liberated from in time. Please observe, though, that I have as yet made no connection between belief and religion.

There are subtleties in Plato: riddles in the language that run down towards suggestive subterranean depths. Let's go back to those Greek words I have been carefully bracketing. As I pointed out, *dianoia* denotes an active passage into *noēsis*. The Greek words themselves make this plain because the nouns *dianoia* and *noēsis* are both related to the noun *nous* (mind, reason, intellect) and the verb *noeō*, to think or conceive. In the same way, the noun *pistis* is related to the noun *epistēmē* (understanding, scientific knowledge) – the *epi* is a prefix meaning 'upon' – and the verb *epistamai* (to know). All these verbal echoes disturb the sheer vertical ascension of the line. The names for the levels both refer back to previous levels and ahead to levels that will follow, blurring where the boundaries lie. This suggests that true knowledge gathers together belief, reasoning and intelligence. It may even be that true knowledge emerges in focusing the illumination that flickers through the various levels. Either way, belief participates in intelligence. It is not erased as illusion, but endlessly clarified through more abstract cognitive processes. Picking up some of the other connotations of *pistis* that I mentioned earlier, we might say: we come to know that which we believe, trust and are assured to be true. Or even: we believe that we may understand – which seems to be the way Augustine read the Platonic thought available to him in the fourth century CE. The visible world passes into the intellectual world and the intellectual world passes into the visible world. What we leave behind is the image, the reflection, *eikasia*, which can be translated as 'illusion', and which is a word that Plato never uses again.

Now we can enter the cave.

CAVERNS MEASURELESS TO MAN

The levels of meaning in Plato's allegory of the cave are rather like the levels of history archaeologists and palaeontologists uncover in caves like those along the southern shores of the Rock of Gibraltar, facing Africa across the waters of the Mediterranean, whose occupancy goes back 125,000 years. We will be visiting such caves shortly. The narrative of the allegory is familiar: it concerns a man who begins a journey from the bottom of a cave, where he sits with any number of other people, a prisoner since a child, forced to look ahead at a screen on which the shadows of puppets play, but he doesn't know they are puppets. For reasons not entirely clear, he is released and compelled to climb up through the cave and discovers that behind the screen there is both a fire and a track between the fire and the screen, along which 'there are men carrying all sorts of gear [...] including figures of men and animals.' As the man is a prisoner, Socrates reasons with Glaucon, he would believe the shadows were real things. Looking at the fire hurts the prisoner's eyes, but he is 'forcibly dragged up the steep and rugged ascent' until he is brought into the sunlight outside the cave. It is a painful journey, the man objects much, and he cannot face the sunlight because of the glare. He has to adjust slowly, looking first at shadows, then reflections and then on the objects themselves, and finally he is able to 'look directly at the sun itself, and gaze at it without using reflections in the water or any other medium, but as it is itself.'

Glaucon is told that the three examples of sun, line and cave are 'connected', but how they are connected is not at all clear, and the connections have been hotly debated among classicists and philosophers ever since. The journey of the now-named philosopher up through the caves is a moral one: towards the sun as the 'Good beyond being'. It is also a metaphysical ascent from delusion to true knowledge, from shadows to reality, and a social and political passage from slavery to liberation, from ignorant herd mentality to enlightened ruler. Socrates confesses the philosopher would now be reluctant to go back down to the cave to preach liberty to the captives – his desire is to sit and meditate upon the sun. The reluctance goes all the way back down the cave, since the captives themselves would struggle, as the philosopher himself struggled, against the arduous pedagogy of ascending to the truth. No one likes a know-all.

The allegory of the cave does not deliberate over the relationship between belief (*pistis*) and reason (*dianoia*). And it is confusing that, in the move from, let's say, weak forms of knowing to strong ones, there are multiple realities: projections, representative puppets, shadows, reflections, objects in the world and then direct sunlight. What is clear is that the cave is not something that can be dispensed with. It continues to be relevant as a realm over which the philosopher and education must rule. If images in the line are related to the projections on the screen, then we might view the entirety of the cave as the realm of belief. Belief is then active in the operation of reason and the pursuit of true intelligence. The vision of the sun seen directly and 'as it is in itself' indicates a transcendence beyond even the philosopher's gaze.

Socrates called the sun simile the form of the 'Good beyond being', which any number of scholars have, with justification, associated with some notion of an impersonal theism. But belief itself, though perhaps orientated towards this transcendence, has a reality and a function with respect to knowing, being and doing that need not be associated with religion. Believing would be an important and constitutive aspect in the process of coming to know, in the operation of reason and in the pursuit of intelligence. As a mode of thinking and consciousness, belief would not lose any of its claim either to be valid or to participate in that which is universal for Plato. Furthermore, reasoning, intelligence (and therefore knowledge) would be chaotic if they were not organised, generated and given to behold by the form of the Good, the sun: a night in which all cows were black. Any emergence from the cave would be difficult, if not impossible; for the philosopher, though now free, would be wandering still among any number of beliefs. He might stagger, metaphorically, from stalagmite to stalactite, tripping over other prisoners and stumbling into puppeteers. He might free himself from the cave and then be left groping among the objects in the outside world, testing them against his memory of the projections and the representative puppets. He might, like the staff and Fellows in my Winter's Tale, propose ways of resolving the relationship between those things in the world he now sees and those things he has learnt in his journey from deep underground. But it is unclear whether anything would be resolved.

Let me emphasise: Socrates' allegory of the cave is not necessarily an argument for theism. Belief can be kept distinct from religion. The allegory can be, and has been, read in Freudian terms as the journey to consciousness from the dark interiorities of the unconscious, the death and libido drives and the id. More recently, the feminist philosopher Luce Irigaray has interpreted the cave as the rejected maternal womb from which the phallocentric and patriarchal order emerges under the rule of the symbolic Father. Even more recently, Roger L. Huard has reminded us that the context of the allegory is Plato's political vision for a republic. The cave is the key to understanding a political philosophy. The allegory can be read as a social critique of the masses enthralled to virtual, mediatised realities that sedate while entertaining them. The Wachowskis' film *The Matrix* (1999) has been interpreted along such Platonic lines. So we need not speak about religion just yet – though we may have to do so shortly.

It is not without significance that the Freudian, feminist and sociological interpretations of Plato's cave *mistrust* the nature, objectivity, obviousness, truthfulness and even dominance of the knowledge of the world discovered in the light of the sun. This world outside the cave could indeed be one in which what Engels called 'false consciousness' and ideology prevail. In their very different ways, Freud, Irigaray and Huard insist on returning us to the cave, the realm to which I too wish us to attend. Out of their suspicion of ideology, they return us to the polyphony of belief; belief which, as I pointed out in the introduction, is prior to interpretation – even where that interpretation is of Plato's cave as a religious, ethical, metaphysical, psychoanalytical, feminist, political or sociological allegory. It is prior also to instrumental reason (Wolpert). We too need to go back, then, like the reluctant philosopher, down through the archaic levels of the subterranean to that very point where a radical change occurs in, to, and for the one who will become the philosopher. We need to conduct an archaeology, not of knowledge but belief.

I already alerted us to the exact location to which we need to return. It is the point where the philosopher is released, compelled to turn around and begin his journey, his education. I observed that Plato (and Socrates) is coy when it comes to explaining how this volte-face takes place. And yet it is at this very point that the protagonist, not yet a philosopher, is released into the realm of belief. To understand this origin of believing, I suggest, we need to enter a set of rather different caves.

STANDING TALL AND HAVING THINGS TO HAND

The caves we are going to enter are prehistoric. But on entering such caves we need to know what we are looking for. What is a sign that believing is taking place? Later – in fact much later – when we discuss religious belief, archaeologists and anthropologists associate such believing with language, myth, ritual and symbolic behaviour. The clearest evidence for such activity comes either from the depiction of a cat in a cave in Namibia in southern Africa (dated to what is known as the Middle Palaeolithic, around 40,000 to 60,000 years ago) or, much more grandly, the caves in the Ardèche region of France discovered in December 1994 by a team of French archaeologists led by Jean-Marie Chauvet and named after him (dated to what is known as the Upper Palaeolithic, around 33,000 years ago). We will be venturing into these caves in the next chapter, when much more will be said about them. In this chapter we need to descend much further into what is not time but a rhythm of sun and moon, noontime and night, ice and desert, seabeds and mountains, tundra and volcanoes, molluscs, fish, birds, reptiles and mammals. And among these creatures are mammals, apes and chimpanzees, all evolving.

I said in the Introduction that I am defining 'belief', albeit cautiously, as a disposition (because although affect-laden, it is not an emotion), and while belief can be conscious, even rationally justified through a degree of reflective critique, it is not solely conscious. Preconscious belief is then an implicit knowledge. I call it a 'disposition' because, as a form of behaviour, its orientation is 'eccentric' – it looks beyond the individual who believes towards some object or person or condition in the world. It is 'disposed towards' as basic evolution is disposed towards survival and reproduction. The signs of belief, then, are not necessarily dependent upon the evidence of conscious thought that a language expresses and provides, or upon representations of objects in the world on the surfaces of rock. We will have to trace pathways prior to such symbolic behaviour and understand the relation of mind to matter, consciousness to material existence. The 'disposition towards' that is one of the characteristics of believing lies between sentience and *scientia*.

In their book *Philosophy in the Flesh*, the linguist George Lakoff and philosopher Mark Johnson set out to demonstrate the way the body and the brain are inseparably tied to the processes of reason. While recognising and emphasising that around 95 per cent of all our thought processing is unconscious, and viewing this 'unconscious' as the 'hidden hand' that moulds conscious thinking, they point out that 'the peculiar nature of our bodies shapes our very possibilities for conceptualization and categorization':

> Consider examples such as *in front of* and *in back of*. The most central senses of these terms have to do with the body. We have inherent fronts and backs. We see from in front, normally move in the direction the front faces, and interact with objects and other people at our fronts. Our backs are the opposites of our fronts; we don't exactly perceive our own backs, we normally don't move backwards, and we don't typically interact with objects and people at our backs [...] Our bodies define a set of fundamental spatial orientations that we use not only in orienting ourselves, but perceiving the relationship of one object to another.

Developing their argument, Lakoff and Johnson show that English, compared to other languages, is relatively impoverished in its use of bodily projections to conceptualise spatial relations. Some languages use bodily projections as their primary means of characterising such relations. Later in their volume they also point to how temporal orientations are part of these bodily projections, particularly when the body is in motion. But we can already observe the way *in front of* and *in back of* are also temporal categories. To perceive ahead in a motion towards is to conceive a future and to leave behind a past.

What Lakoff and Johnson do not foreground is the bodily phenomenon that makes possible the primary senses of space and time from which their examination proceeds: locomotion. The body is erect and its movement is bipedal (on two feet). As Wolpert points out: 'The first evidence for brain-like precursors is the collection of nerves that are involved in controlling movement [...] Sense organs have only one function, to help the organism decide how to move.' Ramp this observation up over several million years of evolution, and we can recognise how bipedalism was one of the most important physical transformations that separated our early hominid ancestors from apes or chimpanzees. The world looks very different when you are standing upright and walking about; there's a sense of greater orientation in the environment.

The second most important physiological transformation came with use of the hands; with the development of the hand and using hands with a flexibility that can fashion (tools), hold fragile and heavy objects, and carry. Hands can grasp (and there are several Teutonic languages in which 'to grasp' is still related to understanding). Hands can touch – and as far back as Aristotle the sense of touch was seen as the basis of all perception. The clinical neuroscientist Raymond Tallis has drawn attention to the importance of the hand in proprioception – sensing, evaluating and making sense earlier than cognitive perception as such. '[T]he basis for the intuition of the *agency* of our own bodies and the intuition of our bodies as our own and, indeed, as *ourselves*, and hence of ourselves as agents' is all down to the evolutionary development of the hand. The hand is precise, it is sensitive, and it is exploratory. It is, through the index or pointing finger, the origin of gesture and communication. The hand 'instrumentalizes the hominid body as a whole' (Tallis), making possible both tool use and the concept of 'tool'.

As the cognitive neuroscientist Merlin Donald has said, the one who walks tall, moving about and having a world to hand (Heidegger), perceiving the relationship of one object to another, oneself to another, 'transcend[s] the immediate environment.' The world opens out with horizons and vistas; the world in which one dwells becomes a world one surveys. Presumably, the transformation from movement and life on four paws to movement and life on two feet came about because of perceived changes in the environment that the body was informed of and responded to (climate change, scarcity of food, new forms of food, new threats from predators, new challenges to sexual reproduction). But there were risks involved in such a posture – one's body is more exposed and therefore needs more protection.

Nor was standing upright and having two free limbs and a pair of grasping hands a simple matter. Great anatomical changes were necessary in hands and feet, pelvis, spine and rib cage; as movement changes, the nature of breathing changes. The American palaeontologist Stephen Jay Gould has recognised bipedalism (though not necessarily having a world to hand) as the greatest single adaptation in the evolution of humankind. It may have begun 4.5 million years ago, but now on two feet and with two hands, the land can be surveyed ahead and around; the world informs the body and its physiological processes in new ways. The body becomes adapted to and through the manner in which it is being informed and the kinds of information it is registering. The adaptation is necessary because any evolutionary explanation is governed by a notion of continuity. Enter 'Lucy', that partial skeleton discovered in 1974 at Hadar, Ethiopia. The head and neck are similar to a chimpanzee's; the brain and the teeth are also small. But the legs (ankle and knee joints) and pelvis are like ours. Her bipedal kind grew up to six feet tall, and they lived between 3 million and 4 million years ago. And it possibly took up to 4 million years for such a development, since evolutionary anthropologists date the first division between chimpanzee and humans to 8 million years ago (Oppenheimer).

Now we are *Homo sapiens* – and the *sapiens* denotes the fact that we have sophisticated cognitive abilities that make us distinctive, particularly in the development of linguistic skills. But human consciousness has a beginning. That is not to say that animals lack consciousness, as we will see, but their consciousness cannot be the same as ours, because we not only perceive the world differently because of the way we move around it; we also adapt the world to our purposes. Adaptation is two-way: natural and cultural. The landscape is always changing in ways that take little or no account of us: the advance and retreat of ice-sheets, the world of volcanoes and the movement of tectonic plates, for example. But our presence in the landscape also changes the landscape. And the more we change the land-scape, the more that landscape changes us. That co-evolutionary process began with bipedalism and the existence of a number of hominids (like *Australopithecus afarensis*, who lived in the regions around Ethiopia 3.5 million years ago and is probably one of our *Homo sapiens'* ancestors) before a variety of *Homines* arrived on the scene.

BRAINS AND BRAWN

There were a number of other *Homines* before us, and several of them had larger brains! In fact, the size of the *Homo* brain has been decreasing in evolutionary terms. This is important because there has been a long-standing trend relating brain size to intelligence and using it as a benchmark for why *Homo sapiens* are the cleverest. Hubris apart, there are at least two highly questionable assumptions in this correlation. First, that there is such a relation, and the assumption that the brain's evolved function is to produce intelligence; and secondly the idea (based, I suspect, on the way we have come increasingly to visualise the operations of the brain in terms of cybernetics) that the larger amounts of brain tissue provide something akin to greater 'disk space' on a hard drive. Being brainy does not necessarily predispose us to being intellectually bright. Based on a body–brain ratio, for example, mice should be far more intelligent. This might accord well with *Tom and Jerry*, but outside cartoons and Hollywood animations the superior intelligence of mice is not a recognised scientific fact.

The relationship between brain size and body size is not a simple one. The brain does far more than cogitate and process information: it is key to our embodiment, to regulating viscera, and to our metabolism. It is not a one-way conversation. While the head metaphor is deeply rooted in our understanding of political order, the brain is not an absolute monarch. Its relationship to the body is symbiotic: as the body develops over time to reach maturity, the brain adapts to the body. The anatomical changes incurred through standing tall and having things to hand will therefore affect what happens in and to the brain, and vice versa. That does not mean there is nothing distinctive about brain size and being human. Our brains are three times larger than an ape's, and I take it on the authority of biologists that '[h]umans show a greater divergence from predicted brain size for our body size than other species' (Deacon).

Certainly at some point in our past the smaller brains of the 'Lucy' kind experienced a dramatic increase in volume, and this certainly relates to enhanced cognitive and locomotive capacities. It takes place in the development of the frontal lobes, which are concerned with our ability to control movement and manipulate objects around us. But there is a question as to why australopithecines and early *Homo* types (like *Homo habilis* and *Homo erectus*) so dramatically increased their brain size. What was driving this enlargement? It began about 2.5 million years ago, and with the evolution of *Homo erectus* 'these changes moved into overdrive' – or so the expert in DNA studies Stephen Oppenheimer records. Nevertheless, why did these changes come about?

Evolutionary anthropologists and archaeologists dance around the same three variables: the hand/tool capacity (Tallis, Wolpert, Donald); language emerging, probably through gesturing (Michael Corballis, Oppenheimer); increasing social organisation (Robin Dunbar). Some scholars, like Terrence Deacon, plump for what is probably correct: the importance of all three factors, each reinforcing the others and working upon the plasticity of the brain, as expressive of the development of human beings as a symbol-using species. But, for our purposes, the outcome is that belief becomes expressive.

The production of early stone tools is certainly related to the development of the 'hand' as a somatic tool. The earliest tools are Oldowan – sharpened rocks for butchering meat and smashing through bones, dating to around 2 million years ago. The biological anthropologist Terrence Deacon informs us that the making and handling of such tools requires 'an increasing prefrontalization, with a corresponding shift in learning dispositions.' Hence the brain develops what is now called its neocortical areas, particularly the prefrontal lobes. Rather than brains leading to the intelligent design of tools (which cannot account for why the brain develops prefrontalisation), it is now suggested that it was probably the increasing use of tools, and their development, that caused the brain's size to increase. In fact, tool manufacture may have been at the forefront of the evolution of australopithecines into *Homines*. 'Large brains, stone tools, reduction in dentition, better opposability of thumb and fingers, and more complete bipedality found in post-australopithecine hominids are the physical echoes of a threshold already crossed' (Deacon). And that threshold marks the advent of *Homo symbolicus*.

Then there is the question about the development of language. Oppenheimer:

> I argue that language was that unique behaviour shared between the sister genera *Homo* and *Paranthropus* 2.5 million years ago which enabled them, co-operatively and flexibly, to survive the barren cycles of the Pleistocene ice epoch and thus drove their brain growth [...] [T]hey must have had some form of language to start with [...] [I]t is much more likely that we were already communicating usefully and deliberately 2.5 million years ago [...] we suddenly discovered we could talk.

Certainly, as I have said, there is a relation between the hand and the origin of gesturing – at least pointing things out.

But Oppenheimer's argument is controversial and needs refining. We have no access to prehistoric hominid brains. However, the argument is not unfounded. Two pieces of evidence for the relationship between language and brain growth have been offered. The first is anatomical (though based upon fossil evidence); that is, the possession of a hyoid bone, enlarged thoracic spinal cord and an extended opening for connecting the hypoglossal nerve to the tongue. These are all anatomical structures necessary for spoken (though not gestural) communication. It is evident that Neanderthals possessed them, and it has been argued by some archaeologists that earlier hominid forms – *Homo heidelbergensis* and even *Homo erectus* – possibly also possessed them.

The second piece of evidence comes from modern neuroscience and its image mapping of neural activity in which the manufacture of tools also reveals activity in the areas of the brain associated with language. Several attempts have been made to teach primates the rudiments of stone-knapping to produce tools. None of them have proved remotely successful. But when an experiment was done using human beings to create the type of stone tool known to archaeologists as 'Acheulean' – a tool that goes back to around 1.65 million years ago – a positron emission tomography brain scan revealed activity in the premotor cortex related to Broca's area. This is an area of the brain involved in understanding language – although caution should be taken in thinking the brain works in a modular manner, as we will see. The manufacture of such a tool requires significant cognitive abilities – particularly the choosing of the right stone, precise hand-eye coordination, the imaginative projection of the form to be achieved and forward planning. The production of the tool has to be remembered, the operations of its manufacture reproduced and handed down to others – thus sharing the knowledge. The flakes knapped in the shaping of the stone were also used as cutting tools. They are tools closely associated with *Homo erectus* and *Homo ergaster*.

What remains controversial in part depends upon two aspects of analysis employed by archaeologists, palaeontologists and evolutionary biologists. The first concerns the inferences drawn from the archaeological evidence, its age and its location. Dating has become more accurate through technological advances and sophisticated modelling of climate change and biodiversity over millions of years. These new approaches enable us to place specific kinds of hominid within a geographical and temporal setting that points to the conditions necessary for survival and reproduction. The hyoid bone is certainly an anatomical development (along with the decrease in sexual dimorphism that meant male and female bodies became much more similar), for example. But its presence in itself will not deliver speech – though it may well have been an anatomical development that occurred because of the evolutionary need for social communication when gesturing became inefficient or not sufficient. This anatomical development would become necessary as cooperation developed among hominids and societies as they enlarged and became more complex.

Secondly, there is a tendency to project back present *Homo sapiens* abilities, diminishing them accordingly, on to the prehistoric hominids. Wolpert's 'analogy' between primitive development in modern children and primitive causal belief development in hominids is a particular case in point. So, with respect to the language areas of the brain that 'light up' when we moderns try to emulate hominid tool production, it is no surprise that human beings today, who are so profoundly immersed within symbolic thinking, cannot separate the task in hand from symbolic thinking processes. Of course, *for us*, the language areas of the brain are activated in tool production, but for early hominids these areas were probably only just evolving. In fact, it was the very need to survive – achieved by developing tools and early forms of communication – that drove the evolutionary development of the brain in this way. And fortunately the brain is such a malleable organ that development was possible.

A FINAL WORD ABOUT WORDS

Added to these complexities in evaluating the data is just what we are talking about when we use a word like 'language'. Here work that has brought together linguistics, cognitive science, neurobiology, anthropology and archaeology in projects developing the co-evolution thesis considerably assists in clarifying matters. For example, the groundbreaking research of Terrence Deacon has established an important difference between 'communication' and 'language'. Bees communicate: that's how they can fly in the complex pattern of a swarm. Wolves can communicate in order to hunt and forage in packs. Vervet monkeys communicate through a distinct set of different calls that indicate not only the presence of danger for other vervet monkeys but also the identity of the predator – whether it is an eagle, a leopard or a snake. But, as Deacon observes, 'The popular notion that the calls and gestures constituting the communications of other species are like words and sentences can mostly be traced to misconceptions about the concept of reference.' There is no 'intention' behind the communication – only the complex coordination of instinctive behaviours and learnt associations. Although Deacon's detailed analysis, which I will be drawing upon, does not discuss the nature of belief, he is able to define the distinctive character of human beings as a symbolic species and language-user. Furthermore, Deacon has been able to demonstrate how human brains evolve such that we have become a symbolic species. Belief, when given concrete expression – we have already noted in the Introduction that believing is, in part, precognitive and implicit knowledge – is not unrelated to knowledge. We have not explored that relation yet. But belief cannot then be separated from our evolution into a symbolic species, and it may determine it in certain ways.

So, if bipedalism and having a world to hand is a beginning, where do we look for the further developmental stages?

II

Signs of Intention: The Archaeology of Believing [2]

Archaeologists calculate that *Homo rhodesiensis*, who lived in Africa around 1.2 million years ago, already had a brain size that was only 6 per cent short of the volume of a normal modern human brain. It was around this same time, perhaps earlier with *Homo erectus* (from around 1.8 million years ago), that the first exodus from Africa that colonised the globe took place. Locomotion now becomes migration. It was from this line of descent that *Homo antecessor* (1.2 million to 500,000 years ago), *Homo heidelbergensis* (600,000 to 200,000 years ago) and *Homo neanderthalensis* (350,000 to around 24,000 years ago) proceeded. The last three forms of 'human' are all evident in Europe before the arrival of *Homo sapiens*. Because of climatic changes – the cycle of ice ages that concentrated water in frozen glaciers and wastelands, and dried up savannahs, turning them into uninhabitable deserts – these forms were cut off from their African origins, developing independently. An interglacial warm-up around 125,000 years ago probably enabled some migration from the sub-Saharan area of Africa into what is now the Middle East, but by 90,000 years ago a global freeze extinguished these people. It is at this point that we enter our first caves in search of belief.

In the 1930s, excavations in the region of Mount Carmel, close to the Israeli coast and a scene associated in legend with the pursuit of Jesus by the members of the synagogue at Nazareth, found fossil evidence of early modern human beings. Perhaps significantly for latter developments in our study, the location has been a place of both pilgrimage and religious worship in a number of civilisations. There are remnants of a Byzantine church nearby, said to have been built by St Helena. The first part of the Qafzeh cave had been paved and bears the mark of a Byzantine cross. It was a place also known to the Crusaders. The Skhul and Qafzeh caves show that *Homo sapiens* lived here around 120,000–80,000 years ago, in close proximity to Neanderthals. In the nearby Tabun cave, remains dating back to the Middle Palaeolithic age were found (Mousterian pointed hand axes made of flint, for example) and a Neanderthal female dating to around 120,000 years ago. The Neanderthal findings here, along with those at the Kebara cave, where a poorly preserved skeleton of a young Neanderthal male (dated to between 60,000 and 48,000 years ago) was discovered in the 1960s, suggest that the two *Homo* species may have encountered each other. Dating is notoriously difficult. Although there are advanced techniques, such as thermoluminescence and electron spin resonance, most dating is radiocarbon, and this is unreliable beyond 40,000 years. But if they did encounter each other, then they shared a Mousterian technological culture, and it was the Neanderthals who survived as an ice age encroached, turning the land to desert. The early *Homo sapiens* died out around 80,000 years ago.

The remains of seven adults and three children were found in the Skhul cave, and the remains of several others, adults and children, have been recovered from Qafzeh. What is most interesting for us is the perforated beads also found, which may have formed a necklace, and evidence of the deliberate burial of the dead. The remains of what is known as Skhul 5 had the mandible of a boar on his chest; Qafzeh 11, an adolescent, was buried in a pit dug out of the bedrock. The hands of the child had been deliberately placed on either side of the neck and were holding the antlers of a large red deer. As the leader of the excavation has commented: 'It is clearly the most significant grave with intentional deposits in all the middle Palaeolithic' (Vandermeersch). We have now entered the province of explicit belief. What the perforated shells, the boar mandible and the deer antlers 'represented' we do not know, but certainly we have entered into the realm of symbolic activity. And though a long way – geographically, technologically, artistically and historically – from the cave paintings at Chauvet and Lascaux and the Upper Palaeolithic ice-age art of swimming reindeer cut into mammoth tusks, the perforated shells that possibly formed a necklace are evidence of a manufacturing process. This process took place in the Middle East at a time when there were no *Homo sapiens* in Europe at all.

Burials as 'intentional deposits' are a clear indication of belief, but is the capacity to engage in the symbolism of funerals only a characteristic of *Homo sapiens* behaviour? Certainly among archaeologists this conviction was held for some time. But the skeleton of the young Neanderthal male found in the Kebara cave was located in the middle of the living area, where there would have been a lot of social activity. The hominid carcass was not dragged there by carnivorous animals. The remains were also what archaeologists call 'articulated' – that is, they were not scattered about. And the Kebara cave is not an isolated phenomenon.

In the Zagros Mountains of northern Iraq in the late 1950s and early 1960s, nine individual skeletons of Neanderthals were discovered in the Shanidar cave, dating from 60,000 to 80,000 years ago. One of them, an adult (Shanidar 4), was around 30 to 45 years old and had been laid in a foetal position with his head towards the mouth of the cave and his jaws open. Again he was found in the middle of the cave floor in a niche of stones that 'looked like a natural crypt', according to a paper offered to the Smithsonian Institute in 1976 by the main archaeologist of the cave, the American Ralph Solecki. The grave had been covered by stone blocks and was found to also contain the remains of two females buried immediately on top of a baby, all beneath the man. He was 'evidently an important man', and his importance may well be related to the fact that he was surrounded by flowers of several different varieties (or what remained of the ancient pollens found in the surrounding soil): yarrow, cornflower, thistle, ragwort, hyacinth and hollyhock. The flowers were evidently grouped, because of the high densities of mixed pollens – out of character with pollen counts taken elsewhere in the cave.

Now some or all of these plants could have been introduced into the cave by animals, the wind, even the feet of those working with the archaeological investigators, but still much about the burial remains unanswered. For example, all the flowers found were recognised as having medicinal properties used in tonics, diuretics, stimulants and a range of reliefs from 'toothache to poultices and spasm.' Solecki writes:

It could be circumstantial and a happy coincidence, but it is remarkable that all the flowers associated with Shanidar 4 [IV] had additional significance – they may have been selected for their medicinal values. Finally, growing out of this find is the realization that the whole question as to whether or not the Neanderthals possessed a mutually comprehensible communication system, in short a spoken language, must be put to rest in the affirmative.

If some archaeologists questioned the interpretation of these findings, and particularly Solecki's conclusion that the Neanderthals had a concept of spirit and a kind of religious life, then the discoveries made in excavations from 1994–2000 at two sites in Murcia in south-east Spain, in the caves at Sima de las Palomas, cast their scepticisms to the wind. Here, high above a Mediterranean saltwater lagoon, not only Neanderthal but also pre-Neanderthal hominid remains were found. The articulated skeletal parts of two adult Neanderthal individuals and a juvenile or child were excavated here and examined between 2005 and 2007. Their burial dates back to around 50,000 years ago. It was noted that the hands of the skeletons were raised close to the head and, associating this practice with findings elsewhere, the team of archaeologists concluded that 'this is an aspect of burial that some Neanderthals and some early non-Neanderthal humans had in common' (Walker). Alongside the skeletons were the cut-off paws of a panther that may also have held ritual significance. The strapline for the discovery, as reported in the journal *Archaeology* in April 2011, says it all: 'Did Neanderthals believe in an afterlife?' This is speculative, but it 'seems reasonable to assume that the origins of sacred relics may be found in the Neanderthal period' (*Archaeology*, August 2002), especially because, in the Krapina cave in Croatia, the bones of the 70 Neanderthals found had been entirely scraped of their flesh.

There are now well over two dozen discoveries of Neanderthal burials dating from before 70,000 years ago (*Archaeology*, August 2002), and the Neanderthals go back a long way, roaming Siberia, Europe and the Middle East 300,000 years before *Homo sapiens* made an appearance in the same regions. Can we perhaps go back further in the construction of our archaeology of belief? It is important to emphasise again what it is we are looking for. The word 'intention' in Vandermeersch's phrase concerning Neanderthal burial practices, 'intentional deposits', is determinative of more than consciousness. Animals have consciousness, but their actions are reflexive rather than intentional. Intentional action adapts nature to purposeful culture. Chimpanzees have a limited capacity for such adaptation. They can use a stick to dig out termites, and even trim it. They can use a stone to crack nuts. But two further requirements of intentionality seem to be lacking, according to primatologists like Daniel Povinelli and Michael Tomasello. First, they cannot abstract from the process what distinguishes cause from effect and use that information to fashion tools. 'They do not understand the world in intentional and causal terms' (Wolpert). And secondly, as a corollary, they do not pass on their technical skills, nor are they aware of the advantages such skills have for other chimpanzees.

INTENTION

As an indicator of the operation and formation of beliefs about the world in which they live, intention is determinative for archaeologists. They will also speak of hearths and 'intentional fires' (fires used to clear forests, for example, or to cook). *What* is intended may be speculatively imagined on our part. But that there is an intention behind this arrangement is evident, as in the Shanidar cave, where a baby is found buried beneath the bones of two women, on top of which is found the full skeleton of a man in a foetal position, festooned with flowers. There is an order here, a natural order of life represented in a cultural ordering – of death. Views on spirits, shamanism, and an afterlife (all of which archaeologists have thought possible) are imaginative inferences, but the order remains – invoking a prior liturgy, a 'proper' way of behaving towards this dead man, a fittingness appropriate to both the living and the dead. Desecration of the corpse is taboo. Daylight, darkness, shadows, fire, the wind passing down the steep sides of the valley and sighing in the rocky hollow in the mountainside, the mouth of the cave and the open jaws of the dead man: a series of associations, a web of ecological correspondences, only some of which are accidental. All of this announces an acceptance and recognition of an order, a diurnal, seasonal, even cosmic rhythm, within which those who live and are now dead reposed. There is a symbolism embedded within such an ordering – however we interpret it – and a schema of beliefs about bodies, reproduction, life, death and their relations.

In our pursuit of intentional activity before the Neanderthals, we come to the excavations conducted between 1976 and 1995 that revealed up to 15 young male bodies (mainly teeth) in a cave in Pontnewydd in North Wales. The bodies have been dated to around 230,000 years ago and appear to be either an earlier form of Neanderthal or perhaps examples of *Homo heidelbergensis*. Studies of DNA have shown that the Neanderthals did not appear as a distinct species until 400,000 years ago, whereas *Homo heidelbergensis* date from 600,000 years ago and were probably extinct by 200,000 years ago. Much more controversially, a grave containing the fossilised bones of over 28 individuals identified as *Homo heidelbergensis* was excavated in Atapuerca in Spain in the Sima de los Huesos. A recent archaeologist has described the importance of this find for our accounts of being human:

> Around half a million years ago a clan of people lived in the valleys of northern Spain, close to today's cathedral city of Burgos. To all intents and purposes they were recognizably human. They were intelligent, tall, and well built: they averaged 1.75 meters in stature, weighed around 95 kilos, had brains of comparable size to ours, lived in social groups, and were probably able to speak (Finlayson).

Significantly, among these bones was found a carved hand-axe made from red quartzite, rock not found in that area and suggestive of travel and the exchange of goods. The burial and the hand-axe reveal earlier forms of complex, symbolic behaviour and levels of self-awareness. Because of the importance of the pit for our accounts of human evolution, it was declared a UNESCO World Heritage Site. But that was before a controversy arose in the early months of 2012 over the dating and identification of the remains. Professor Chris Stringer, an expert in human evolution, claimed the bones are not 600,000 years old but 400,000, and that they are not examples of *Homo heidelbergensis*, but instead are early Neanderthals. Stringer also casts doubt on whether the site was a burial ground, since there is no other evidence this early of 'ceremonial behaviour' (the *Guardian*, 10 June 2012).

I do not need to demonstrate 'ceremonial behaviour' – only 'intention' – though the attention paid to the evolution of hands and feet and an overall physiology capable of exploiting both cannot rule out early forms of communication through gesture and dance. Even so, ceremonial behaviour associates believing with vague notions of religion, the sacred, the liturgical, etc., and I do not wish to move too quickly to such an association. We can allow that the 'human' transcendence of environment takes conscious form, consciousness of transcendence itself. Other primates do have limited versions of such a consciousness: they can recognise themselves and other primates, form alliances and even develop (with human assistance) protolanguage skills (David Premack). But 'transcendence' is taking on a character shared with no other animal. Early in the evolution of human beings the capacity of and for belief enters the field of the religious. At this point in our archaeology it is intention that is paramount as an indicator of creative consciousness, forward planning, instrumental reasoning and shared understanding. The bodies were not placed in the pit in Atapuerca by natural occurrence, and the quartzite hand-axe still remains. The value of such an axe to a group of hunters is incalculable. Its burial with these remains is an 'offering', a 'sacrifice', even a 'gift' – but to whom and for what is hidden from us. It raises the question of the transcendent Other. The scientists can wage war over dates, but somewhere between 600,000 and 400,000 years ago an early species of human being acted intentionally. And this displays cognitive capacity.

Belief requires cognitive capacity for its expression (even while its operation still remains hidden) – the same cognitive capacity evident in the shaping of hand-axes and the development of language. It is a different cognitive capacity from that belonging to other animals and our nearest primate cousins. Animals, as I have already said, do not *make* tools for a specific purpose. It has been known for primates to recognise the death of one of their members, even grieve for them. Sometimes they carry the corpse around for a couple of hours, but they do not *bury* their dead. In a safari park in Botswana a female elephant has been photographed holding on to the trunk of her dead mate and guarding the body from being ransacked as a food source by vultures and hyenas. But human beings take the honouring of the dead in intentional burial to another level entirely. Although in ape society there is some food-sharing, no ape or any other animal *makes* fire and employs it for keeping warm, cooking and clearing land. Animals can anticipate – if they do x then y will or should follow. Such anticipations are learnt and become automatic, reflexive actions conditioned by past experience. But their anticipations are short-term; they do not plan for a future that is more than a brief span of present consciousness. Some anticipations have been taught to chimpanzees, but even when memorised, these anticipations have a short temporal span with respect to their employment. The evolutionary psychologist Merlin Donald, adopting a term originated by Tulving (1983), calls this cognitive condition 'episodic'. The behaviour of apes,

> complex as it is, seems unreflective, concrete, and situation-bound.
> Even their uses of signing and their social behaviour are immediate,
> short-term responses to the environment [...] Their lives are lived
> entirely in the present, as a series of concrete episodes, and the high-
> est element of their system of memory representation seems to be
> at the level of event representation.

Chimpanzees can make connections in this visual environment because they can represent the event presented to them, between cardboard-boxes, say, and a banana suspended from the ceiling. They can problem-solve and conceptualise in a way indicative of an ability to anticipate a solution through associating objects and employing them instrumentally. They register objects within a context and can draw an inferential relation. But the number of objects remains limited and they do not seem able to project their anticipations – that would require imagination and a more expansive, even different, memory capacity. In other words, apes can react but we (and the 'we' here seems to include various species of *Homo* from *Homo erectus* and their Acheulean tool-making onwards) can model and invent.

SEEING AS

Let me take this more slowly. Why have I related anticipation to projection? To answer this question and show the contribution of anticipation and projection to human action, I need to take one step back into non-conscious processes. Some of these processes *become* unconscious; that is, certain actions now may need little in the way of conscious attention because they have been learnt such that they are automatic. If I fall into a river I will swim or try to swim – the response is not now a conscious one. Lessons and practice have become habit; they have worked their way down into many different forms of embodied memory. But those of us who have learnt to drive a car recognise a further level of complexity to automatic responsiveness.

Driving requires a high degree of motor-control and coordination: of hands, feet and eyes. Spatial awareness, and its representational mapping, is decisive. These abilities for control, coordination and spatial awareness are automatic. None of these actions are the subject of introspective reflection. But into this non-conscious process is fed: a) an awareness of other vehicles on the road, beside the road, emerging into the road or backing up from the road; b) an awareness of pedestrians who may be at the kerb watching the traffic and waiting to cross, cyclists overtaking on the inside or the outside, a ball-game being played by children up ahead; c) an awareness of the closeness of the car in front and the distance of the car behind; and d) an awareness of traffic signs like an approaching zebra crossing, a give way sign or a one-way sign.

I failed my second driving test because the instructor asked me to drive in accordance with the traffic signs, and in driving straight on, through a one-way sign that directed traffic to the left, I entered a street for oncoming traffic only. End of test. I had stopped reading the environment and was relying totally on the automatism of a great deal of practice. The fourfold awarenesses listed require anticipation and projection, and I will not be a good driver if I rely simply on automatic piloting.

Sentience means that the body is continually receiving an input of information, but anticipation is directing and focusing that information in specific ways. As I noted earlier, only a small percentage of what is being received is adequately lit by our consciousness. In being lit, anticipation disposes what is received through the senses such that the excitation passing through numerous neural networks can cognitively map the various spatial awarenesses of the environment.

Now this is where we have to take enormous care, for reasons that will become more apparent in Chapter VIII when I speak about various invisibilities. Put briefly: at this point, I have no access to anticipation processes as such, nor neural processes, for that matter, nor cognitive mapping exercises. I am describing these 'events' from their visible effects (on my driving) and an introspection of my feelings, intuitions and perceptions. All of which means that the metaphorical description simplifies the activity in ways that can be misleading. Sentient reception, for example, appears remarkably passive in my account, but there is no pure reception as such. Perception is always being actively processed across a trillion synaptic gaps and through the same number of electrochemical discharges. Anticipation with respect to these processes appears, controlling or taking a lead in the direction and nature of the processing. In turn that puts 'disposition' into the driving seat as if it was some innate inclination. And that that is the case is not demonstrable. Anticipation also emerges from the processing of sentience; and because sensing is not a passive activity, anticipation is involved too in what is sensed in the environment and what is not. Recall the person who jumped into the river *before* understanding how critical the situation was for the child who couldn't swim. The disposition is not necessarily innate, and it is not necessarily fully determinative. It has been learnt at some point in the evolutionary process and recognised as an important capacity for survival, because it looks ahead, assessing the possibilities for risk, in a number of creative ways that plot possibilities. The work of the three cell biologists, James E. Rothman, Randy W. Schekman and Thomas C. Südhof, who shared the 2013 Nobel Prize for medicine, treats the inner workings of the cell and suggests disposition towards the future operates at the cellular level. We discuss this in Chapter IV.

On the basis of stored memories and evolved capacities, anticipation concerns 'what may happen' (with that ball being kicked by those excited children) and 'what will happen' (as the road approaches a roundabout).

Adjustments to behaviour and control of the car are modified in the light of these anticipations. Furthermore, spatial awareness while driving is made more complex and three-dimensional by having always to look in mirrors, above the windscreen and around the wings of the car. Anticipation 'predicts' possible scenarios for what will happen (as you approach traffic lights) and what may happen (a child running after a ball that has bounced into the road). From a complex set of visual stimuli, anticipation that is not necessarily conscious generates a variety of future possibilities that, for the alert, can be translated into motor activity (braking, hitting the horn, swerving, etc.) if necessary. When this predicting or prescripting by anticipation (which is for the most part nonconscious) is projected, then it becomes conscious or available to conscious introspection.

The represented environment, cognitively mapped, is a temporal and temporary one. It is changing all the time as one drives up the street. But perception produces images, consciousness selects from those images, the neural networks of association link those images to previously stored ones, and cognition maps the representation of those images. Anticipation, which has been involved in what is sensed and is part of the processing of what is sensed, generates associative narratives, and this imagining of other possible and future trajectories of possible events and actions rides seamlessly with conscious recognition and the reading of signs. They are coordinated with the motor functions of the body that respond (hopefully) accordingly. This association is learnt. Even the coordination is learnt. But the human body has multiple forms of memory, some which are formed through the evolutionary process itself, that inform spatial awareness, its cognitive mapping and its imaginative projection.

Anticipation and projection require both cognitive abstraction from a set of changing conditions, rules for how things work in the world (based on the memory of how these things have worked in the past) and also the instrumental application of these abstractions to construct multiple, coexisting representations of 'what could happen'. Belief is evident not only in these projected possibilities – the belief of their possibility based on previous occurrences which are not simply recalled in order to predict. It also determines how what is seen is seen. Furthermore, belief also resides in the abstraction process itself – the construction of how things work in the world. More fundamentally, belief is evident throughout the cognitive processes in ways that inform both the disposition to anticipate and the projection of possibilities. If animals, including the most advanced mammals (like apes), cannot project these anticipations, and through introspection be conscious of them as anticipations and projections, then it is difficult to claim that they have the capacity to *believe* or *have beliefs*. Anticipations and their projection depend upon the ability to associate one phenomenon (whether an object, the memory of an object, or an abstract rule for the way certain objects behave) with another and draw an inferential association. But the disposition to the inference that is drawn may not be a conscious one. Chimpanzees can be trained to make associations, but they cannot *freely* associate in ways that not only break down a visual event into its multiple constituent parts (pedestrians, children playing, traffic signs, the cars in front and behind, the map of roads entering and leaving the main carriageway, etc.), but also project any number of different templates for possible actions given a change to any one of those constituent parts.

The cognitive ability to process information in this way, and the belief in the world (and oneself as an agent within it) that is represented on multiple levels, returns us to brain size. Why? Because the growth in the size of the brain in hominids and *Homo sapiens* is an 'increase in size and complexity [...] especially prominent in the cortex, cerebellum, and hippocampus; and within the cortex, it is most evident in association areas' (Donald). We will have more to say about the physiology of these brain regions and their relation to the prefrontal cortex in the next chapter. What is important for now is that what we are witnessing in early forms of intentional behaviour (burials, hearths and the production of hand-axes) is the emergence of symbolic consciousness *in which belief plays a significant and fundamental role*. To appreciate more fully the critical role belief plays, we need to understand more how consciousness is always a seeing *as*. Because perception is always woven into a neural network of images, associations, memories and affects, we never see *as such*. As Terrence Deacon remarks: 'We live in a world that is both entirely physical and virtual at the same time.'

Observe: this negotiation with an environmental context and social conditions when driving a car need not relate to language. The mind need not verbalise any of the perceptions and responses involved in driving up the street. An experienced driver may be verbalising an entirely different script to him- or herself. This is a phenomenon well known to psychologists: the ability to relate in a number of complex social interactions requiring a working memory, sense of oneself, scripting possible actions, representing the environment, understanding and assessing the context – all without language (Donald). Anticipation and projection can, of course, be verbalised – but much of association and coordination is non-verbal or stored in ways that do not require a language system and symbolic form. Nevertheless, the negotiations, and even manipulations of situational events in driving, though non-verbal, are communicative. I am communicating levels of intention and intelligent control – to other drivers, to pedestrians, to traffic police. There is an act of social communication that is evident. The communication is gestural (albeit the gestures are enhanced and amplified by the prosthetic extension of the vehicle itself).

Now, to a certain extent, this non-verbal communication is imitative. I have learnt to drive in this way by copying other people, including my driving instructor. I have been trained to behave in this way. Chimps can be trained in a similar way to manipulate signs that communicate intention and intelligent control. What is different is that my driving instruction, however detailed, cannot prepare me for all the eventualities I might encounter and have to negotiate in any act of driving down a street. I can make links or associations between phenomena visualised beyond any imitative behavioural training. I can, as I said above, *freely* associate rather than just perform the associations I have been taught through various forms of behavioural reinforcement. Apes have been known to generalise from a series of perceptions of a situation and interrelate them, but only in accordance with either the training they have been given or by imitating what they have seen others do. They can only do this reactively. But I can generalise freely, and so have a spontaneity in my intentional communicative acts. Not only can I figure or model what I am doing (driving) to myself, but I can also refigure or remodel that driving according to any number of possible templates for action that the circumstances throw at me. And all this cognitive activity does not necessarily require speech, even internal speech – though it is representational as an activity. Mental figuring and re-figuring, and its somatic correlations, means I can generate a number of possible options should a pedestrian step into the road, or the car in front suddenly brake and reverse.

As phenomenologists from Edmund Husserl onwards have recognised, human beings *perceive* intentionally. They *see* meaning. 'Chimpanzees lack [...] intentional gazing and pointing: the ability to realize the intentions of others' (Donald). This ability to perceive intentionally is crucial to social interaction, and it has been recognised by evolutionary anthropologists such as Robin Dunbar that the extension of social interaction was a significant factor in brain-size development. A greater intellectual ability follows from this, because it requires working within an increased number of relationships and cooperating across levels of increased social complexity. As I have said, the move to standing upright and negotiating the world on two feet has been seen as bringing untold disadvantages to survival (it requires more energy to start with and therefore a different diet, for example), unless other anatomical changes not only compensated but also enhanced the possibilities for flourishing (Lovejoy).

SMALL TALK

To return to Oppenheimer's claim that hominids began to talk from around 2.5 million years ago: the date is probably taken from the earliest known stone-tool technology (Oldowan). The tools are crude – little more than modifications made to pebbles – and best used for smashing bones. The real breakthrough came a million years later with *Homo erectus*. The manufacture of Acheulian hand-axes is a sign of some form of social hunting and gathering configuration (which it no doubt is), and social configuration *requires* talk. But 'talk' is too graphic a word for what was possible at this time. To 'talk' as we know talking demands access to a pre-existing symbolic language system and a sophisticated anatomical development of vocal apparatus (known as the supralaryngeal vocal tract). In his book *The Biology and Evolution of Language* (1984), the American evolutionary biologist Philip Lieberman pointed out that human vocalisation was dependent upon a descended larynx and that the primate mouth was long, narrow and taken up mainly with the tongue. Although early hominid development saw the descent of the larynx, it was only with

Homo sapiens that the vocal apparatus enabling talk was fully formed. Nevertheless, with increasing social complexity, communication far more sophisticated than that available through gesturing is required. Our first indications of stable social grouping come from discoveries of hearths and the intentional use of fire.

QUEST FOR FIRE

There are a number of things wrong with Jean-Jacques Annaud's 1981 film *Quest for Fire*. The setting, for example, is 80,000 years ago – and we know the domestication of fire goes back much much further than that, to somewhere between 300,000 and 1.5 million years ago (Wolpert). The work done between 1953 and 1954 on what is known as the 'Cave of Hearths' in the Limpopo province of South Africa traces the intentional use of fire back to level one occupation – from 250,000 to 200,000 years ago. The film also portrays various encounters with different human species. There are early *Homo sapiens* who live in organised groups under a leader, use body-painting, have mating rituals, a developed verbal language, elaborate mythic costumes, sophisticated weaponry and an understanding of how to *make* fire. Alongside these are what appear to be heavy-browed Neanderthals – not nearly so developed physically, with the rudiments of vocal calls and gesturing that is not yet a language, basic tools and a lack of technological know-how such as how to make fire and why it is necessary to keep it from water. It is the Neanderthals who are trekking across the Kenyan landscape looking to steal fire from another group. There is also a more primitive collection of *Homo erectus*, still with the body hair of apes, who initiate the storyline by raiding the Neanderthal camp and stealing their fire. The coexistence of various species of *Homo* is recognised by the archaeological and palaeontological evidence – though the kind of relations between them can only be guessed at. There is considerable debate among archaeologists and anthropologists about interbreeding between hominid and human species – but the dominant opinion is little, if any, took place at all. There were no Neanderthals in Africa, as far as we know.

But Annaud was working with the evidence available in the late 1970s; more sophisticated analysis and spectacular discoveries have followed.

Even so, there are some very interesting scenarios in his film that can help us in our archaeology of belief. They take us beyond the anticipations and projections that we examined earlier to add a further cognitive and very human feature: recognition. We can see *as*, we can see *intentionally,* but meaning is shared.

Meaning is obviously shared in a common symbolic language. We are born into such systems. But if, as I have been arguing, belief at a dispositional level is implicit and non-verbalised – which is its profundity because it predisposes to know before there is knowledge – then how is that sharing possible if it is a distinctively human trait, sharing in but greatly superseding the various gestural, vocal and indexical communicative skills of other animals? And why was it necessary to evolve such complex, nuanced forms of communication *before* the advent of a shared symbolic vocabulary and grammar, while species of human and hominid groped towards languages as we understand them? How was belief shared such that what was meaningful could also be registered not as madness but illumination, shared understanding?

Recognition becomes fundamental here. I am using this term in a manner expounded by the nineteenth-century German philosopher G. W. F. Hegel in his groundbreaking *Phenomenology of Spirit* (1807). Himself something of an early anthropologist, the word he used was *Anerkennung.* The German word is subtle. *Erkennung* is 'knowledge', but the prefix *an* lends that word an incompleteness. It is 'almost' knowledge or 'on the way to' knowledge, pre-knowing, intuitive, in ways that bear some similarities with what many neuroscientists refer to as 'emotional knowledge'. Nevertheless it announces a cognition regarding what is outside the ego, the one perceiving. It is as if from an external stimulus the self provokes a knowledge that is not quite knowledge within itself: a déjà vu. Hence the translation 'recognition'. The other and external provides the possibility for a self-awareness, a consciousness of what was not fully known previous to the encounter. 'Recognition' speaks of a further application of what I called earlier 'projection': from a consciousness of myself I come to an understanding of the other, myself *and* the relation of meaning binding both other and self.

So, in the film, although there is no shared verbal communication possible between the Neanderthal man and the *Homo sapiens* woman, each recognises something about the emotional state of the other that communicates and illuminates each with respect to the other. This recognition inaugurates a new kind of relation between creatures that differs dramatically from the relationship between a human being and another animal. Both the other and the self become meaningful for each other. 'Recognition' involves the reciprocity of a meaningful or semantic relation now understood. Intention is now perceived in oneself and is attributed (projected on) to another.

In the final scene of *Quest for Fire* the Neanderthal man sits staring at the moon and the woman draws close to him, nestling against his body in a new sociality that we might call 'love', but is certainly intimacy and trust. There is a new peaceful coexistence for both of them; an abatement in the restless turmoil of survival. And this is the origin of conscious belief: the going out of oneself – that's the projection – towards a recognition of communication with the other that makes the self also understand something about itself. These two forms of being human recognise something in each other and affirm that recognition. They *believe in*; they *believe that*. Terrence Deacon has proposed – and this scene fits in with that proposal – that the evolutionary leap into the symbolic realm arose out of reproductive needs 'to negotiate mate choice and pair-bond maintenance.' Only such a cultural drive will force people, and their mental abilities, to foster ways of communicating that belief in each other upon which mutual trust can be founded. 'Belief in' and 'belief that' are cognates of 'trusting'. Of all animal species, not only are human beings the only one to have punched their way through to and honed symbolic practices, but they are also the only species that establishes such mating alliances with each other. To begin with, '[s]ymbolic communication was likely only a small part of social communication [...] The first symbol systems were also likely fragile modes of communication: difficult to learn, inefficient, slow, inflexible, and probably applied to a very limited communicative domain' (Deacon). Attention has to be fixed upon 'higher-order, more distributed associations and away from those based on temporal spatial correlations.' This takes an enormous and patient investment in time to learn 'associations which aren't much use until the whole system of interdependent associations is worked out.' The need for such a radical shift in communicative strategy and focus of intellectual energies came from the need to select the right mate in the game of survival, to extract more information about physical states' 'resource defence capabilities, care-giving abilities, and likely fidelity [...] Evolution will favor mechanisms for avoiding getting stuck with an incompetent, unreliable, or unfaithful mate.' Belief, its communication and its sharing, concern that which we can come to trust. Its process of knowing is emotional and relational before it is rational.

If we analyse the pair-bonding in the last scene of Annaud's film, then certain cognitive conditions for such belief become evident: a focus of attention on that which is other and exterior; a new level of association; a sharpening of perception because of its semantic weight; an ability to store such affective and cognitive memories; self-awareness, self-consciousness, and then the projection of this awareness to become not just an awareness of the other, the exterior, but also the meaningfulness of the other, the exterior, for oneself and for itself. Belief is a relational category. From the memory and accumulation of such memories new inferential and predictive powers can emerge.

Chimps have been shown to be self-aware. Coloured stickers have been placed on their foreheads and the chimps have been placed before a mirror. They will first reach out to touch the surface of the mirror. They begin by thinking there is another chimp in or behind the mirror. And then they touch the coloured sticker on their own heads in recognition that it is they who are standing before the mirror. But chimps cannot take the next step: the projection beyond oneself to recognise the meaningfulness of the other, the exterior. They are capable of affection and responding to affection. Like pets, they can be trained in their dependence; a training reinforced behaviourally and rewarded. They are not capable of love – a relationship of mutual independence in which there is understanding, affection, forgiveness, trust, continual recognition of the other and the projected investment in the truth of what has been in part discovered and in part revealed. They cannot make the semantic leap that makes an exchange of glances meaningful one to another.

Why call this leap 'semantic'? Because the glance 'refers'. As a communicative sign, it does not simply have sense (the perception registered by the intentional dilation of the pupil and exercise of the muscles around the eyelids); it has reference. 'Reference is not the difference between alarm calls [by animals] and words,' Deacon informs us. But in human communication there is a qualitative relation between the sign and what it signifies – a relation that produces a mutual understanding. Signs abstract from the immediacy of a situation, establishing themselves as markers independent of that situation, and usable in other situations to those who have learnt the sign. So the sign refers to, and expresses, a world of shared meaning. An animal can be trained, as a computer can be programmed, to decode signs, but this is not to understand the meaning they bear. A sign has to be more than an index of an object, an index that can stand in for the object. It has to have this abstract independence. 'Establishing such social-sexual relationships cannot be accomplished by indexical communication alone,' Deacon informs us.

Self-love is primary in such reciprocation, and we can only wonder whether the founding moment of conscious belief was first encountered and understood when a hominid gazed at themselves in the reflections in a pond, a rock pool, a boggy tarn or a lake and recognised the meaningful-ness of being who they were as a species different, distinctive. Raymond Tallis associates early conceptions of agency with the use of the hand and the concept of the tool. And this may well be true. But while this notion of agency may be registered inchoately, the self-consciousness of agency needs self-recognition. Did this arise in the shock, wonder, one might even say illumination, of a face peering into water and beholding its own utter distinctiveness?

We will have more to say about belief and the origins of the self in a later chapter. For the moment it is important to understand how the self-belief that may have arisen from the wonder of beholding oneself in some reflected surface is primordial to recognising that same self-recognition in another person. So perhaps Plato was not too far wrong, after all. Perhaps consciousness *does* arise from reflections of objects (*eikasia*) that become self-reflections. Self-consciousness dawns with wonder. With the world and other people in it becoming – being recog-nised as – meaningful comes the ability to dwell, in Heidegger's sense of that term; that is, to create a world. The restfulness with which *Quest for Fire* concludes emphasises a new sense of belonging to the world and the world to us. As a recent phenomenologist has written: '[I]nteriority does not close off the world but allows the world to penetrate us more deeply' (Terence C. Wright).

RELIGIOUS INTIMATIONS

The closing sequence of *Quest for Fire* shows that mutual *belief in* and *belief that* is prior to any developed or shared symbolic language; nevertheless, that conscious believing is the foundation for the social contract. The origins of belief are not themselves necessarily religious. Put tersely, there has to be self-awareness *before* there can be any awareness of God – though there is a question still of how that self-awareness emerges, how it is revealed. We will leave that for a later chapter. Belief at this point concerns the quality of a semantic and social relation; a quality governed by personal investment in reciprocated dependence. From this foundational and conscious *belief in* and *belief that*, other investments in believing can proceed. Belief can be interpreted religiously only with an entry into a socially recognised symbolic order – and we are on the threshold of that here.

Nevertheless we need to pause and observe the possibility, even at this embryonic stage of consciousness, that there is an inner association between the interiority of belief, the wonder, the love, the investment of oneself in the meaningfulness of what is other and exterior, the dwelling and sense that one belongs, and religion. The world now exists *for us* and we exist *for* the world. The worlding of the world, as Heidegger would put it, is our creative project. And if that sounds anthropocentric, it's because it is; that anthropocentrism is key to the advance of our understanding as an animal species now distinct and different. But in the necessary projection of an investment of oneself beyond oneself, there is an element of transcendence that issues from a discovery of something new and a disclosure of what was not understood or clearly understood before. There is a moment in that complex interface between discovery, disclosure and creation in which there resides the intimation of a primordial givenness. To refer once more to Heidegger and the German language: in the elemental 'there is' (in German *es gibt*) lies a sense of a gift (*es gibt* can also be translated 'it gives' from the verb to give, *geben*). What gives is at the heart of the questions that remain, though some anthropologists venture to suggest that it is 'plausible to suppose, although beyond demonstration's possibilities, that religion's origins are, if not one with the origins of humanity, closely connected to them' (Rappaport). And Deacon notes, as a corollary of the association he makes between symbolic learning, language and pair-bonding, that we are on the cusp of ritual and liturgies of marriage. The movement from the concrete to the more abstract, which entry into the symbolic requires, is an investment in a 'higher' meaning and an entrustment to 'ideas' – which are invisible. In intimacy there arises a religious intimation.

Even so, let us be clear about a difference, a difference based upon belief as more primordial than religion as such. In the interface of discovery and disclosure there is also creation; there is also human fabrication. The meaningful, which is the living flame of the semantic leap I mentioned earlier, is not just what we discover or what is disclosed; it is also what we create as we dwell, as we world our worlds (and all the possible alternative worlds). Religion, and therefore religious faith, emphasises the discovery and the disclosure: it is the world that is meaningful, ordered, and structured as accommodating to human apprehension. Belief makes no such semantic claim: it allows for the creation of what is meaningful, it informs the way we see the world *as*, but the world may not be intrinsically meaningful. There may not be meaning 'out there' – nevertheless, because of belief, we who dwell within the world and respond to it will *make* it meaningful *for us*.

The difference here is crucial because belief can be qualified or even disqualified by unbelief or disbelief. Unbelief and disbelief are parasitic upon believing, but they reside within its operation. With the development of a symbolic system of language, the massive potential of disbelief reveals itself, not only in the conflict of interpretations but also the intentional deception of lying – the *making* of belief, the *making of meaning* with the intent of deceiving the other. But we have not yet entered the symbolic realm; the shared understanding and the sense of belonging is still gestural. The gesture is referential, but as an index of a socially reciprocated recognition. It is on the way to becoming a symbolic sign that can be abstracted from the concrete and detached from what it signifies. That detachment, as we will see, literally *makes* a world of difference and the possibility of different worlds.

To clarify this, allow me to return to a distinction I drew earlier on the basis of the work undertaken by Terrence Deacon: a distinction between 'communication' and 'language' – with language being the provenance of the symbolic. If I am right, then my own conclusion would suggest belief is between these two evolutionary stages: more cognitively advanced than the former, more primitive than the latter. Merlin Donald described this 'in-between', in which 'words don't substantially change the nonverbal elements of exchange', as mimetic. Others talk of protolanguage (Bickerton). Donald views mimesis as forming the core of an ancient root-culture that is distinctly human. Beyond the imitative, mimicking and conditioned responses of the animal world, 'mimesis rests on the ability to produce conscious, self-initiated, representational acts that are intentional but not linguistic'.

We can in fact view such acts in *Quest for Fire* itself, since much of the film is not communicated by language but manual gestures, bodily posture and facial expressions between the characters, and camera shots and editing by the director Jean-Jacques Annaud. Only human beings have an extensive range of facial expressions, though they do have (and human beings still retain) what some neuroscientists (Ploog, Sutton and Jurgens) have called 'limbic speech' – phonetic utterances which relate immediately to primitive emotions processed through the oldest parts of the brain and its connection to the nervous system: the limbic sphere. Such vocalisations cannot be controlled. Learning plays no part in their articulation because they are reflex-like in the immediate relation they have to perception and production. These are the cries of pain, fear, pleasure and surprise, and their immediacy of production is mirrored by the immediacy of response they can invoke. That's why most limbic speech is 'infective'. But it is '[s]elf-conscious action [that] is [...] the basis of mimesis' (Donald). And this introduces a whole new level of motor (rather than visceral, limbic) control over mimetic production, because they are 'voluntary' (from the Latin *volo*, 'I will'). Donald demonstrates that such mimesis is more efficient than language in communicating emotions, elementary skills and modelling social roles because it is more direct and so less open to ambiguity and a conflict of interpretations. Belief is not produced by such mimesis, but the circulation of belief in and through mimesis does operate to create, sustain and control social relations. Furthermore, belief is reproduced and reinforced by mimesis. Mimesis (as Donald represents it) *and* belief are at the root of ritual.

SUMMARY

Our archaeology of belief has led us back to the evolutionary development of *Homo erectus*: its migration beyond the frontiers of modern Africa; its ability to adapt to different climatic, geographical and geological conditions; its venture into advanced tool manufacture; its intentional use of fire; and, at some point, its burial of the dead. We are beginning to appreciate also the architecture of belief: its relation to cognitive capabilities like anticipation, projection, recognition, memory, association and communication. But to understand this architecture of belief more clearly we must now explore (as so many recent archaeologists and evolutionary psychologists have in their attempts to understand human development), its biology and psychology: how matter becomes mind, and how minds come to be conscious of themselves.

III

Emerging from the Cave:
The Architecture of Believing [1]

n the dark, the total dark, the subterranean dark, there is nothing. I once
experienced such a darkness, whilst potholing in Yorkshire, England. As
we were passing single file down a narrow limestone passage a hundred
metres or so below ground, wading through an icy stream that seemed to
flow even deeper into the tunnel ahead of us, the group were instructed
to stand still and turn off the lights on our helmets. The guide, twenty
metres ahead of us, held a torch shining upwards onto his face and warned
us what he was about to do. He then turned off his torch, and we were
all engulfed. The darkness was like nothing I had experienced before:
endless, but not empty. In fact, it was full of the echoing sound of water
flowing, plummeting somewhere, roaring. But the 'somewhere' was not
locatable. The sound crashed and ricocheted around us. I gripped the wet,
slimy walls of stone, pressing my hand more and more firmly into the
damp, cold surface. In letting go there was a dizzying sense of floating,
of movement. Not of being *one* with the water, but certainly being *akin*
to the water – liquid, formless – and one with the darkness. It is not just
states of perception that are altered in the darkness; states of consciousness are also altered.

   In altered states of consciousness, believing is accentuated because the
stability of what is perceived – which is stable only because it is in accord
with what is familiar, the recognition of which has become habitual – is disturbed. We enter the realms of the 'uncanny': in German *das Unheimliche*,

a word which, as Freud understood, is the destabilisation of all that we have come to know as home (*Heim*), homeland (*Heimat*) and customary (*heimatlich*). But as Freud also pointed out in his essay 'The Uncanny' (written in 1919 in the wake of the upheavals and devastation of the First World War, particularly in Austria), the uncanny is not something totally alien or even opposite of what is familiar, domesticated in and through dwelling. *Heimlich* also describes that which is secret, hidden. In common usage, he notes *das Heimliche* has been extended into its opposite, *das Unheimliche*, but there is a 'secret nature of the uncanny [...] for this uncanny is in reality nothing new or foreign, but something familiar and old – established in the mind that has been estranged only by the process of repression.' What the uncanny effects is an effacing of the distinction between imagination and reality. But in Freud's own account of the psychopathology of the everyday, reality is itself fragile and fabricated. The uncanny calls our attention to the brittle nature of our certainties, the ego's fathomless insecurities, the invisibility that haunts the visible, the unknown out of which the known is carved. We dwell still within the caves of belief.

Several of Freud's analyses of the uncanny take the form of observations on literary texts, particularly the tales of Hoffmann, as in the earlier study of the uncanny in the 1906 essay by the German psychiatrist Ernst Jentsch ('On the Psychology of the Uncanny'), which Freud draws on. We shall investigate the literary nature of believing, and the alterations of consciousness that aesthetic appreciation initiates, in Chapter VI. But Freud also recognised the uncanny as intrinsic to 'primitive man' with his 'primitive beliefs' – beliefs that, for Freud, were comparable to the fantasies of an infant; fantasies we can never really rid ourselves of, however grown up we become.

> It would seem as though each one of us has been through a phase of individual development corresponding to that animistic stage in primitive men, that none of us has traversed it without preserving certain traces of it which can be re-activated, and that everything which now strikes us as 'uncanny' fulfils the condition of stirring those vestiges of animistic mental activity within us and bringing them to expression.

The effects of the uncanny ripple down through prehistory, when human beings did not have 'homes' as permanent places of dwelling, and then into history. As with those early human beings gathered in a cave described towards the end of Freud's *Totem and Taboo*, circled with fears of the forbidden and the stews of incestuous desires, we are today still living out the psychosomatic impacts of our evolution. The uncanny, which alters our consciousness of things that can only ever be perceived *as*, awakens believing that is more primordial. Freud had read Émile Durkheim, who also wished to return to the caves of prehistory in order to understand *The Elementary Forms of Religious Life* (1912).

If now we take a tentative step towards religious believing, it is not to focus on religious beliefs as such. That would be too presumptive. We still need to understand something more about believing itself.

One archaeologist who has done much to enable us to understand the relationship between altered states of consciousness and caves is the South African scholar David Lewis-Williams. With Lewis-Williams we're in safe hands, even when handling representations of religious belief. He doesn't believe in religion anyway: it's all in the mind, or rather it's all a matter (literally) of the electrochemical flows through synaptic connections, transmitting information from cell to cell through the dendrites (inputs) and axons (outputs) that govern neural activity.

CAVES AND CONSCIOUSNESS

Lewis-Williams covers a major period of human flourishing which takes place in the Upper Palaeolithic and Neolithic period, in particular between 77,000 and 6,500 years ago, between a piece of ochre carefully incised with geometric patterns, found in a rock shelter at Blombos on the South African coast, and curious statues found in 'Ain Ghazal, close to Amman in Jordan, with their staring eyes outlined in bitumen. In between these dates his most concentrated work focuses upon the rock art in the Volp caves of Ariège, the Chauvet cave of Ardèche, also in France, and the Altamira cave on the Cantabrian coast of Spain. What he is attempting to access, as he examines this diverse range of work from different locations, and the portable works of art like a spear-thrower carved in the shape of a leaping horse, or the carving of a bison out of mammoth ivory, is 'knowledge about the universal foundations of diversity [...] We need to ask: What anchors facets of human behaviour that turn up in culture after culture? What leads to these commonalities?' His answer is the neurological structure of the brain and the mind or consciousness it gives rise to. But most importantly for Lewis-Williams, the consciousness is not one thing: it is a spectrum.

Lewis-Williams builds on the work of another cognitive archaeologist, Steven Mithen, who we first met in Chapter I. Mithen was one of the first to attempt to construct an 'architecture of the human mind' and describe its evolution, using fossil evidence from the australopithecines down to *Homo sapiens*. Mithen depicts the human mind as a cathedral. The central nave is given over to general intelligence, and he credits many forms of animal with such intelligence. But then there are add-ons – in particular technical intelligence (how to use and make tools), natural history intelligence (know-how about the natural world and its physical phenomena), social intelligence (working with and relating to others) and linguistic intelligence (the ability to convert cognitive representational mapping of the world into symbolic re-representation of that world, and then communicate it).

Each of these cognitive competences is like an antechapel nestling in an alcove sealed off from the main nave of general intelligence. Mithen accounts for what he calls, with self-conscious irony, the 'big bang of human culture', through the modular development of these competences (particularly by *Homo erectus* and his descendants the Neanderthals). The development is modular because each antechapel is kept sealed off from the others. Subsequently, around 40,000 years ago (though others offer an earlier date), after the appearance of *Homo sapiens* and plastic image-making, the antechapels start to speak to each other and interconnect as associative and analogical thinking develop and there is the emergence of 'cognitive fluidity'. One of the major aspects of such fluidity is the ability of the mind to be creative – that is, give rise, in the confluence of technical, social, and linguistic intelligence of the natural world to religion, art and science.

As we will come to observe, much contemporary cognitive and neuroscience rejects this modular architecture of the human mind, even when it comes to language where two regions of the brain (Broca's and Wernicke's) have long been associated with language production and comprehension. Nevertheless, there are things we can learn about the architecture of the human mind as Mithen constructed it, and Lewis-Williams develops it – even though Lewis-Williams has his reservations, most particularly about the central figure of 'rationality' in defining intelligence. The prominence of 'consciousness of rationality' is viewed as 'Western' and scientific in its bias. Mithen's architecture reflects 'an historically situated notion [of both intelligence and consciousness] within a specific social context'. Lewis-Williams proposes an alternative based upon the work of two cognitive scientists (Colin Martindale and Charles Laughlin): a spectrum of consciousness that, at a certain point, subdivides.

THE SPECTRUM OF CONSCIOUSNESS

Consider a lazy day on vacation: the sun is high, the sky a clear duck-egg blue, and you set off for an ambling walk to the beach. First, there is a lunch to think of and plan. A simple lunch of bread, cheese and pickle chosen from among a number of different foodstuffs in the kitchen. Lunch prepared, you look at the fruit bowl and decide to take an apple. Then you remember you will need something to drink, so hunt for a suitable plastic bottle. There are the remnants of some lime cordial in one, but you can pour much of this into a cup so as to not waste it, and you fill the bottle (with some cordial still in it) with water. You set off with your map and a book and walk for some time, making observations on the trees and hedgerows, recalling the last time you were here, thinking of friends and family back home, cursorily dwelling on problems at work that are yet to be resolved, imagining what it would be like to stay here by the sea and retire early, enacting in your head little scenarios that might occur when you tell your family and the people in the office of your plans. You find a path down to the coast, checking it against the map. The path is marked but overgrown, and a fence has to be negotiated. On the other side of the fence you pick up the path, and follow it as it wends towards the sea. At one point it disappears and you find yourself in a boggy area without the right footwear. But there's a large piece of driftwood you can use to cross the worst of it, and some semblance of a path is picked up further down. At the beach you find a good sheltered spot in the sun, with rocks to your back and the sea creeping up the sand in small waves. You sit and decide to read for a while – a novel about a New York detective in the latter part of the nineteenth century investigating a series of brutal murders in which the bodies are being buried in the foundations for the pillars in the construction of the Brooklyn Bridge. The sun is warm and you doze off, dreaming of waves and huge iron girders, the steep descent down a rugged bank towards the Hudson River, where you encounter your boss…

What we have in this scenario is a spectrum of normal modern consciousness over a given stretch of time. Images, narrative, focused attention on objects being perceived, all flowing easily and seamlessly into a single stream. Consciousness seems holistic, but it is also variegated: moving across past, present and future, moving between observation and problem-solving, slipping the fictitious into the factual, imagined places into real places, etc. At points you are alert, concentrating on what you are working at (making lunch, reading a map, relating the map to the landscape) and problem-solving (finding a suitable water bottle, negotiating a fence or a boggy patch). At points you are daydreaming, fantasising, recalling scenes and snatches of conversation from the past. At points you are reading imaginatively, engaged in someone else's fantasies, conjuring up people, places and incidents far removed from your own situation. At points you are in a hypnagogic state when the words on the page blur in the warmth of the sun, and as your muscles relax, images fluidly come, go, fade, melt and transfigure. You begin to dream, and in your dream unconscious elements surface, like the workplace which you have been trying hard to avoid, being on vacation, and its problems, focusing upon your boss.

I stated that the holistic nature of the stream of consciousness was only a *seeming*. The holism may not be the nature of consciousness itself, as we will see, but the way consciousness works to cut, paste, edit and delete in order to present a single stream. One can imagine writing an account of one's morning or telling someone on the phone that evening of how pleasant the day had been in ways which script the narrative and its details differently and bring about new emphases, new perspectives.

Charles Laughlin calls what I have been describing the 'fragmented consciousness': over a period of time, particularly when we are relaxing, we move in and out of a shifting set of mental representations, some of which are orientated to the external world and some of which are orientated towards our interior state. Martindale, whose work researches the states of mind between wakefulness and rapid eye movement sleep (REM – a state that precedes deep sleep), charts six stages of everyday consciousness along a spectrum running from alert to autistic, which Lewis-Williams charts horizontally along a line from problem-solving to daydreaming, hypnagogic states, dreaming and the unconscious. The significance of this horizontal plotting will become evident in a moment.

If this is normal fragmented consciousness, in which what we are conscious of at any given time is shifting and being altered, then what happens when that consciousness is deliberately manipulated? For example, Martindale does not put 'reading a novel' into his spectrum, but for many of us reading a novel, watching a film, tuning into a radio station or turning on the TV are part of our deliberate manipulation of the fragmented consciousness. Furthermore, if I had decided not to take the bottled water on my picnic but a can of beer instead, the alcohol would also have impacted upon that shifting consciousness, heightening for a time certain external and internal representations. The gates between external observation and internal fantasy, external and internal stimuli, open towards each other. It is at this point on the mainline of everyday consciousness that a branch line emerges, orientated towards a deepening interiority. This branch line is not just the result of psychotropic substances; it can emerge through sensory deprivation (fasting, pain, tiredness, being in the dark) and sensory overloading (the rhythmic beating of a drum, the drip of water, rocking or swaying back and forth). In both of these states, what Martindale calls the brain's 'stimulus hunger' feeds off its own inner workings.

This branch line of consciousness Lewis-Williams calls the 'intensified trajectory'. It branches off the main line around the hypnagogic point and, for him, it reaches its terminus in hallucinations. There are two stages in between: stage one is entoptic phenomena, and stage two is what he vaguely names 'construal'. Entoptic (from the Greek *entos* 'within' and *optikos* 'visual') phenomena are those visual sensations produced within the eye itself (rather than the brain) – dots, grids, zigzags, meandering lines, etc. – viewed even when the eye is closed. They are networked into our nervous system and arise because of the patterns of electrical connections between the retina and that part of the brain that receives visual signals (the striate cortex) relayed by one or both of the lateral geniculate nuclei on the right and left hemispheres of the brain. These inner visual phenomena, when intensified, become sketchy forms that are associated with objects in the world the perceiver is familiar with. As Lewis-Williams puts it: 'A visual image reaching the brain is decoded [...] by being matched against a store of experiences.' This is what he means by 'construal'. But then he adds a hiatus between this second stage and the third stage, hallucination. He calls this the 'vortex'. The vortex is that dizzying, vertiginous slide, experienced sometimes as floating and sometimes as flight, into the hallucinating trance. It is currently under investigation by those examining near-death experiences, where entry into a tunnel is frequently reported. It is the portal to another world, with similarities to the hypnagogic condition just prior to REM dreaming.

THE PSYCHOBIOLOGY OF ALTERED STATES

Lewis-Williams proposes on the basis of these 'architectures of belief' a psychobiology of altered states of consciousness which, he argues, provides a) all the types of rock art he comments upon, and b) the shaman narratives of the three-tiered cosmos that he employs to unpick the meanings of what is figured in this rock art, with a universal condition: the evolved human body, its brain and its nervous system. And so the horizontal depiction of the spectrum of human consciousness is mapped onto two-dimensional plans of the Volp, Lascaux, Gabillou or Chauvet caves. The caves themselves are entrances to the spirit world underground. At their entrances the community share a common daily life. There is a wider chamber in which certain members of the community participate in rituals, a vortex negotiated by certain specified initiates and, finally, the culmination in a vision quest.

This culmination is most spectacular in the second of the Volp caves, Les Trois Frères, where in a chamber called the Sanctuary the initiate encounters the painting of 'the Sorcerer'. This is a painting situated on a high rock ledge, arrived at through a narrow tunnel. The legs of the figure painted are human, but the face is more of an owl's topped with the antlers of a red deer, and the figure has a horse's tail. This 'therianthrope' 'suggests belief in a powerful chthonic being whose transcendence of the human: animal dichotomy people emulated in altered states.' The figure is the climax of a process of transformation in which animal becomes human, and human animal, and the spiritual material and the material spiritual. In sum:

> Caves became the models of, and locales for, transcosmological journeys. People interacted with the immutable forms of the caves. We can see evidence for their religious beliefs and practices. We can also infer the kind of mental experiences that led to and accompanied those beliefs and practices. Importantly, the experiences, beliefs and practices that we can detect fit together to form a logical, coherent whole – a religion.

The walls of the caves are considered to be membranes, so that 'for Upper Palaeolithic people, touching the rock was touching a powerful, perhaps dangerous cosmological interface.' The animals themselves are integral parts of the rock surface and are viewed as mediators of the different cosmological levels. Their representations show no ground surface or natural habitat, so the figures float. In the flickering lights of a smoking torch they would have shape-shifted and have more of the character of hallucinations. My own experience of altered consciousness during a blackout in the cave at the start of this chapter concurs with this possibility.

In brief, the unity of both religious belief and human social experience is neurologically generated. So the cave for Lewis-Williams, as in Plato's *Republic*, is the mind, and the journey undertaken is a psychobiological one into the depths of the unconscious. This psychobiological condition is the constant in all manifestations of religion (and art). It is institutionalised, and therefore experienced, in any number of ways, from cave painting and portable ice-age art to the Neolithic tombs at Newgrange in Ireland, the fifteenth-century painting by Hieronymus Bosch, *The Ascent into the Empyrean*, found in the Doge's palace in Venice, and the nineteenth-century depiction by Gustave Doré of Dante's vision of the route to the Empyrean.

EXPLAINING RELIGION AND
EVERYTHING ELSE

Given that most of the representational work that Lewis-Williams examines has been viewed as associated with beliefs with a religious significance, he then joins a long list of 'reductionist materialist atheist[s]' (Wolpert) in showing the significant role this universal neurological condition plays in 'explaining' religion. All religious representation, ritual and myth-making is a product of this somatic and neural activity, even though the activity itself is given local and contextual colour through associating and interpreting an interior state alongside external experiences. Here we are provided with the cognitive origin and evolution of religion (as the subtitle of Lewis-Williams' most recent book phrases it). These Palaeolithic peoples

> merely had to deal with the weird, non-real experiences that their brains sometimes generated. And they did so by accepting the existence of a parallel realm where all this was happening [...] Belief in a supernatural realm thus formed in parallel with conscious perception of the material world [and] symbolic thought.

But this insistence on scientific and reductive materialism is to some extent at odds with the way Lewis-Williams wishes his spectrum of altered human consciousness to supplement Mithen's Western and emphatically rational architectural model. Because Mithen's model is supplemented by taking account of non-rational elements – elements which remain hardwired into the kind of mammal we are and the minds we have evolved to possess. He conjures a world imbued with the mythopoeic, and points to how it emerged, then cultivated and dominated thinking and sensibilities. But the wonder, awe and terror expressed, he claims, is now difficult to appreciate 'because our sense of causality and our categories of thought' (the scientific and reductive materialist categories) are different. He tells us that caves that were no longer dwelling places for human beings became cosmic theatres evoking and possibly teaching beliefs. Participation in whatever rituals took place in these caves reinforced the beliefs, and the paintings of the animals, which used the faults, fissures and nodules of the rock face to accentuate the form and movement of their representations, may indeed have been participations themselves in the mythic world of the caves. Pieces of bone are found pushed into the crevasses of the rocks like votive offerings. Prints of hands and silhouettes of hands are found throughout these caves as indices of cultic participation. And yet this interpretation of the caves and the beliefs they invoke is an *appreciation* of the irrational and mythopoeic.

Let me put my irritation and puzzlement more precisely. To an archaeologist and anthropologist examining ancient rock art and megalithic burial sites, these archaeological works reveal minds very different to the minds shaped by Western rationalisation. Agreed. And yet, ultimately, Lewis-Williams as that archaeologist and anthropologist wishes to explain away the irrational and mythopoeic by referring it to the most recent explorations by Western rationalists: the electrochemical functioning of the brain. He conjures the magical literally in his writing in order to account for it through the researches of cognitive- and neuroscience. The logic of his method is all very curious and circular. Beginning and ending with the superiority of Western rationalism, its rejection of religious experience and its erasing of the sacred from the secular, Lewis-Williams' work seems to reinforce the dominance of Western rationalism – at the highly reductive cost of all the fabulous and imaginative treasures he has presented to us. *Logos* triumphs over *mythos*. The evocative richness of these products as prehistoric belief is reduced to so many side-effects of physiology. What certain philosophers of mind would call his 'eliminative materialism' explains (away) everything.

And yet the power of his conjuring remains. That is why he is read, and the plaudits by academics attest to the 'fascinating' and 'powerfully evocative' character of his 'adventure in the archaeology of religion'. The weird, the uncanny, the paranormal, the supernatural still fascinate – and he can give no account of that continuing fascination *in the face of* his atheistic materialism. Lewis-Williams does not confront his own belief systems, his own belief-biases – the superiority of his secular and enlightenment liberalism. The institutions of his own social and cultural context somehow transcend and support the universalism of his psychobiology – as if that very psychobiology itself was not a product of such a context. For him, it is the neurological that gives rise to the cultural, so, for example, Hildegard of Bingen's twelfth-century mystical visions are the result of a migraine. Lewis-Williams may persuade himself and others that he has explained the experiences and behaviour of the shamanic seer, but he fails to account for his own seeing. He is a certain scientist seer. That's all. And Mithen has a similar view: the architecture of the human mind is the origin of art, religion and science. Plot the architecture and you can then observe how communication between the different chambers or antechapels gives rise to Buddhism, Michelangelo and Einstein.

WHAT IS MISSING?

Both these views fail to account for two important aspects of human evolution. First, nature does not give rise unilaterally to culture. There is a co-evolution. Put simply: believing moulds the neural networks of the brain *for* belief. Believing gives rise to behaviours that, in turn, modify the psychobiology of the human beings who believe. That is why we needed to account for the unprecedented explosions of encephalisation first with the ascent of *Homo erectus* and then around 500,000 years ago with *Homo heidelbergensis*. It is not the case that we evolve the capacity to shape tools and carve mammoth tusk. These tasks instead mould the brains and bodies we have. We don't just biologically adapt to our landscapes, we shape and impact upon those landscapes in ways which require us to readapt. Today, if your internet connection doesn't work for a week, you recognise how you have adapted to living with email, for example. But the interruption is not just a damn inconvenience as you rush off to some internet café to access your account. The interruption, the frustration it causes, and the anxieties – about having missed something important or not being able to respond to something important promptly – all have physiological effects. The situation can only have these physiological effects because you have adapted physiologically to having easy access to electronic communications. They have not only made your life easier, but in making your life easier the autonomic biological regulation of your living accommodates itself to that ease. Ergo: the relationship between the mental experiences necessary to create the paintings in the caves (like belief, thought, forethought or planning, consciousness and a sense of agency) and brain processes is not one of simple cause and effect. As Terrence Deacon explains: 'In fact, probably the vast majority of brain processes contributing to our moment-to-moment behavior and subjective experience are never associated with consciousness.'

Secondly, and as a corollary of the first point: in co-evolution the world is not simply the given to our senses such that our bodies become organic receptors of information. The objective and external nature of the given as such is a myth. The world is given, created, discloses itself to and affects us. It is through this impossible-to-divorce association of the inner workings of the body, the productions of the mind and the external environment that a certain fittingness or accommodation comes about. As embodied creatures with an expanded prefrontal cortex we receive, adapt and modify. This raises a question that we will need to examine further. Natural selection as it is conceived from Darwin to Dawkins is a blind, accident-driven process. It is non-teleological. How then does the driven and teleological nature of 'disposition' and 'intention', even at the organic level, relate to the non-teleology of evolution? Adaption *is* purposeful: to find the best ecological 'fit' between corporeality, mind and circumstance that will better facilitate survival. How does teleology emerge from the non-teleological? We have to leave that question hanging for the moment.

There is yet a further complication with the correlation of cave-clambering and an odyssey through the spectrum of consciousness. The cave remains material; so do the representations of the animals on the walls, however thin the membrane separating us from the other world. Scraping one's knees in negotiating a tunnel, banging one's hand on a low-hanging stalactite, tripping over the skull of a bear will always be reminders of the cave's materiality. Consciousness is not material. It may be motored by neurological feedback and feedforward loops and somatic affects, but it remains invisible. No one perceives another's consciousness. So a radical disjunction still remains between the cave and the mind, however much one may affect the other. The difference cannot be collapsed into a single causal, one-way logic. As we saw with belief in the last chapter, mind is not the same as matter. That's why the archaeologists and anthropologists sometimes define us as *Homo sapiens sapiens*: we are conscious of our minds within and distinct from the materiality of worlds we create.

Now, mind not being the same as matter raises the shadow – and indeed it is a shadow – of dualism. And, despite the phantom in our opening

Winter's Tale, I am not wanting to produce a ghost in a machine. But I am not wanting to produce zombies, either – biologically programmed machines in which there is 'no one at home'. We need more complex models of the relation between matter and mind, and we will go on to develop a more complex model in the next chapter. For the moment, where do the architectonics of Mithen and Lewis-Williams leave belief? Back, I suggest, in the cave and the power of its suggestion. Certainly, to ask about the *making* of belief is to ask questions about the human mind, its somatic relations to the brain, the viscera, the spinal cord, breathing, blood and body tissue. We need to move, then, from cognitive archaeology to cognitive architecture. We have learnt that belief is bound up with a number of evolved rational competences (Mithen) and a consciousness spectrum that can be altered by environmental or self-induced conditions (Lewis-Williams), but it cannot be reduced to these competences or conditions. Belief can submit itself to technological, social, linguistic and natural historical processes: that will give it expression. But belief is prior to these. It can surface within consciousness and must do so in order to be given expression. But it is prior to consciousness. We believe more than we know – and there are certain experiences of consciousness that enable us to understand that. What we need now is to explore that psychobiological territory between what Lewis-Williams depicts at the limits of consciousness – the unconscious – and the transcending invisibilities of our mental life.

LATERALISATION

Despite much work done by neuroscientists, neither Mithen nor Lewis-Williams writes about the lateralisation of the brain. Consciousness concerns the prefrontal cortex, but neither mentions that there are two frontal lobes – the left and the right – and that they do two different but complementary and interrelated things. In the last two chapters I wrote about belief as preconscious and implicit. It comes to the fore in 're-cognition', but the extent to which it is cognitive remains unexplored. It is the burden of Iain McGilchrist's groundbreaking volume – *The Master and His Emissary: The Divided Brain and the Making of the Western World* – that the purely cognitive functions of being human belong to the productions of the left hemisphere of the brain. McGilchrist, who is a British psychiatrist, informs us that the right hemisphere has perceptual awarenesses of its own – creative, intuitive, emotional, imaginative – and much of it is preconscious. That is not to say the right hemisphere doesn't think. It does – but in a much more inchoate, diffuse, 'big-picture' manner.

We share this division within the brain (lateralisation) with any number of other animals, but it is a division in human beings that the evolution of the frontal lobes extended. Lateralisation, for McGilchrist, has profound cultural implications. The second half of his book charts the historical swings between the dominance of the two hemispheres to the point where, in the modern world, the left hemisphere, which should be the emissary that decodes and illuminates the messages from the right, informing the whole body, has now usurped the place of the master, the right hemisphere. To be fully human requires that we address this imbalance and recover the wealth of creative understanding produced in the right hemisphere of the brain. To continue to neglect this hemisphere will have co-evolutionary consequences: because the brain is so plastic, those associated links within the brain which are underused will not be strengthened – so imagination weakens, and likewise the capacity to be creative and to respond intuitively to the environment. An extended citation will assist here:

> Belief is not to be reduced to thinking that such-and-such might be the case. It is not a weaker form of thinking, laced with doubt [...] Since the left hemisphere is concerned with what is certain, with knowledge of the facts, its version of belief is that it is just absence of certainty. If the facts were certain, according to its view, I should be able to say 'I know that' instead. This view of belief comes from the left hemisphere's disposition towards the world [...] So belief is just a feeble form of knowing, as far as it is concerned.
>
> But belief in terms of the right hemisphere is different, because the disposition towards the world is different. The right hemisphere does not 'know' anything, in the sense of certain knowledge. For it, belief is a matter of care: it describes a *relationship*, where there is a calling and an answering, the root concept of 'responsibility'. Thus if I say that 'I believe in you', it does not mean that I think that

such-and-such things are the case about you, but can't be certain that I am right. It means that I stand in a certain sort of relation of care towards you, that entails me in certain kinds of ways of behaving (acting and being) towards you, and entails on you the responsibility of certain ways of acting and being as well [...] It has the characteristic right-hemisphere qualities of being a betweenness: a reverberative, 're-sonant', 'respons-ible' relationship in which each party is altered by the other and by the relationship between the two, whereas the relationship of the believer to the believed in the left-hemisphere sense is inert, unidirectional, and centres on control rather than care.

This account takes us back to *Quest for Fire*: belief is relational; it concerns 're-cognition' that is also responsive (and bears that responsibility). It is implicit knowledge rather than knowledge *as such*.

McGilchrist is careful not to construct a binarism here between the left and right hemispheres (although his work helps us to understand how such binarisms can be constructed and pass themselves off as true and natural).

[T]he right hemisphere, though it is not dependent on the left hemisphere in the same way that the left is on the right, nonetheless *needs* it in order to achieve its full potential, in some sense to become fully itself. Meanwhile the left hemisphere is dependent upon the right hemisphere both to ground its world, at the 'bottom' end, and to lead it back to life, at the 'top'.

So there are myriad and subtle ways in which they can and should inform each other, although the 'controlling' character of left-hemisphere thinking can assert an overriding command and be convinced of its autonomy. Hence, as I have suggested, believing should be understood as a mode of cognition, a mental activity, imbued with the affective – summed up in McGilchrist in the term 'care' as a disposition towards the world. 'Cognition in the right hemisphere is not a process of something coming into being through adding piece to piece in a sequence, but of something that is out of focus coming into focus, as a whole,' McGilchrist writes. Right hemisphere believing is more directly in contact with the world. That is why it is more primordial, both anthropologically in terms of prehistory (our archaeology of belief) and neurologically in terms of brain/body processing (our architecture of belief). The right hemisphere does have its own cognitive and therefore conscious capacities. It does have a place therefore within the spectrum of consciousness we explored above. It apprehends, though not always in a fully conscious way, more quickly than the left hemisphere – by a full half-second, according to certain neuroscientists. It is, particularly, the production site for the creative imagination, whilst simultaneously related more directly to the emotional life of the body and its autonomic responsiveness. But the articulation, evaluation and analysis of belief are more left-hemisphere activities because the left hemisphere governs calculation, cataloguing, language production and the instrumental, abstractive processes of ratiocination.

Working together, the left and right hemispheres of the brain make believing a mode of cognition associated with imagination, motivation, desire, intuition and feeling. It captures the provisionality and elusiveness of knowing. By motivation here I mean the energies that swirl within embodiment itself, fed by air and water and various foods, orientated by appetite – Spinoza would say *conatus* (the self-protective drive to live) – and desire (which is more than appetite, deeper than appetite, because it longs for what it cannot name). The Slovenian philosopher Slavoj Žižek, following in the wake of the French psychoanalyst Jacques Lacan, speaks about 'the abyss of the Other's impenetrable desire'. The word 'motivation' is from the Latin to move, to motor. If, as has been suggested in Chapter I, consciousness emerges with movement and locomotion, then it is also related, through consciousness, to motivation. And motivation is associated with disposition, orientation and intention.

Belief is unavoidable; it is fundamental to that economy spoken of in the last chapter of anticipation–projection–reception–recognition–response. Because we live in the world, because the world lives in us, we relate to it and we make sense of it. In McGilchrist's term, we care. As such *credo* is not necessarily and immediately linked to a calculus of probabilities and 'causal thinking' (Wolpert), but rather to relational categories like trust, loyalty and empathy. Drawing attention to the etymological association of truth and belief, McGilchrist writes:

The Latin word *verum* (true) is cognate with a Sanskrit word meaning to choose or believe: the option one chooses, the situation in which one places one's trust. Such a situation is not an absolute – it tells us not only about the chosen thing, but also about the chooser. It cannot be certain: it involves an act of faith, and it involves being faithful to one's intuitions.

A CRITICAL PAUSE

Now we need to pause here in McGilchrist's advocacy for the recovery of the right-hemisphere believing – rather than the left-hemisphere certainty – as the deliverer of new possibilities for moral, social, philosophical and aesthetic development. It is the alignment of belief with choice that creates room for the pause. For who is doing the choosing? Belief as an unalienable disposition towards the world, an anthropological a priori, would not be simply a matter of personal choice, not unless we could choose that towards which we wish to be disposed. Such choosing, such decision-taking on the basis of being 'faithful to one's intuitions' would involve left-hemisphere activity. McGilchrist is certainly arguing that the left hemisphere should serve, as emissary, right-hemisphere mastery. We must enquire then about belief *and* acting on the basis of an articulated consciousness of what is believed. It is not that belief has nothing to do with choice, but we need to be clearer about the relation between them, and they cannot be the same thing (despite what etymology might indicate).

The question of their relationship is highly significant with respect to religious faith, which we will discuss in Chapter VIII. McGilchrist flattens any distinction between belief and faith in a way that returns us to what is troubling, or at least making a pause necessary, in the association of choice and belief:

Some people choose to believe in materialism; they act 'as if' such a philosophy is true. An answer to the question of whether God exists could only come from my acting 'as if' God is, and in this way being true to God, and experiencing God (or not, as the case might be) as true to me. If I am a believer I have to believe in God, and God, if he exists, has to believe in me.

This is stylistically neat, with an echo of Meister Eckhart, but for a religious believer it actually drives a wedge between belief and faith on several grounds. First, that characterisation of believing as acting 'as if' is rather condescending; for from what exalted level can one judge another person to be acting 'as if' what they believe is true – rather than acting in conviction that this is indeed true? The logic of 'as if' here introduces into belief a degree of untruth, a degree of being true that is less than the true. Of course with belief there are no certainties, but the motivating force of some beliefs (I haven't defined what might characterise such beliefs yet) would not admit that one's experience of the world was just a matter of optatives and subjunctives, hopeful wishes and may-bes. Secondly, to what extent does anyone 'choose to believe'? I can think of one parallel to such a situation which does actually treat 'choosing to believe' 'as if' something were true. It is a scene from the Wachowskis' film *The Matrix* (1999) in which Cypher, who has betrayed Morpheus, Trinity, Neo and the others who exist outside the simulated world created by the intelligent machines, sits in a restaurant with the agents who have been trying to track down the felons. He stares at the steak on his plate, lifts his knife and fork, and tells the two agents that he knows it is not real, that the Matrix has engineered this simulacrum; nevertheless, he gives himself up to enjoying the illusion. But the nature of such believing has the pathological logic of sadomasochism; that is, the satisfaction of a desire knowing the true object of that desire has been substituted for an illusory one. And so pleasure is taken in what desire knows is lacking. This is the logic of the 'as if... but nevertheless'. Agreed, there is a choice, and Cypher articulates that choosing very clearly; but it is a perverse choice and a perversion of choice, for this is the freedom to choose the form of one's bondage. Slavoj Žižek immensely enjoys such symptoms.

Belief disposes, even orientates, but it does not determine; and so there is room for assent or dissent by a 'self' we have not even begun yet to examine. We will tackle the notion of selfhood and go some way to erase any notion of an inner homunculus in the next chapter. For the moment, what is troubling in McGilchrist's description is the 'as if' element which associates believing with wishful thinking. We can still legitimately explore the question of choosing what one believes, omitting the 'as if'. In fact, such a liberty is the basis of rational-choice theory. I can choose to be a materialist, to take McGilchrist's example, or a Marxist. Actually it does not necessarily follow that my actions and behaviour are dictated by such a choice. There are materialist atheists like Daniel Dennett and Richard Dawkins who accept that every organism is a disposable machine for the transmission of DNA – only DNA survives; everything else is used to ensure that survival. But, really, is that how they perceive their loved ones and how they respond to the corpses of children who have been chemically exterminated in the dusty suburbs of Damascus? That's some acute form of cognitive dissonance! And I have known several self-proclaimed and even celebrated Marxists with a very keen eye for a capitalist contract. Still, I can choose to believe that, rationally calculated, materialism or Marxism best fit the facts as we have them. But this form of believing is much more akin to Locke's account of knowledge that we will detail in the next chapter; it is believing very much in service to the probability calculus of left-hemisphere thinking. It cannot be equated, as McGilchrist does, with faith.

Certainly, there is a circularity about believing in God that is an important aspect of a pious pedagogy: the more one submits to faith, the more one is confirmed within that faith (though still allowance has to be made for very ordinary periods of what mystics in a more elevated sense called the dark night of the soul). But I do not choose to believe in the same manner that I choose to vote Labour or grow rhubarb rather than radishes. In fact, choice here is far too locked into the assumption of a Cartesian, monadic ego who does the choosing; an ego that is not so prevalent in right-hemisphere activity because of the concern for relation. There are religious accounts, some of them holy texts prescribed by the monotheistic religions, which bear witness to an experience not of choosing God but being chosen by God. Such a re-cognition is based in something familiar, something half-known, known intuitively, known in the very substructures of our being human. It returns us to one of the moments in self-consciousness I drew attention to in the last chapter: the givenness of things. In seeing *as* there is always a moment of what is given in seeing. Seeing *as* is not the same as seeing *as if*. In creative imagining there is always a moment of consciously imaging what is disclosed to us. There is in the 'there is' (in German *es gibt*) what is given. As such, in McGilchrist's characterisation of believing, choosing and the 'as if', neither does justice to the rich complexity of belief in a creator God nor fully describes the disclosive nature of what comes with such a belief.

CONCLUSION

All I have said does not invalidate McGilchrist's important observations on belief. It simply helps us to clarify the difference between belief and faith that will assist us later. To recap: at this point I am treating believing as distinct from the religious form belief may take, while drawing attention to an association between belief and religion that I will examine later. Nevertheless, on his analysis of the relation between choosing and belief, McGilchrist does seem to slip from either right-hemisphere activity or the coordination of right- with left-hemisphere activity, into purely left-hemisphere ratiocination. Right-hemisphere belief is inchoate and implicit knowing (which is active and concrete, unlike the abstractions of 'knowledge'). It is the basis for moral responsibility, empathy and a generous acceptance of what is there. On this basis, McGilchrist constructs a history showing the increasing dominance of left- over right-hemisphere thinking. What should have been the emissary has become the master. So today we are in need of an 'unworlding' of the world that has been made in the left hemisphere's image.

Let me add something now about the advocacy for this 'unworlding', which will be taken up and developed in Chapter VIII but which relates to the architectures of belief we have been examining in this chapter. The 'unworlding' is most keenly pursued in the penultimate chapter of McGilchrist's book, where he presents the modern and the postmodern world view that has issued from the slide into the predominance of left-hemisphere instrumental rationalism. Lewis-Williams' functionalism is an example of such rationalism. The twentieth- and early-twenty-first-century culture of the West is characterised by 'a loss of meaning in the experienced world', which inaugurates a certain schizophrenia. In fact, for McGilchrist – who adheres to co-evolution in which the operations of the brain not only constitute and adapt to the world in its own image but the world in turn informs and develops the operations of the brain – an analysis of the world of a schizophrenic provides us with insights into the world that we live in. In this schizophrenia, while there is an increasing drive towards certainty, transparency and the immediacy of knowing, there is also, simultaneously, a drive towards 'derealisation' in which the world is 'robbed of its substantiality'. As such the world is increasingly unworlded by left-hemisphere predilections because it is increasingly emptied of 'its human resonance or significance'. And so we have fragmentation, aliena-tion and reductive abstractions on the one hand, and the crass appeal to the self-evidently material on the other. In rather telling phrases, McGilchrist writes about how 'the left hemisphere interposes a simulacrum between reality and our consciousness' and this leads to the '[i]ncreasing virtuality' of human experience. These terms 'simulacrum' and 'virtuality', and the acceleration in their production, are exactly what change the architecture that organises our understanding of knowledge, and therefore the nature of believing.

What McGilchrist's analysis suggests is that there is not only a history of cognitive contention installed by lateralisation, but that this history is part of the co-evolution of human beings and their cultures. It provides an alternative and less rationalist account of Mithen's 'cognitive fluidity' in which belief plays an important part. A number of critics of Mithen's architecture of the human mind have drawn attention to the weak link: that process which breaks down the compartmentalising walls between different conscious know-hows (technological, social, natural historical, linguistic). Mithen places all the weight for the breakdown upon the development of language, but McGilchrist's model of brain operations and consciousness suggests that the communication between the know-hows concerns media-tions between left- and right-hemisphere operations. The development of successful (in evolutionary terms) social knowledge, for example, is much more a right-hemisphere activity, as is natural historical knowledge (the intuitive association of prints and faeces with particular animals to be hunted, for example). Technological knowledge is much more the remit of left-hemisphere processing, along with language competency, abstraction, categorisation and symbolic activity. If cultural history *does* reveal to us a cognitive contention, with evolutionary consequences for adaptation (and we are still co-evolving), then it demonstrates the way the human brain works, like the human body, towards a homeostasis or the right ordering of right- and left-hemisphere activities.

This historical perspective has a further corollary for the architecture of belief: its changing structure; its historical and cultural contextualisation. We will begin to see more of this changing structure of the believable and the unbelievable – and its relation to the values of certainty, trust, relationality, motivation, intuition – when we investigate our two other sets of questions: what makes a belief *believable* and what *makes* a belief believable.

Before adding two more levels of our architecture of belief, and concluding this chapter and our investigations into the first set of questions concerning what *makes* a belief, let me recap what McGilchrist's work has enabled us to recognise. Three points are salient. First, believing not as a weak form of knowing but a faithfulness to one's intuitions that will always remain somewhat inchoate, even if resonant with meaning, is a right-hemisphere cognitive and affective activity. It is a faithfulness to pursuing those intuitions, seeking to understand them; it makes religious faith possible (but not necessary). Secondly, modernity is driven by the need for true and certain knowledge discovered, measured and evaluated through instrumental reasoning that requires faster and increasingly more efficient forms of technology, bureaucracy and surveillance to filter out untruth and illusion. This drive expresses the betrayal of the Master (right-hemisphere activity) by the emissary (left-hemisphere activity). Thirdly, by cutting itself off from the experiential grounding, concern for context and time, and caring and empathetic attentiveness of right-hemisphere activity, modernity increasingly generates an image of itself (upon which it increasingly reflects), convinced that what it views in the mirror of its representations is the truth about all that is. Hence in the staggering overproduction of simulacra and virtual realities, another form of believing emerges from this left-hemisphere tyranny that is not the same as the believing that issues from right-hemisphere activity.

I will have more to say about belief and virtual reality in the Conclusion; for the moment we are still not free from the cave. But we have begun the Platonic journey towards the sun, and as the work of Lewis-Williams on rock art informs us, the cave now is no longer a home. Dwelling is outside the cave, the rock-shelter: the caves, tunnels, galleries, grottos and the elaborate paintings and parietal art – of bison, horses, aurochs, woolly mammoth, deer and felines – of Altamira in Spain or Lascaux and Chauvet in the region of Ardèche in France, dating from around 32,000 years ago, are some form of sanctuary rather than a home. The difference between the dwelling place and the religious sanctuary may indeed be complex – entry into the uterine darkness might have been understood as admission to a deeper, more primeval and cosmic sense of 'home', but nevertheless there is a separation. It is as if, on Lewis-Williams' spectrum of altered consciousness, there is a human recognition that, for the most part, life is lived in and through everyday consciousness. But everyday consciousness is far from being a simple matter.

IV

A Deep Mind Odyssey:
The Architecture of Believing [2]

'*Will you take a leap of faith, Cobb? Or will you die as an old man?*' With these questions, the plot begins to plant the seeds of an idea and another form of behaviour deep in the subconscious of Robert Fischer, in Christopher Nolan's film *Inception* (2010). The idea for the film was Nolan's own, inspired by the neuroscience on lucid dreaming in which someone falls immediately from a wakeful state into a dream state, close to what Lewis-Williams defines as the hypnagogic condition prior to REM sleep. But in lucid dreaming there can be both consciousness that one is dreaming and also false awakenings. Nolan was also inspired by the science fiction idea of 'dream stealing'.

The idea, planted several levels down in Fischer's mind, is to change his father's dying wishes and to divide an energy empire. 'An idea is like a virus,' Cobb tells another member of his team, 'highly contagious.' (Nolan has obviously been reading Dawkins on 'memes'.) The inception team must build, through a 'dream architect', levels of consciousness to fall through in enough detail that the subconscious of the dreamer completes the construction. Each level of dream moves through a plastic, malleable space in which time bends downwards, slowing. What is one week one level down is six months two levels down, and ten years three levels down. The danger is of becoming trapped in even deeper levels of the mind and never being able to re-emerge; of living within one's own manufactured dream world. That danger, but also the seduction of living in a dreamtime, is part of the film's questioning of the real. What begins as creating a dream within a dream within a dream (three levels) becomes the manufacture of a dream within a dream, within a dream, within a dream within a dream (five levels). Knowledge becomes highly questionable: 'You keep telling yourself what you know. But what do you believe? What do you feel?' At the deeper levels of dreaming it is not knowledge but belief and feeling that orientate. In the final scene, when Cobb returns to his family, the audience is faced with a question about its own collaboration with the film-making: is this family reunion real, or just a level of dream that Cobb's mind has generated? There is much to suggest we, like Cobb, never emerge from the dream-state; that the real is not available; and that all of us, individually and collectively, are implicated in odysseys generated by our imaginations and their commitment to symbolic activity.

HOT, HORS, HOP AND HOE

This could have been the title of an eighteenth-century novel describing something akin to Hogarth's *A Rake's Progress*, only set in the Kent countryside. But the words are actually acronyms for a number of related theories of consciousness based upon 'higher-order representations' (HORs). Why might these hierarchically organised levels add significantly to our architecture of belief? Well, the accounts of consciousness according to both spectrum and lateralisation offer two-dimensional maps of complex neural operations. In particular, what the architectures of consciousness in either Mithen or Lewis-Williams lack is an appreciation of how 'thick' this consciousness is. Higher-order accounts of consciousness offer depth, gradations, scales, degrees of awareness, all hierarchically arranged. The combative labours of those engaged in developing 'higher-order perception' (HOP), 'higher-order thought' (HOT) and 'higher-order experience' (HOE) models of consciousness demonstrate that everyday consciousness, even with a spectrum that moves from alertness to dreaming and unconsciousness, is multi-layered. An appreciation of both that multi-layering and levels of awareness provides the psychobiological architecture of belief with significant detail. Why? Because HORs, in all their variety, treat 'dispositional states' – and so belief.

CONSCIOUSNESS AND THE BRAIN

But allow me to take a step back to better prepare us for these analyses of mental states and sketch very broadly the understanding of consciousness to date.

Consciousness emerges in some way from neural activity. 'In some way' is vague, and I have left it vague for a reason. The reason is: we have not yet treated the relation between mind and matter that my question on teleology arising from non-teleological processes alerts us to. Neither have I said anything about the 'self' – the one who has consciousness, who directs their mind towards purposeful (that is, teleological) activity, and the one who believes. Nevertheless, at this point we can say consciousness as a neural, molecular and ionic process operates in and across both hemispheres of the brain.

The brain works globally. There are certain regions of the brain more involved in the emergence of consciousness than others, and this gives us insight into the evolution of consciousness and the extent to which other animals may also be conscious. For example, the emergence issues from the area around the upper brainstem, one of the oldest cortical areas. Anatomically, the brainstem is surrounded by three areas: the cerebellum, the temporal lobe, and the area in the midbrain carapaced by the cingulate gyrus. When brains first evolved, these were the areas that were developed. I spoke about the encephalisation process in Chapter II – when the brain suddenly expands in volume and the frontal lobes are formed as the neocortex. The important point here is that consciousness is not just a product of the neo- or cerebral cortex, but of the whole of the brain. The brainstem nuclei are responsible for wakefulness in general, and they are connected to the thalamus, which operates 'as a way station for information that's collected from the body and destined for the cerebral cortex' (Damasio). The thalamus not only collates, connects and delivers this information it configures by inter-associating it; the ability to associate – the key to perception, seeing-as and belief – also has its origin here. The cerebral cortex then maps all the informational signals that the thalamus provides it with, often creating, associating and multiplying images, and so from the material brain mind emerges. Profound connections to the oldest parts of the brain, then, root consciousness in our affective nature (Panksepp) – and we will have more to say about that connection in the final section of this chapter.

What we can appreciate from this architecture is that consciousness is not a thing. It is not even a steady state. It's a continual process of adaptation and adjustment, involving the complicity of body and mental states. As such it has attracted major attention from philosophers, psychologists, cognitive scientists and neuroscientists since the 1970s. What each pursues – and there is no consensus that has yet been arrived at – is an explanation of its nature: to dispel some of consciousness' ancient mystery (a mystery associated with the 'soul') and understand the relationship between brain and mind.

On the whole, many of these scientists and philosophers of mind work with and against notions of the soul that are allied to the Cartesian *Cogito*. Here the 'soul' is conceived as the mastermind of the self, sitting in some black leather executive chair directing a theatre of the mind and controlling the proceedings of body, brain and mind, unifying them in some hard-lined construal of the self, the ego – rather like the little alien found in the head of the psychotic killer in the film *Men in Black*. Each, in their own way, removes this homunculus, the seed pearl of the self (what Descartes understood as the centre of the mind in the pineal gland), and attempts to reconstruct the workings of the brain and the creation of mental states on the basis of the way we have evolved as primates. Conclusions drawn by the philosopher Daniel Dennett, in his book *Consciousness Explained*, illustrate a fundamental (though certainly not uncontested) position:

> each act of discrimination or discernment or content-fixation happens somewhere, but there is no one Discerner doing all the work [...] What there is, really, is just various events of content-fixation occurring in various places at various times in the brain. These are nobody's speech acts, and hence they don't have to be in a language, but they are rather *like* speech acts; they have content, and they do have the effect of informing various processes with this content.

To understand these various electrochemical events, and the representations they give rise to in mental states (Dennett: 'the representation of presence is not the same as the presence of representation'), is to unravel something of the evolved engagement of our embodiment and the world. It is also to recognise that as human beings, as *Homo sapiens*, if we have some capacity (and this is highly contentious) to transcend the world, we are nevertheless profoundly part of that world; our brains and bodies are adaptations to that world.

Where does belief register with respect to consciousness? Dennett: 'Seeing *is* believing' (my emphasis). In other words, and bringing in McGilchrist's work on the lateralisation of the brain, the right hemisphere does not deliver beliefs to the left hemisphere across the fissure of *corpus callosum* to be turned into knowledge, like the dwarf bringing Rapunzel straw to spin into gold. Rather: belief goes all the way down. All reality is virtual.

I'm turning to HORs at this point in my investigation to provide something of an intellectual dyke against being overwhelmed by a tsunami of conflicting intellectual currents, because theories and accounts of consciousness are so manifold that the field of enquiry is as vast and badly lit as the mind itself. There is much debate and contestation: Nicholas Humphrey's, Marvin Minsky's and Daniel Dennett's explications of consciousness (not themselves without inner debates) conflict with those of Thomas Nagel, Roger Penrose, Raymond Tallis or John Searle (again there is no neat homogenising of projects), for example.

Each of the first set of distinguished figures believes that conscious experiences can be identified with the information-processing undertaken by the nervous system and the brain. Consciousness is a by-product of this processing; the brain is the mind. They represent the materialist camp. Each of the second set of thinkers believes there are severe limitations to any explorations of consciousness in terms of neuroscience or artificial intelligence – for how can the subjective experience of consciousness, the phenomenology of consciousness, be 'explained' by the objective physiological architectures of the brain or the hard- and software of a computer? Isn't consciousness foundational? After all, aren't all our constructions of the physiological or the computational structures themselves a product of that consciousness? There is a spectre of a yet-to-be-explained and yet-to-be-eliminated dualism in this camp. The work is ongoing, and across several highly specialised intellectual disciplines.

RETURN TO BASE CAMP

We need to return to basics. Belief, I have said, is a disposition. It need not be a cognition, but unless in some sense its presence is registered – even after the conscious mental state announces itself and can be submitted to further, meta-introspection – we could not speak about it at all. I may believe in democracy, freedom and human rights without actively being engaged in thinking about those subjects and my beliefs in them. These dispositions can therefore exist and remain unconscious biases. 'Unconscious' here is not some dark abyss because I cannot gain access to or become conscious of these dispositions. Like Kihlstrom and his 'cognitive unconscious', HORs (both of the HOP and the HOT variety) offer theories both 'of the distinction between mental states one is aware of being in and mental states one is not aware of being in' (Lycan). However, dispositions have been configured (and in an account of seeing *as*, we recognise their formation is inevitable) by evolution; that is, by adaption: learning by trial and error. These configurations can be retrieved from what some have called deep mind in the same way in which well-trained athletes have developed muscle memory enabling them to react to a tennis serve, for example, without consciously placing the racket anywhere.

I repeat: only a small percentage of what we process in terms of information about our environments and our body states is available to us: perhaps 5 per cent at most. Our bodies are continually responding to internal and external stimuli and making readjustments accordingly. Our autonomic systems – which regulate pulse and heart rate, body temperature and blood pressure – work ceaselessly in ways that, generally, we are unconscious of. That's why high blood pressure is often called the 'invisible killer' – we only come to know it is too high when we experience a haemorrhage or have a stroke. What is commonly called 'access consciousness' is a foreground consciousness of our mental states. At base, belief is a mental state (where 'state' can cover 'thought', 'perception' and 'experience', all of which are dynamic, not static conditions), but not all mental states are brought to consciousness. That does not mean that mental states are disassociated from sensory perception – our beliefs have arisen from somewhere – though there is a continuing debate

about the extent to which sensing itself has – technical term coming up –
intentional content.

The word 'intention' relates back to its use by archaeologists (Chapter III),
but its referential scope is widened. Intention is target-driven. So 'intentional
content' is purposeful. Every cell has a mindless, biological intention – a
natural will, if you like – to survive. If poked, a cell withdraws. It seeks to
keep its membrane intact. It seeks to survive, to gain access to resources
that will enable it to survive (nourishment) and to reproduce. The single
cell develops a tail function to swim, just as birds develop wing functions
and human beings self-conscious minds. The single cell gains movement by
this function so it can avoid predators and forage for food better.

Is 'intentional' a metaphor when used descriptively of a cell's behaviour?
Is it a piece of anthropomorphism? Certainly there is no 'consciousness'
involved in its purposefulness. But there are evidently levels of awareness
deeper than consciousness that are related to the evolved design and biological function; awareness that is the precondition for response, and response
that is purposeful, directed towards learning from and adapting to. From
this 'teleodynamic tendenc[y]' (Deacon), both biological and psychological
functions will emerge. As Ruth Millikan writes on the relation between
biology, language and semantics:

> the mechanism through which goals are projected by conscious desire
> and reason are undoubtedly mechanisms that our genes have been
> selected for engendering. The mechanisms are still with us because
> they have sometimes – often enough – produced behaviours that
> benefitted human genes in the past.

Here the 'teleodynamic tendenc[y]' is itself a product of natural selection.
But it could be – and Deacon has argued this – that the 'teleodynamic
tendenc[y]' is 'preserved and tested' by natural selection (Deacon). The
tendency then exists prior to and determines the process of natural selection.

It may be that the myriad collections of cells that make up every aspect
of the human body – cells that have come to work not just individually
but collectively – amplify this evolved design in which awareness and 'teleodynamic tendencies' become inseparable from intentionality. But when
it comes to consciousness, these levels of intention – or some of them (we

have no access to our cellular levels of intention) – get mapped across neural networks that communicate with each other. And the mapping creates brain events in which intention manifests its purpose-driven meaningfulness; intention becomes semantic. Hence Millikan's philosophical biology spawning a school devoted to examining 'teleosemantics'.

Some cognitive scientists have wanted to distinguish mental states that have intentional content from those that just have phenomenal content; that is, states having either directed or semantic content from states having only sensory perception. When I see colour (red), when I hear a noise (discordant), when I touch a tree (rough), these states have phenomenal content, as does pain. What is at stake in the controversy over intentional and phenomenal content in mental states is the relationship between perception and thought. Is there anything that can be just perception or does perception, because it sees *as*, always involve the search for understanding? There is a difference, but of what does this difference consist? I am not going to take us to the thickets of such discussions. Suffice it to say, for the moment let us acknowledge that beliefs have intentional content – they direct and inform other judgements about the world. They are not directly perceivable by the senses, though they may be, as I said earlier, affect-laden, and they cannot be divorced from perceptions because the stimuli for their associative activity comes from somewhere. Because they are directive, they can become objects of consciousness. They become 'thoughts'.

To some extent 'higher order' theories of consciousness return us to the hierarchy in Plato's cave. Beliefs (or desires) are viewed as first- or lower-order nonconscious, dispositional states that when brought into thought become an object of thought: second- or higher-order states. If these thoughts direct action of some kind and find expression or representation – in a gesture, in speaking to oneself or to another, in a cave painting – then they become third- or even higher-order states. For some cognitive scientists, like David Rosenthal, and evolutionary psychologists, like Merlin Donald, there are 'metacognitions' – that is, judgements about one's mental states (whether these states are conscious or unconscious). Donald views metacognition as the basis for our sense of self-governance. It is only at this judgement stage that beliefs can be recognised as 'propositional attitudes' (see Introduction).

Not all those involved in investigating HORs find the attention to cognitions, concepts and thoughts convincing. Hence the exponents of HOEs and the HOPs, who wish to emphasise perceptions and 'feels' (*what it is like* experiences). This allows for nonconceptual content of first-order experience. For example: 'Any occurrent mental state M [...] is conscious = M is disposed to cause an activated belief (possibly a non-conscious one) that I have M, and it causes it non-inferentially' (Carruthers). If there is anything ambiguous about 'disposition' here, it is a matter of where the disposition lies: in the mental state (M) or with the belief that gives rise to the mental state. I say 'if', but one could explain this account of HOEs as implying that disposition lies both in the belief and the conscious mental state of the belief (of a second order). This is sometimes known as dual-content: the first-order perception and the second-order experience of the perception is given in the same state, M. As Carruthers has explained it elsewhere, these mental states of 'feel'

> will be both world-representing (or body-representing, in the case of pain and touch) and experience-representing at the same time. In such cases it isn't just the world that is presented in a certain way to us, but our own experience of that world will also be presented in a certain way to us.

The words *in a certain way* characterise the dispositional aspect of *making sense* of the world (and our selves as perceivers/experiencers of such a world). The disposition here is teleological; it bears an intrinsic causal character – though that does not mean one could not misrepresent (at the second and third levels) a first-order experience of feeling. Some exponents of HORs, like Rosenthal (whom we have already cited), cannot accept any unconscious sensory states – because these always need accompanying thought; others, like Carruthers, affirm that not all that enters into consciousness makes itself available to higher-order perceptual attention. There can be unconscious or nonconscious sensory states that can actually impact on our sensory-motor abilities (like driving a car on automatic pilot), but they are not experienced as such while we are unconscious of them. It is being allied with belief or, more widely, dispositional systems (like desire) that enables them to become experienced states of consciousness. But all accept that conscious seeing (whether conceived in terms of thought and cognition or sensory perception and its experience) is seeing *as* (Churchland). We live within our believing. And this shows us that HORs only provide more systematic and cognitive detail to what Pope John Paul II observes in *Fides et Ratio:* 'the one *who lives by belief*', which is an analogue of an observation made by Ludwig Wittgenstein in his book *On Certainty*: '[m]y *life* consists in my being content to accept many things.'

Sometimes what the world gives us and we are disposed to experience in ways that make sense – in ways governed by our belief and disposition systems, and therefore think about – takes time to attain a higher order (a third order) of consciousness associated with verbalisation. Take, for example, the following dialogue between an interviewer (Int.) and a French archaeologist (Arch.) exploring the caves at Chauvet for the first time:

ARCH.: The first time I had a chance to enter Chauvet cave I had five days. And it was so powerful that every night I was dreaming of lions. And every day was the same shock for me. It was an emotional shock. I mean I'm a scientist, but a human too. And after five days I decided not to go back in the caves because I needed time just to… relax… and take time to…

INT.: …to absorb it?

ARCH.: to absorb it. Yeah. Yeah.

INT.: And you dreamt not of paintings of lions but of real lions.

ARCH.: Of both. Of both definitely. Yeah.

INT.: And you were afraid in your dreams…

ARCH.: I was not afraid. No. No. I was not afraid. It was more… a feeling of powerful things… and deep things. A way to understand things which is not a direct way.

The dialogue was conducted by the German film director Werner Herzog for his documentary film on Chauvet, *Cave of Forgotten Dreams* (2011). The dialogue reveals the movement from 'a feeling of powerful things… and deep things' to consciousness of experience (first- and second-order HOP) and then from conceptual analysis of that experience, 'No. I was not afraid' (third-order HOT), to an inchoate 'metacognition': 'A way to understand things which is not a direct way.' There remains a struggle to verbalise the powerful nature of that experience. This is a struggle within disposition itself, akin I think to the struggles of those people at Peterhouse who could see the effect of the mysterious event upon College staff members they knew well, but could not process their perceptual experiences with respect to what they believed. The struggle evidences a dissonance.

We are most often accustomed to understanding cognitive dissonance when what is experienced can be understood in very different ways. Wittgenstein's famous duck-rabbit example comes to mind. The illustration in his *Philosophical Investigations* can either be of a duck or a rabbit, but the mind cannot see it as both simultaneously, though the mind can register the presence of both meanings because it recognises both the figure of a duck and the figure of a rabbit are present. But cognitive dissonance, if we take the example of the French archaeologist, can occur when what is perceived does not fit easily into patterns of previous perceptions or dispositions to believe. It not clear from the interview with Herzog whether the archaeologist ever did 'absorb' his experience of being in the cave. The experience was certainly processed, but the paintings of lions morphed into dreams of real lions and *vice versa*. Consciousness and subconsciousness interacted. The dissonance was registered as affect ('a feeling of powerful things… and deep things') remote to consciousness and understanding. The dissonance is not resolved. Rather, to employ a psychoanalytic term, the dissonance was sublimated. Concrete objects, in this process, lose all distinctive characteristics. These characteristics dissolve into the abstractions of 'things' with profound affective (and therefore psychosomatic) effects. The body will remember them. Other experienced events may trigger that registered disturbance, restructuring the disposition to believe. Perhaps, indeed – and we will explore this further in Chapter VII – this is why myth can affect us at levels beneath the cognitive. There can be feelings about an event that cannot be fully assessed; feelings that don't hook up with dispositions of belief available to higher-order thoughts but disturb them deeper down. We need to explore these 'deep things' and their association with believing.

THE FEELING OF WHAT HAPPENS

The neuroscientist Giacomo Rizzolatti and an associated team have been conducting work into what they call 'mirror neurons'; that is, neurons involved in imitative behaviour such that when I perceive and experience an external action my body and brain mimic, to some extent, that same activity. It is possibly the activation of these neurons that triggered a transferral between the paintings on the walls of the cave at Chauvet and the French archaeologist examining them. Mirror neurons are an important aspect of a biology of belief. They write the 'as if' of belief into our physiologies because they evoke the 'simulation, in the brain's body maps, of a body state that is not actually taking place in the organism', amplifying the 'functional resemblance' (Damasio). In this way, and with the help of what another neuroscientist, Antonio Damasio, terms CDZs (convergence-divergence zones at the microscopic level that assemble neurons within feedforward–feedback loops of information) and CDRs (convergence-divergence regions located at strategic areas in association cortices where major pathways for information come together), belief is not only embodied but inseparable from the capacity to imagine. The critical contents of the conscious mind are thereby organised. Fundamentally, the emotions are engaged in this 'body loop' as the areas of the premotor-prefrontal cortex (involved in compassion), the amygdala (involved in fear), the somatomotor complex in the rolandic and parietal opercula, and the insular cortex deep within the brain are engaged. Damasio conjectures that this activity is the basis for empathy and the recognition of comparable body-states in other human beings.

We are returned to that final scene of *Quest for Fire* – the moment of a communication that is unspoken, but shared. This is the evolved biological context for social relations: knowledge of others and a means of communicating with others aids collective adaptation and survival. Believing is then not passive: it is rooted in 'a preactivation of motor structures'.

Damasio takes this emotional fundament for consciousness further. It is important to sketch his conclusions, because in nearly all the models of consciousness we have been concerned with in this and the last chapter, only McGilchrist's work has treated the centrality of the emotions in right-hemisphere activity in recognising the way the right hemisphere is associated most closely with the older areas of the brain. The champions of HOEs refer to 'feel' as an important aspect of disposition, but Damasio's neuro-anatomical work peels back the layers of cortices to show how thoughts are triggered by feelings, as the patterns of association generated by memory and image production are fired by neural and hormonal transactions. This triggering brings together (in CDZs and CDRs) the oldest parts of the brain (the tractus solitarius and the parabrachial nucleus in the brainstem, the thalamus and the insular cortex) with the neocortex that developed in the encephalisation process. 'The anterior cingulate cortex tends to become active in parallel with the insula when we experience feelings'.

The tractus solitarius and the parabrachial nucleus are the first recipients of signals about the body-state, and integrate information across the whole of our embodied interior. 'The upper brain-stem machinery in charge of body mapping interacts directly with the source of the maps it makes', and in this way all thought has its origins in emotion, even 'late cognitive reactions to the emotions under way'. The emotions are understood then as programmes for action as the body-state changes due to either internal or internalised external stimuli, such that these early emotion maps 'constitute the substrate of a composite, multisite image'.

Rizzolatti's and Damasio's work helps to explain the transmission of belief through simulations or 'as-if feeling states'. The French archaeologist's response in the Chauvet cave, then, is in part (because we have no direct access to the semantic content of these cave paintings) an embodied response to a prior set of beliefs being mimicked by an observer. We will encounter a similar situation when we turn to the question of making a belief *believable* and examine the 'suspension of disbelief that constitutes poetic faith' (in Chapter VI). The act of trying to 'absorb' the experience and the time it took for this 'absorption', which the archaeologist emphasises, are products of higher-order thoughts and perceptions. The brain records the manifold consequences of the body's interaction with the stimuli and the emerging sensorimotor patterns seek associations with previous memories of comparative and analogous situations. Higher-order consciousness can only emerge from this activity, and the associating processes are highly selective since our 'memories are *prejudiced*, in the full sense of the term, by our previous history and beliefs'. In treating this selection procedure, Damasio adds to our understanding of 'dispositions'.

Damasio's analysis of dispositions provides another level of excavation in the biological foundations of belief. He takes us back to the early evolution of the brain, and indeed to cell biology. I spoke earlier of how even the single cell can be said to have 'intention' in so far as it has a desire to prevent its boundaries from being broached, and to receive nourishment to survive from the competitive environment in which it is placed. It is also able to extend its capacities by coupling with and binding itself to similar cells to form a collective, a nucleus. These innate responses are prior to any consciousness or even a process of mapping where the object impinging from the outside is represented. Damasio informs us that the early brain responded in the same way to external stimuli. 'What seems to have been represented by these brain ensembles [of neurons] is not maps but rather *dispositions*, know-how formulas'. He goes on:

> For a long, long time in evolution, brains operated on the basis of dispositions [...] The dispositional network achieved a lot and got to be more and more complicated and wide-ranging in its achievement. But when the possibility of maps arose, organisms were able to go beyond formulaic responses and respond instead on the basis of the richer information now available in the maps.

The older parts of the brain developed internally and synergistically with the newer cortices such that '[l]ater, the dispositional, nonmapping networks would join forces with the networks that created the maps, and as they did, organisms achieved an even greater management flexibility.'

Human beings have inherited, during the evolution of the brain, many of these networks of disposition. They manage our internal autonomic systems at a basic biological level, but, combined with our more sophisticated neural mapping abilities, 'maps can be recorded in dispositional form'. This can be seen as a space-saving device, since past perceptions and representations are then encoded as dispositions rather than needing to be memorised as such. Damasio calls this a 'dispositional space'. It is a knowledge base that allows for very rapid reconstruction of knowledge in recall. This is implicit knowledge. While the contents of images can be accessed by consciousness, we can never have direct access to the contents of our dispositions. They are encrypted and dormant. Nevertheless, this dispositional space is

> the source of images in the process of imagination and reasoning and is also used to generate movement. It is located in the cerebral

cortices that are not otherwise occupied by the image [mapping] space (the higher-order cortices and parts of the limbic cortices) and in numerous subcortical nuclei.

The point of all this for an architecture of belief is that the foundations for the very edifice of believing itself lie in a knowledge base that is implicit, encrypted and unconscious.

There is a question – and we should raise it now because it has consequences for any notion of transcendence – as to whether this hierarchical ordering of consciousness is *extrinsic* to the brain or *intrinsic*. The question is key to materialist understandings of the brain/mind relationship: is there some kind of teleology that leads sensations and experience into conscious states (the intrinsic view), or is there a lack of such a teleological association, meaning that the architecture of mental states operates with a certain autonomy from neuroanatomy? I will leave this question hanging at the moment, because until we discuss the nature of the 'self', the subjective nature of conscious experience, then what is involved in this question is oversimplified.

We exist in, adapt to, modify and compose continually, environments of belief. Some of these are personal, but most are shared and cultural – like our belief that the bodies of dead human beings should be treated with respect, as they evidently were in the Shanidar cave visited in the last chapter. The disposition to believe is varied, because it is shaped and coloured by other secondary dispositions like desire, yearning, expectation and hope. That does not mean we are forever immured within Plato's cave. It does not mean that we cannot ascend to Plato's daylight world of truth. But it does mean that when we ascend, the Platonic Forms of true knowledge are abstractions of our beliefs. The believing doesn't stop, certain knowledge (instead) dawning. We emerge into higher-order beliefs. Beliefs that are articulated, debated and contested, verified, maintained, amended or discarded. We emerge with another set of questions about making belief *believable*; that is, by what means the representation and articulation of beliefs win wider social and cultural support. We must turn now to *that* set of questions.

PART TWO

Believability

V

Sense and Sensibility:
The Unbearable Lightness of Certainty

f we still remain in Plato's cave of belief, we are not as in the dark as
once we were. *Homo sapiens* came out of Africa on the second long
expedition, this time across the straits at the mouth of the Red Sea as
it opens into the Indian Ocean. The time is a matter of conjecture about
weather systems, middens of empty shells on raised beaches in Eritrea,
the depression of plankton with sea levels dropping 80 metres below
present conditions because of another ice age, and the genetic drift of
mitochondrial DNA. But if the human species *Homo sapiens* emerged
in Africa around 125,000 years ago, then around 85,000 years ago they
began a beachcombing migration along the coast of the Indian Ocean.
Several groups continued, and even reached Australia (before they reached
Europe). Some stopped in what is now India, and in an interglacial age,
around 50,000 years ago, a warm spell, perhaps lasting 'only a few thousand
years' (Oppenheimer), formed a green belt down the Indus Valley and the
Fertile Crescent of Iraq. This allowed migration from the Arabian Gulf
into the Middle East. The first Europeans were of South Asian origin. As
the ice sheets retreated, they penetrated into the steppes of Siberia and
the regions around the Caucasus Mountains. From there, around 45,000
years ago, they infiltrated what is now western Europe. By that time, as
the cave at Chauvet shows, they no longer permanently occupied caves
and rock shelters. These places were used for other purposes, or left to
the wild bears. Here was the most adaptable species of *Homo* to date:

inventive, curious, restless, talking, and not just conscious creatures, but self-conscious creatures: *Homo sapiens sapiens*.

They emerged from cave life and, if Chauvet was indeed some kind of sacred place, they began to develop semi-permanent habitations, communities and a cultural life expressive of their symbolic sophistication. They may still have remained predominantly itinerant, pitching skin-tents over mammoth bones and moving seasonally with the herds of animals they tracked and hunted. It was not until around 10,000 years ago, in the Neolithic period, that stone and mud were used to establish permanency. The first cities were built in what is now Turkey and the Middle East, and an agrarian society emerged. We are not going to pursue this history, but with the successive representations of the contents of their minds and imaginations (in monolithic and portable forms of art, carvings and paintings), the systems of their beliefs found increasing expression as their symbolic activity and proclivity developed. Human beings began living with the invisible while adapting themselves to a hundred different material landscapes, climates and habitats. They accommodated themselves to the material in and through the immaterial. And this immateriality concerned not just gods, mythic animals, magic forces and inscrutable cosmic powers, but also the immateriality of ideas, stories, images and icons, some of which now were being stored and transmitted through symbolic representation. Our believing is now inseparable from this symbolic activity in which the natural and cultural drive forward our evolution, our civilisation.

This fact is crucial to our examination of belief, because in providing belief with an archaeology with respect to the evolution of the genus *Homo* (in Chapters I and II) and an architecture with respect to their, and our, psychophysiology (in Chapters III and IV), we have not explained belief. Something yet remains which words like 'invisible', 'immaterial' and 'consciousness' point towards. That something still remains to be explained. Since at least the meditations of René Descartes, philosophy has turned its attention to consciousness and knowledge. Epistemology came to the forefront with attempts to explain human understanding and its relation to the sensations of the material world. The work of Locke, Berkeley, Hume and Kant followed, and set the philosophical stage for the dramatic debates between empiricism, idealism and phenomenology. The modern understanding of belief was created in and through these debates.

The debates continue to the present day with materialist accounts that argue consciousness is directly produced through sensation (Humphreys, Dennett, Kirk). Consciousness here is a by-product, an epiphenomenon of the neural activity engendered by the sensory cortices. Consciousness itself is passive – it simply mirrors what is out there in the world. It is non-functional and has nothing to do with what is meaningful. The meaningful and the valuable are only illusions to those who wish to pare back our minds to our bodies and our bodies to the cells (and even subatomic particles) of which they are constituted. We are all preprogrammed by our evolved biologies. Preprogrammed indeed since the Big Bang itself, beyond which no further reduction is possible – if the Big Bang can account for (as in explaining) anything at all.

As Thomas Nagel points out:

> Our beliefs about the properties of the physical elements and their constituents are based on what is needed to account for their contemporary observable behaviours and interaction and the results of their combination into molecules and larger structures [...] This is a very large assumption.

Such reductive explanations remain, in the end, just 'our beliefs'. But they are beliefs that, in being expressed, represented to and believed by others, are shared. In being shared they announce a collective judgement about how things are: a judgement by consensus. This judgement operates as a general norm for the ways things behave. In this way we achieve what Nagel defines as 'justified beliefs about some [...] objective truths – though some of those beliefs will probably be mistaken. [Nevertheless] those beliefs in combination can directly influence what we do.' The norms that constitute a belief system should be open to evaluation since they are aiming at maximal logical consistency. Well, within science, anyway – because science seeks to understand the way things are objectively.

I'm far from sure that people are orientated towards attaining maximal logical consistency among their beliefs, although there is a certain physiological and mental stability about consistency, and I am aware that was the goal people were supposed to pursue as advocated by the Enlightenment *philosophes* under the aegis of Reason. The continual negotiation of beliefs that informs scientific rationalism is abstracted from subjective emotion and affect. That is not to deny that we make rational choices on the basis of observations and evidence confirming or denying what we suspect to be the case. But we cannot simply conflate this rationalism and scientific rationalism and say they are the same. That cannot be. Not without at least recognising and accommodating an important difference. We realise in our individual and social living that in seeking answers to our existential situations we are ourselves part of the problem; we cannot abstract ourselves from it. It is our experience and how it has arisen that is the evidence with which we work. And what counts as evidence is the way I have seen *as* and the experience of living with others who also see *as* and whose perceptions, motivations and cognitions are not transparent to me.

The human pursuit of happiness and well-being in relations is not governed by the scientific rationalism (*pace* Wolpert). There are elements of a calculus of probability at times; there is also the complete surrender of the compass of such a calculus because of deeper convictions. It is no coincidence that at a zenith of Enlightenment thinking in Britain, the novelist Jane Austen could so humorously and ironically play with the differences between rational and emotional intelligence in her *Sense and Sensibility*. The adventures of Marianne ('eager in everything: her sorrows, her joys, could have no moderation') and Elinor ('this oldest daughter whose advice was so effectual, [and who] possessed a strength of understanding and coolness of judgement [...] and enabled her frequently to counteract [...] that eagerness') lead to the conclusion that both qualities of mind (acute sensibility and forensic common sense) are needed to understand human behaviour.

By the light of the materialist belief system we are all utterly determined automatons, and the 'we' here includes any number of other animals that also have consciousness in so far as they also have perception, emotional responses to their perception, and appetites, since we do not know what has consciousness and what does not. Now this is where 'explanation' (which is based on 'a very large assumption') becomes political: human beings in this belief system have no special place in the order of creation. There is no order – that too is just an illusory by-product, because both the eye and the world are incessantly in movement. *We* manufacture a stability. So human rights and animal rights exist on a level playing field.

GOING MENTAL

Then there are the advocates (numerous and distinctive) of non-materialist construals of consciousness, like Nagel, Penrose, Tallis, Midgley, Sorel and Galen Strawson. These usually begin with what the materialist accounts cannot explain: the subjective experience of the world and the mind with respect to the world. I said above that reductions to the material are based upon beliefs orientated towards a calculus of probability that aims at consistency: the goal of such consistency-seeking is a unified explanation of consciousness. But to be unified, to even continue the quest, such beliefs must be open to being modified if something arises which does not fit with the system of that consistency. What is characteristic of the debates between the materialists and their opponents is that they are very good at pointing out the errors in consistency or gaps in the explanations in each other's positions. But on the whole they remain adamantly, and polemically, on one side or the other. The evidence of what does not fit either system is not adaptive such that a new system with a better and more unified grasp of consciousness comes to the fore.

The non-materialist advocates of consciousness share a concern with the materialists not to capitulate to the dualism that would only place a ghost in the physiological machine. But they also reject a computer model for the biological programming that runs a physiological machine. And so we enter the realm of 'panpsychism' and 'neutral monism', in which the material is already imbued with the mental. Let's go back to a word I used in the last chapter to describe the reaction of a single cell to invasive activity: 'intentional'. The advocates of panpsychism and neutral monism construct a metaphysics on the basis of the 'protomental': that from the beginning the properties of all matter have contained a 'protopsychic' element that, ultimately, led to the creation of consciousness and creatures who are conscious of the fact they are conscious. Us. The biological dispositions that intend – that is, target-drive a cell to reproduce, associate itself with similar cells and protect itself from dangers to its living integrity – demonstrate the possibilities of more developed and complex forms of intention. But whence this 'intentionality' in a non-metaphorical sense of the protopsychic? Now wherever it comes from, this protopsychic element is another matter. And the pun's intended. But unless it relates back to the material, then this 'belief' system has not explained very much. Intelligibility remains questionable, and hypothesis has an explanatory form but lacks considerable explanatory content.

Furthermore, such accounts of the protomental rely upon a notion of causality that has been on the wane since the advent of modern science: teleology. There have been a number of attempts among philosophers to rein-state teleology. The movement towards complex forms of self-organisation is recognised by the materialists, but it is a blind process resulting, presumably, from millions of failures and some fluky successes in the evolutionary drive for survival and adaptation. This movement is not teleological because it lacks the intention, the purpose of self-organisation. For Aristotle, teleology is final causation – final because it aims at the completion and perfection of a state; the potential in the material becoming actual form – the form it was always meant to be. Many working in the panpsychic and neutral monism camps develop an account of teleology that shaves off values associated by Aristotle with 'completion' and 'perfection'. They tend to go for a narrower view of 'intentionality' as a motivated agent designing something – rather than intention as 'target-driven' such that we can say even the cellular has 'motivated intention'. But by adopting this narrower view of intention, it stops short of accepting anything like a theistic design argument. So this account distinguishes intention from teleology that is a natural bias.

Sometimes the panpsychic account allies itself with theories of 'emer-gence'; that is, there can be a natural bias towards complex but neverthe-less highly organised systems such that these systems themselves in their complexity enable new, unforeseen possibilities to appear: like conscious-ness from biological material, the psychological from the physiological. 'Emergence' might account for the appearance of a number of such unfore-seen possibilities – that is, what is understood to be possible knowing what we do *at this point* about the properties of certain things and how they behave. There is, for example, the transformation that made the physical properties of a fragment flung out by the Big Bang into the biological prop-erties that engender life and trigger the evolutionary process: the possibility of changing rocks and metals into cells.

There is not a *teleos* as such in 'emergence', but what Deacon calls a 'teleonomy', and if it has a direction, well, we are still trying to discern it.

It is not predictable; that is the point. But it seems to be disposed towards higher forms of value – though that may be from an entirely human perspective. For us, it does seem better to be a plant than a rock, a badger than a microbe, and a human being with rational capacities to make judgements and pass laws than a badger. Put briefly, to have life is more valuable than to be inanimate and lifeless (if indeed rocks are lifeless). One philosopher has called it a 'bias towards the marvellous' (White) and Nagel 'the universe gradually waking up'. To avoid over-optimism here I think we have to understand the word 'marvellous' in terms of its use in the circus: something never seen before; something never imagined. And it is not clear to me how such an evaluation can divorce itself from the strong notions of intentionality without becoming either incoherent or leading directly to a theistic hypothesis of design.

To go back to uncials for a moment – if we call a cell's target-driven nature its 'good', and we don't wish to be metaphorical about such an ascription, then this teleology is more Aristotelian (and metaphysical) than it wishes to admit. Natural teleology, based upon emergence, can only say that the laws by which we explain things now may not be the laws by which we explain things in the future; things may change, dramatically, within the very immanent processes that science is attempting to understand. The universal may only be the historically particular, though 'historical' here has to be understood in cosmological time frames. Such a natural teleology cannot predict, and therefore ascribe value to this process by utopian culminations in 'the marvellous' or the universe 'waking up'. Such projections are simply beliefs. The laws of entropy predict an altogether different and dystopic finale.

So back to base, Scottie. Those panpsychic explanations of consciousness, which see mind going all the way down – sometimes to the protomental – have not explained anything by saying consciousness emerges from matter. Like the materialist explanation, the panpsychic explanation has a form but it does not have a content. Like emergence itself, such accounts of consciousness cannot explain *how* it occurs – *how* one complex and highly self-organising, self-replicating and self-regulating system morphs unpredictably into something new. And until the mentalist account or the emergent account *can* answer the question *how*, it is not in itself an answer to the mind–materiality problem. Though, as some philosophers have pointed out, such a teleology does posit a law behind the change (even if we cannot predict the operational direction of that law), and it announces a probability in all those changes – though it is a probability in the *longue durée* of its development. It is not the probability intrinsic to the material elements themselves which is the basis of efficient causation.

The panpsychic and neutral monism accounts draw attention to the unaccountable leap from material electrochemical discharges across different regions of the lateralised brain to the immateriality of ideas; from neural networkings between brainstem nuclei, subcortical and neocortical structures to the creation of mental maps, pictures in our head and representations that constitute consciousness (to say nothing of the impact and effects of the contentless unconscious upon this consciousness). The leap is not without precedent. It's an ancient hiatus: the leap from the mouth of Plato's cave to the reality of the forms themselves. This is a qualitative leap. We know something about cells and particles and how, over geological and evolutionary time, they become organised and form complex interdependent creations. But, as Nagel also points out:

> we have no comparatively clear idea of the part-whole relation for mental reality – no idea how mental states at the levels of organisms could be composed out of the properties of microelements, whether those properties are similar in type to our experiential states or different.

That there is a relation is a 'belief' also. The materialist reduction to the efficient causality of the elemental cannot explain reductively enough – but then neither can the nonmaterialist reduction to teleology and emergence.

BEYOND BELIEF?

Interestingly, and maybe not insignificantly, Plato's philosopher king never wanders in the landscape of the ideal forms that opens before him from the ledge of his rock shelter. He is forced to return down into the deep shadows of the cave of belief to release other prisoners. Belief remains, and though we have no wish to resort to the magical, the explanations founded upon these beliefs remain enigmatic: open to answers yet to be disclosed; open to what is still to come. So our anthropological, neurological and philosophical investigations continue. There are 'gaps', and we should be hesitant to fill those gaps with God or the soul or anything religious too quickly, if at all. Aristotle, and more recent philosophers such as Alvin Plantinga, wanted to push teleology outside of the natural order, and they end up with some form of creationism: God as the intentional creator. Then all the laws of nature, known and emergent, work together to actualise that pinnacle of creation that can understand and respond to the creator God. Such a position, embracing what is called the 'anthropic principle' – whereby all things cosmic fit together to make conscious, rational human beings possible – is not in itself a solution: it pushes any solution towards the mystical.

Whatever God is (or may be) is a name we give to what we don't understand. Such a bold creationist view helps neither science nor religion, nor the conversations conducted between them. Besides, such a cosmic architect (as Kant called him) could well be a *wanderlustig* alien from another dying planet, such as in the opening sequence of Ridley Scott's 2012 film, *Prometheus*; some creature who descends and kick-starts the DNA process. If in Scott's film the alien doesn't leave but dies, bequeathing his 'life' through allowing the DNA in his own decomposing body to be dispersed into the waters of a great river, the picture remains that of the Newtonian divine who, having begun the chain of efficient causality, leaves it to its own devices and withdraws. As Nagel observes: 'A creationist explanation for the existence of life is the biological analogue of dualism in the philosophy of mind.' Creationism too is a belief that puts the full stop somewhere in a cosmic sentence. So believing remains, until given concrete expression, as the invisible (as thoughts are) substrate. And even when given expression, the signs themselves (open to manifold interpretations) are only standing in for something not present in and of itself. Although, bearing in mind our French archaeologist's experience of being in the cave at Chauvet, something is communicated that has profound psychological and physiological effects. The invisible is not divorced from the concrete and material. The virtual deeply informs the real – as anyone with a valid bank card knows. Belief, both in its prehistory and its implicit unconscious dispositional space, is marked by a certain constitutional absence.

We have to keep this in mind because it maintains belief (and thought more generally) as something irreducible to both materiality (either in terms of evolutionary biology or neurophysiology) or consciousness (the cognitive operations of rationality). The accounts of mental processes as electrochemical transmissions of information rely upon metaphors often drawn from computing circuitry. The metaphorical nature of the discourses reveals the gap between the physicality of the processing and the mental account whereby we come to an understanding of this processing. Such accounts then already go beyond the physical properties of the things they are defining. They involve ideas divorced in some way from the processing; divorced because otherwise we would have to admit to mind, ideas, beliefs, causally effecting these processes – processes that, on these accounts, give rise to and are therefore the cause of mind, ideas, representations, etc. Terrence Deacon observes: 'even if all physical processes involve some tiny hint of protomentality, we would still need an account that explains why two equally complex physical processes can differ so radically in this respect.' If we don't have such an account we are left with Cartesian dualism, which admits occult, transcending and invisible forces distinct from the immanent workings of the natural world. The irreducibility of belief to the physics and chemistry of the brain draws our attention to a lacuna that cannot be disassociated from the lacuna of consciousness itself. We cannot account fully for belief, and belief cannot fully account for itself. We don't always (possibly most of the time) know believing's secret operations, its secret selections among our memories, emotions and understandings.

I recall a Christian couple whose daughter married a Muslim. Their first grandchild was a girl, and all the Christian friends of the grandparents thought it was wonderfully liberal that the child should be brought up a Muslim. They were happy for the girl and the marriage that had made this possible. The second grandchild was a boy, and suddenly the questions to the Christian parents from their Christian friends became much more quizzical, even serious. He too was going to be brought up a Muslim. Indeed, he would have the mark of being a Muslim in his flesh – in terms of his circumcision. Somehow, in the little girl being a Muslim the faith she was to be brought up in was practically invisible; the little boy being a Muslim made the faith he was going to be brought up in all too visible.

What disquieted the Christian friends was not that this was an awful state of affairs theologically. What disquieted them the most was the fact that they were disquieted. As liberal-minded adults they had not expected to be disturbed at all. They accepted: that was one of the moral basics of their liberalism. That is how they understood themselves. That is how they believed themselves to be. And their beliefs were now being challenged by emotional convictions that they really didn't understand the basis of. There was a dissonance.

This story is not as unusual as it might first appear. How many white people never recognised their whiteness was an ethnic marker, viewing other people as having ethnicity, until the transmigration of peoples became more frequent? How many men in the twentieth century, and maybe even today, see gender as a women's question, not seeing themselves as gendered? To understand oneself as gendered raises all sorts of destabilising questions; disquieting questions. Something was made to appear that had been in operation for many many years. It had become a habit of mind of which they had been completely unaware.

The secret operations and mind-bending powers of belief probably account for why belief is so powerful, as we will appreciate more in a later chapter when I discuss the myths and metaphors by which we live and the politics and religions that institutionalise them. There's no getting behind or beyond belief, so for the moment we have to settle for a paradox – a paradox of belief – expressed in terms of a series of questions. If, as I have been arguing in the previous section on the making of belief, belief is more foundational than knowledge, if it renders both itself and all knowledge virtual, then how do we forget that to the extent that we then construct systems of knowledge, sciences? How do beliefs become believable such that we forget they are beliefs – and credit them as truth, as the way things are, as even self-evident and scientific in a way that denies (or at least downplays) their association with belief? How can we get behind (or beyond) belief – to explain it – without this not simply being a belief itself, and an act of believing in being believed? Why is the Emperor of assured knowledge *seen* to be wearing clothes? As one recent biological anthropologist and philosopher has written, in defence of some of the ideas I have expressed in the opening to the second of our investigations, in terms of what he calls 'our enigmatically incomplete nature':

If the most fundamental features of our human experience are considered somehow illusory and irrelevant to the physical goings-on of the world, then we, along with our aspirations and values, are effectively rendered unreal as well. No wonder the all-pervasive success of the sciences in the last century has been paralleled by the rebirth of fundamentalist faith and a deep distrust of the secular determination of human values. (Deacon)

We flee from the insecurities of scepticism to the rigours (still intellectual, still the products of the invisible workings of the mind) of certainty. We deny the cave and live in what we believe (yes, *believe*) are the sunlit, shadowless certitudes of reality: life in a halogen glare.

I will argue that all our attempts to make beliefs believable – baptising beliefs as hypotheses to be tested, for example – are a means of assuring ourselves that the worlds we create and inhabit are a great deal more stable than in fact they are. And already in using those two words 'in fact' and, indeed, in constructing an argument, I am myself (and I confess it) engaging in the process of making what is unseen into a currency that can be acceptably exchanged in the market of ideas.

BELIEVABILITY

Let's return to those Christian friends faced with a certain dissonance between what they believed themselves to be and a response that made them recognise their existential discomfort in accepting the beliefs of others. There are several ways of dealing with that dissonance. Denial, for example: I do not feel uncomfortable. Or self-recrimination: I should not feel differently towards this boy from the way I feel about this girl. Or rejection: it is wrong for both the boy and the girl to be brought up Muslim. They should both be brought up in a household free of religion until they reach an age at which they can decide for themselves. The options for dealing with the dissonance focus our attention on what is the central subset of questions with which this section of the argument is concerned: the believability of belief. What makes a belief *believable*? This is not just a question of identifying why you believe what you believe or why you might be persuaded to believe in something else. It also concerns what I call the structures of belief. And these structures change – with time, with geography, with cultural difference. To understand this structural aspect of belief, let's start from a basic and contemporary example.

E.ON is a leading supplier of energy in the UK to the domestic and industrial market. I'm going to stick with domestic use, but industrial use is only an expanded version of the same (with discounts for 'bulk'). On its website, in this time of financial austerity, there is much about the customer being in 'control' of the energy they use and there is a link to a separate set of pages concerning the saving of energy and detailing how to make those savings. What we the customers infer from this is that

a) energy has sources (fossil fuel, oil, water, wind, sunlight, etc.);
b) E.ON has acquired considerable stores of these sources;
c) energy is a commodity the company therefore has and is wishing to sell on (to us);
d) we have a need (for heating, lighting, and to power any number of household gadgets) for this commodity;
e) the commodity is measurable because we can purchase (and save) a certain amount of it; and
f) when that amount of the commodity purchased is used up, we can buy some more.

Now all of these assumptions about the nature of energy we simply accept. The majority of us probably do not even realise that this acceptance entails a number of *beliefs* about the nature of energy. Few will know that this understanding about the nature of energy is a product of eighteenth- and nineteenth-century science (the way it came to 'explain' what the nature of energy was) and its astonishing application in the Industrial Revolution. But, as physicists in the mid nineteenth century, from James Clerk Maxwell and his laws of thermodynamics onwards, discovered: a) energy does not have sources (fossil fuels, water and wind do not 'contain' quantities of something called 'energy'); b) if it does not have sources, then it cannot be extracted from these sources and 'stored', and so there is a question concerning what companies like E.ON actually *have* that they wish to sell on to us; c) if energy does not have sources, it is not a commodity either, and so this raises questions about d) what we are using when energy powers our heating, lighting and domestic appliances, and e) what is being measured as 'used' such that we can f) use it up, require more or save it.

The physical facts of the matter (as twentieth-century physicists have shown) are: nothing is stored or used up with respect to energy. Of course, there are material substances involved in the transference of energy (fossil fuels, water, wind, sunlight, etc.) in and through a physical–chemical reaction, but energy is never depleted. The molecules involved in one substance get translated into something else, and in being translated into something else there is a dissipation of the physical power in and between the molecules. In being dispersed it is not necessarily possible to retrieve or reverse this molecular dispersion, but there is no such thing as 'energy' loss in so far as this is the nature of energy. To take up an observation made by Mary Midgley that we will develop further in a later chapter: 'many of the visions that now dominate our controversies are ones which look as if they were based on science, but are really fed by fantasy.'

The point is: this is not how we perceive or have come to perceive the nature of energy – and there are reasons why we have come to perceive (and still perceive) it in the way companies like E.ON market it to us. And there are reasons why we might well come to view energy differently in the future (as our understanding of its nature is more widely understood). Now what I wish to examine here is twofold. Taking a cue from those good old-fashioned structuralists, but on purely heuristic rather than metaphysical or semiotic grounds, I want to examine the synchronic and diachronic axes of believing. It is these axes that structure our believing and what is believable.

SYNCHRONIC AXIS

We have recognised, from our examination of the psychobiology of believing, a mental, somatic and affective architecture of belief. In the structure of belief, aspects of this architecture will take on specific functions. What then are we examining in this structure? Namely, the normative conditions operating in any culture that support and reinforce the believability of a belief. These conditions, I propose, constitute what Foucault would call a 'grid of intelligibility' that makes certain beliefs either believable or unbelievable. Although in any given historical period, in the particularities of any given social and cultural situation, the values assigned to these normative conditions may vary, my claim is that the norms for explicit believing themselves are a priori: they enable the operation and transformation of believability. As we have seen from the first part of this essay, there is an implicit, dispositional believing upon the basis of which explicit beliefs are founded. But we have been turning our attention in this second part to explicit forms of believing. The transformation of believing becomes appreciable when we consider the diachronic axis. But, as we will see, it is often in the transformations of believability within the particularities of any given culture that we have access to the synchronic grid that makes believing (and disbelieving) possible. The branch of philosophy concerned with knowledge and understanding (broadly, epistemology) frequently concerns itself with articulating these normative conditions, although in extracting them from the particularities of their historical and cultural embeddedness they take on the metaphysical weight of *what is the case*. We will examine this later in the work of John Locke.

For the moment, we will return to our example of energy supplies by E.ON, and begin sketching the synchronic structure of believing by drawing attention to how *a discourse about* plays an important role in the way we currently are conceiving energy as a measurable commodity that has specific sources and can be used, stored or saved. 'Discourse' covers a wide range of linguistic activities. First, it describes an object (energy, in this case). Secondly, since any specific discourse is a product of a certain way language is used, then discourse is implicated not just in a passive description but an active dissemination of that description through various media and agencies. I looked online, but other media are used to advertise a product, from TV and radio to distributed mailed pamphlets. Thirdly, these modes of dissemination are themselves discursive – they communicate through a variety of signs (digital, pictorial, vocal, printed, etc.). Active dissemination (advertising, promotional material, etc.) increases the levels of communication of the passive description.

The way we describe the phenomenon of energy, even when, as I said, scientists have been showing us since the mid nineteenth century that this is not how the phenomenon actually is, develops a habit of mind. And this mind does not simply belong to individuals; it is intersubjective in the same way that any specific discourse is not owned by any one person. It becomes a shared habit of mind. We begin to see energy *as* this type of commodity because the phenomenon is symbolised in ways that facilitate its conception as, and therefore its perception *as*, a measurable commodity.

The believability of a belief is then related to discourses that persuade us to imagine an object in a certain way. But discourses do not arise spontaneously; they are authored. So another aspect of the synchronic axis for believability is related to a cluster of ideas around authoring, authority (the social standing of an author) and authorisation (how that social standing is culturally published and legitimated). E.ON is not the author of the view of energy it employs and encourages, but is an accredited agent in the dissemination of this view of energy. Its accreditation comes from two different sources. First, it is registered as a public limited company in the UK. It has a registration number and a VAT number. But this alone would not suffice for accreditation as an agent in the buying and selling of energy. Any number of companies are registered by the state in this way. So, secondly, the accreditation issues from the size of the market in energy that E.ON has secured. In what seems a tautology, numbers count. We are informed by its promotional material (which is another form of discourse) that five million people receive electricity and gas for both homes and work from this supplier (in 2013). As such it is one of the leaders in the UK energy market. Being a recognised leader also counts; that is, it is credited with social power – at least over those five million customers.

The promotional material does more than just establish E.ON's prominent and therefore authoritative presence in the field. It seeks to win confidence and trust in this authoritative presence. It does this by appealing to the shared cultural concerns of the present, assuring customers and potential customers that it is 'always looking at ways to make energy cleaner', 'improving [its] gas, coal and oil-fired power stations', 'producing more energy from renewable sources like wind and water', making energy not just cleaner but 'simpler', with 'single-sheet bills and fewer tariffs that are easier to understand', and 'doing more to help customers save energy and money'. There is a sales charter and a commitment to investing in communities. As the promotional material states, the aim here is to be perceived as 'a company people can trust'. The authority of E.ON, then, rests upon winning this trust (which if successful will give it an even greater share in the market), but the trust first has to be inspired by listing what it is doing to improve things and associating such improvements with an unstated but implicit moral claim: we care.

Now part of what is making the belief believable here belongs to the diachronic axis; that is, present cultural values (renewable energy in the face of the insistence that resources are being rapidly depleted, and saving money in a climate of financial austerity, for example). And these cultural values can change. But when we are examining the synchronic structure of belief, we are paying attention to the normative conditions that make a belief believable: the trust in the authority of those authoring the discourses that persuade us. However, it is apparent that disseminating and maintaining descriptions in which energy is a commodity certainly assists E.ON (or any other energy supplier): it creates a market for energy.

The strategies for gaining that trust rely also on providing empirical evidence for each claim: cleaner, improved, simpler and more cost-effective energy consumption. E.ON provides percentages per year for fuel mix (x per cent coal, y per cent oil, z per cent wind, etc.) and amounts in euro that have been or are to be invested in the generation of renewable energy. The evidence acts as a public testimony guaranteeing the validity of other claims made for what the company is doing. Of course, the public has no access to how these figures are arrived at or, indeed, their accuracy. So the trust in the figures, the assurance that they are facts, is a vicarious trust placed in other mediating agencies.

These mediating agencies might be competing companies, which would challenge these figures, or agencies, like the UK Advertising Standards Authority (ASA), which monitors the relationship between persuasive discourses and the facts of the case. If externally verifiable facts fly in the face of the promotional claims, if complaints are raised, then investigations can be made and remedial action taken when necessary. Appeals can also be made to law courts, where companies can be sued for publishing mislead-ing information and settlements made to those affected. Furthermore, in many countries, there is the office of the ombudsman. This is an official appointed by either the parliament or government to act as an independ-ent agent serving public interests. There are then institutional authorities accrediting or discrediting other institutional authorities. Processes of legitimation emerge in and through the cooperation of these institutions. Of course, these institutions, their number, their distinctive work, are also subject to diachronic change. They rise and morph, amalgamate, subdivide and even disappear over time.

Often these agencies are managed by or employ 'experts' – people qualified and experienced in specific fields and therefore able to assess the veracity of claims entering the public domain. Their assessments, authorised by other authorised companies, are viewed as authoritative. The fields of expertise change in parallel with the rise or fall in the hierarchies of knowledge; in any culture, intellectual expertise is arranged according to its wider social or cultural value.

Scientific knowledge has risen to be prominent in many contemporary cultures because of its usefulness, its success at problem-solving, its inventiveness in making seemingly labour-saving devices for domestic consumption, and its ability to generate income through various industries. In a number of internationally known universities it is the reputation of their scientific research, their medical, law or business schools, even their sporting prowess, that is valued far higher, institutionally, than their humanities faculties. None of the top ten universities in the world boasts of its Classics department or its achievements in religious studies.

This hierarchy of knowledge is subject to cultural change. In part, the change comes about internally as the different intellectual fields jostle competitively to demonstrate their public value. As Michel de Certeau reminds us concerning the rise of lawyers in the early seventeenth century: 'These laymen were ordained to a priesthood that takes over where the clerics left off.' Near the origins of modernity the professions cultivated expertise, educated and authorised it. The professional bodies compete with, ally themselves to, and demote each other, so gradually, in seventeenth-century France, the lawyers, medics and eventually scientists take over and become the new priest-class. Their discourses are recognised to have great powers to explain the world in which they have emerged as 'the ones who know and understand it'. The hierarchy of knowledge is based upon this explanatory power, which can account for the past and present experience of a phenomenon, and predict its future. Explanation is as much about control, and control through understanding, as knowledge. But that control is not a professional given. It is a professional achievement: most of the dominant professions today emerged from murky reputations in the past, with business and management only shaking off its low-born commercial status after World War II.

Again, we are sliding towards a diachronic view of the structure of believing – which is inevitable and important: the structures of believing become most manifest when they are undergoing a transformation. But attention to the synchronic structure allows us to recognise that the believability of a belief depends upon models of both knowledge and understanding. It depends, that is, upon the epistemological conditions that prevail within any given culture. And these models of knowledge and understanding – for there are numerous ways in which one's experience of the world can be explained – cannot be disassociated from their evaluation in any particular cultural hierarchy.

In mediaeval times, a metaphysically and theologically conceived world view was dominated by an Aristotelian understanding of causality that was fourfold (material, formal, efficient and final causation). As we have already seen, in modernity the explanatory power of science was harnessed to a Newtonian understanding of efficient causality. Both formal and final causation dropped out of the picture as unnecessary. The success, in terms of technological developments and their subsequent economic and social consequences, popularised a model of explanation based upon a description of material and efficient causes and their predictable effects. It also popularised a model of knowledge – still with us today with every management invocation of the need for transparency – based upon the mutual reinforcement of what we might call the three Cs: clarity, certainty and calculation. This translates into: Is it easy to understand? (Complex explanations score lower here than sound bites.) Is it proven to be the case? And are there metrics verifying that this is the case?

However much Enlightenment aspirations to objectivity have been shown to be myths masking various levels of human interest and cultural bias, moves away from the subjectivity of opinion towards the maximal objectivity of a standpoint still have currency. In the nineteenth century, two competing models of knowledge and understanding – one based on empirical sensation, perception, thought and judgement, the other based upon intuition, feeling and imagination – brought about a division between the natural and the human sciences; a division that, in the competition for resources and authoritative backing (from the State, for example), still leaves the humanities fighting to define their importance compared to the financial leverage of the 'hard' sciences. There are plural models of knowledge and explanation, but belief in the superiority of one model over any of the others is enmeshed in any number of culture wars fought over the credibility of belief.

Again it is the diachronic shift that has revealed the synchronic structure. But any model of knowledge and understanding orders and allocates value to a set of other variables: the status accorded to belief, imagination, feeling, conviction, personal experience, etc. So the wider horizon within which a culture's epistemological conditions prevail is intimately associated with what that same culture understands of what it is to be human. The epistemological conditions both determine and are determined by a prevailing anthropology. A conception of what it is to be human involves judgements concerning agency, choice, freedom; judgements related to evaluations of human willing, desiring and the ability to reason. In a culture in which human beings are valued as being rational above being emotional or imaginative; conceived as being free individuals with a will to choose between various options; recognised as moral agents to the degree that they discipline desire for the sake of duty; respected for their abilities to consider any number of arguments and arrive at a considered judgement of what is the case – then belief is viewed as a weaker form of knowledge, mere opinion. And the patina of the scientific is lent to such knowledge that reasons according to a mathematical calculus concerning the probable. But there are many indications that this anthropology and the epistemological conditions it reinforced – or these epistemological conditions and the anthropology it reinforced – are currently undergoing a major transformation. More of that anon.

THE DIACHRONIC AXIS

Like a child's acceptance of Father Christmas and fears of the bogeyman, the objects and expressions of belief change over time. Once scientists believed in an element called phlogiston and the impossibility of a vacuum; some now postulate (that is, believe possible) parallel worlds and alternative universes.

Belief and imagination endlessly refract what may be and what is always and only seen *as*. Belief in angels is thought to be one of the first victims of scientific rationalism, but as the social historian Callum Brown points out in his subtle rejection of any standard secularisation thesis: 'One of the great mythic transformations of the early nineteenth century was the feminisation of angels', so that 'by the early Victorian period angels were virtuously feminine in form and increasingly shown in domestic confinement, no longer free to fly.' Angelic figures haunt literature and iconography throughout the nineteenth and early twentieth centuries. The American sociologist Robert Wuthnow, writing in 1998, lays out some significant empirical facts about angels in the last quarter of the twentieth century in America:

> Overall, the number of books on angels (according to the Library of Congress) rose from 20 published between 1971 and 1975, to 31 between 1976 and 1980, 34 between 1981 and 1985, 57 between 1986 and 1990, and 110 between 1991 and 1995. During the last of these periods, total sales of angel books were estimated to exceed five million copies.

1995 was declared the Year of the Angel by no less than Hillary Clinton, then US first lady. And Wuthnow's material does not cover the films and Broadway shows over that time and since, from Wim Wenders and Luc Besson to Tony Kushner's *Angels in America*.

The changing objects and expressions of belief are why any synchronic structure that articulates conditional norms for believability has to be supplemented by a diachronic account of the temporal contexts in which those conditional norms are evident. As was evident above, while the conditional norms may be abstracted from their temporal contexts, the abstraction is only heuristic; it enables us to model the conditions for believability in a way that puts to one side the concrete beliefs themselves. It is frequently, as I said, only when the temporal contexts change that the epistemological, discursive, social and anthropological model of the normative conditions becomes clear.

Analogous to the changing beliefs in an individual, and the cognitive dissonance this often sets up prior to and driving forward the change, are the cultural shifts in belief. Again, we can use Michel de Certeau's work on the possessions in seventeenth-century Loudun to illustrate this. The old ways of believing, promulgated and policed by the Church through discourse and the institutions of that time authorising and legitimating that discourse (and the power it could exercise), were being challenged in the light of new discourses, new ways of believing, and institutions gaining public authority. Overall, the clerical authoritative monopoly was in the process of being replaced by a lay authoritative monopoly. Ecclesiastical hierarchy was being replaced by the new political hierarchy of the State that increasingly championed a political over a religious discourse. This change was signalled within language itself; that is, the shift from an authoritative language (Latin) – which remained a *lingua franca* above the ebbs and flows of any number of particular national languages – to the predominance of the vernacular. At the same time, the State fostered (because it required) any number of secular professions, all of which were developing their own institutional power bases and the discursive dissemination of the ways they saw things (their beliefs).

New forms of 'knowledge' appeared as new forms of seeing, understanding and examining the world: medical, philosophical, legal and political. The consequence of this 'passage from religious criteria to political ones, from a cosmological and celestial anthropology to a scientific organization of natural objects ordered by the scrutiny of man' (de Certeau) was a cultural cognitive dissonance that is given expression in the ineffable cries of the mystic and the possessed. The cries, which are not discursive but punctuate all discourses with pain and distress, announce the need for and also the movement towards new forms of cultural therapy; they are symptoms of new cultural conditions, new struggles in believability that demand new epistemological, anthropological and social forms of healing.

In his monumental work, *A Secular Age*, the philosopher and social theorist Charles Taylor provides us with a thick account of this cultural shift in the West, the cognitive dissonance that announced its crises, and the way in which it found its 'healing' in secularisation and the birth of the 'modern'. While de Certeau works on a micro level in which he takes one event (the exorcisms of the possessed) in one location (a French country town), Taylor works on the epic historical level that employs classic terms familiar to sociologists and historians of modernity. He writes, after Max Weber, of the movement from the enchanted sacerdotal world of

Christendom to the disenchanted world of technical and scientific analysis and instrumental reason. He writes, after Émile Durkheim, of the movement from a world in which people are embedded within a religious (and therefore cosmological and celestial) community to the 'great disembedding' and the disembodied world of atomised individualism.

Belief is absolutely at the heart of these movements. Taylor, on the whole, confines the word 'belief' to religious believing, and names the opposite of religious faith 'unbelief'. The challenge I am posing in this book is that such 'unbelief' is itself a belief because religious faith is only one of the many forms believing takes. Taylor's is a story of the unity of belief in Christendom, its fissuring under the pressures of the Reformation and the Wars of Religion and its supernova explosion in modernity, which correlates with an expanding universe of unbelief. It is not simply that the world is imagined in a different way, or that faith in God now faced an atheistic humanism, that people lost their faith and found 'new niches or spaces for unbelief'. More significantly, the world no longer made sense under the aegis of the old beliefs.

> Now what has happened is that for many, even most people in our civilization, the whole way of understanding things has fallen away. The world for them shows up as disenchanted. It's not just that the cosmos theories are no longer believed; they are even no longer fully intelligible.

There are questions here about who 'we' are in the phrase 'our civilization' (and who is excluded), what that 'civilization' is comprised of (and excludes) and why Taylor suddenly makes a distinction between a 'them' and, presumably, an 'us' – but these are questions we need not pursue here.

My intention here is only to point to two prominent accounts – both accepting the hegemony of the secularisation process – of the diachronic axis of believing and the way the synchronic structures of believing come to prominence in crises of belief where the intelligibility of the world is thrown into profound doubt. The secularisation theory on which they rest is an old one formed in the late eighteenth and early nineteenth centuries (Brown) and largely discredited as a myth (Hoelzl and Ward; Ward; Brown). We will explore this myth in Chapter VII along with the other myths that have shaped the ways we see, examine and understand things today. But for the moment, these two accounts enable us to see more clearly a particular set of epistemological conditions (and its anthropology) that provided a new intelligibility that existed throughout modernity. And I wish to present this new intelligibility because part of what I am doing in this essay is pointing to how this way of understanding the world, and the hierarchy of belief and knowledge in which it is invested, is passing away. We are entering another period of cultural dissonance that is challenging the hegemony of secularisation that is fundamental to the accounts of both de Certeau and Taylor.

SENSE AND SENSIBILITY

The syncopation of the synchronic and diachronic structures of believing are quite clearly evident in the opening chapter of John Locke's *Essay Concerning Human Understanding* (1690). They order and foster a dominant trend in the habits of believing still with us today. Although, on my analysis, this is a trend receding more and more into 'what is no longer intelligible' (Taylor). Here Locke lays out the purpose of his work: 'to inquire into the original, certainty, and extent of human knowledge, together with the grounds and degrees of belief, opinion, and assent.' He takes up belief specifically in Book IV in an examination of knowledge and probability. There he defines knowledge as

> the perception of the agreement or disagreement of two ideas. Knowledge then seems to me to be nothing but the perception of the connexion and agreement, or disagreement and repugnancy, of any of our ideas. In this alone it consists. Where this perception is, there is knowledge; and where it is not, there, though we may fancy, guess, or believe, yet we always come short of knowledge.

Knowledge is the connection between ideas, and ideas are the representations of what has been perceived through the senses. In Chapter I, section 9, where he examines two kinds of 'habitual knowledge' – truths laid up in memory and truths of which we are convinced but concerning which we have forgotten the proofs demonstrating them – Locke writes about believing the memory rather than really knowing, associates such believing with something 'between opinion and knowledge' and examines 'a sort of assurance that exceeds bare belief'. Then finally, in Chapter XV on probability, he defines belief:

> Being that which makes us presume things to be true, before we know them to be so. Probability is likeliness to be true, the very notation of the word signifying such a proposition, for which there be arguments or proofs to make it pass, or be received, for true. The entertainment the mind gives this sort of proposition, is called belief, assent, or opinion; which is the admitting or receiving of any proposition for true, upon arguments or proofs that are found to persuade us to receive it as true, without certain knowledge that it is so. And herein lies the difference between probability and certainty, faith and knowledge, that in all the parts of knowledge there is intuition; each immediate idea, each step has its visible and certain connexion; in belief, not so. That which makes me believe, is something extraneous to the thing I believe; something not evidently joined on both sides to, and so not manifestly showing the agreement or disagreement of those ideas that are under consideration.

Here we have laid out for us all the modern understanding about the epistemology of belief and believing. All cognitive activity takes place in the receiving and receptive mind. The world is 'out there' and the senses deliver it to us such that the mind becomes a theatre of intellectual representations or ideas of what is out there. The mind 'entertains', and sometimes its ideas connect to what is out there immediately and sometimes they don't. Either way, the epistemological problem is based on the dualism of world and subject (a subject who is like a homunculus operator). Because knowledge is organised in and around this 'problem' of how what goes on in the head hooks up to what is out there in the world, then belief is related to: a) a calculation on the basis of likelihood, itself based on a series of pre-established certainties with which we are familiar; b) the reception of a persuasive argument (and therefore, implicitly, trust in the authority of the supplier of that argument); c) the absence of certain knowledge based upon the immediate relation between idea and thing; d) the absence of 'steps' that might make the 'connexion' between intuition of the thing and certainty; and e) the separation between the object of belief and that 'which makes me believe'.

The implication of e) is that with certain knowledge there is no separation between the object and my perception of it – there is no 'extraneous' persuasion. That is why there is certainty, and we should apply ourselves to garnering certainties, rather than beliefs, if we are to understand. Belief and faith, in this section of the *Essay* at least, are synonymous with and remain distinct from knowledge. But one can see that – with the association of belief with opinion, fancy and guessing, the variety of possible degrees between probability and improbability, and the notion of there being 'bare belief', which is presumably (for Locke does not develop the idea) an opinion, fancy or guess; that is, both weakly persuasive and without any proofs or demonstration – in such a semantic field, Locke, a Christian believer, would have to distinguish between belief and faith. At best faith becomes a Pascalian wager, a leap beyond reason.

The language of assurance throughout Locke's treatise, and the cool, lucid prose with which he delivers that assurance of what is true, are telling here. Such assurance is an effective counter to fear. And what is feared? Historically and socially it is the return to the civil wars of religion that Locke had heard far too much of from his father and his family. His father was a captain who fought for Cromwell and the Protestant Roundheads in the first civil war (1642–46). In 1652, Locke went up to study at Christ Church, Oxford. The College, his College, was notorious because between 1642 and 1646 it became the palace of the exiled and later executed king, Charles I (1600–49). In the late 1680s, when he came to write his *Essay*, religious disputes were still a long way from abating. A prose elegant in its clarity and reassuringly unpolemical in its tone was needed to pave the way to a new political future. The philosophical fear here is scepticism. It is doubt. Recall the pre-gothic horrors of John Bunyan's Doubting Castle in *The Pilgrim's Progress* (published only twelve years earlier than Locke's *Essay* and with a far wider circulation that points to an inflamed pustule that still remained unlanced in the popular imagination). Doubting Castle is occupied by the feudal tyrant, the Giant Despair, and Pilgrim very nearly succumbs to madness during his imprisonment and torture there.

The word 'doubt' haunts Book IV of Locke's *Essay* and certain knowledge offers assurance (and reassurance) because it keeps doubt – and the spectre of scepticism that is always epistemology's *bête noire* – at bay. Furthermore, 'proof', although associated with mathematics and the theory of probability, is shifting historically at this time towards 'supported by evidence', because probability is a matter of 'what counts'. The new cultural movement begins to distinguish between the evident and evidence, a shift which gives rise to experimental science in which repeatable results constitute, on the grounds of probability and evidence, support for or disqualification of a theory or hypothesis (Peter Dear). In Book IV, even though Locke is discussing ideas in the mind and not facts as such, there are numerous references to 'evidence' (especially the self-evidence of maxims) – though at this point in the transmission of ideas 'evidence' plays a secondary role to rational proof and demonstration.

In Book IV, Chapter II, on the degrees of knowledge, Locke comes close, in sections three and four, to defining a hierarchy in which proof comes first, then demonstration and finally evidence, which, in certain forms of knowledge (even where that knowledge is established by proofs), 'is not altogether clear and bright'. This hierarchy is related to there being three degrees of knowledge – the intuitive, the demonstrative and the sensitive.

There is a curious slippage here in Locke's language, indicative of things to come. The slippage is from proof based on self-evident maxims and evidence (the empirical data used to support the truth of the demonstration made from the proof). We can observe the slippage best by tracing back the language of self-evident maxims, which in mediaeval scholasticism were known as *per se nota*. These were the first principles that organised knowledge (*scientia*) as mediaeval scholasticism interpreted Aristotle. They did not concern the empirical and so bore no relation to evidence. The questions that followed deductively from the first principles of a science concerned not *that* something is the case, but *why* something is the case. In the words of Frederick Bauerschmidt, on Aquinas's understanding of *scientia*:

> The modern scientist might make field observations of a whole host
> of right triangles and draw the correct conclusion that the sum of
> the square of the two sides of a right angle is equal to the square

of the hypotenuse, but this knowledge remains uncertain, since one has not examined all right triangles. Someone who has Aristotelian *scientia* of the Pythagorean theorem, however, knows with certainty that $a^2+b^2=c^2$ because he or she will know *why* it is true.

Locke's language of evidence slips between the self-evidence of deductive proof on the basis of *per se nota* and inductive demonstration on the basis of evidence. But more clearly than the character of belief, the character of what is certain knowledge emerges as that which goes beyond persuasion, the rhetorical process of *making* me believe. It is founded upon what Francis Bacon called 'true axioms' and the demonstrable connection between the proposition and these axioms.

The goal of this epistemology and the cultural politics that followed from it is pronounced: we should aspire to knowledge 'altogether clear and bright' – certainty, transparency, daylight forever; a realised eschatology (without God and without judgement) in which there is no shadow of belief or opinion: angelic truth. It is this mystic truth that colours the imaginations of later modern architects like Le Corbusier and Mies van der Rohe. It dreams a new sublime, and all the skyscrapers since that time – from New York's Woolworth Building to London's Shard – articulate this aspiration for angelic transparency, halogen-lit with certainty.

Philosophically, the logical positivists shared the same habits of belief as the Bauhaus designers. But while liberty was being carved from light, space and limpid prose that related verifiable objects with concrete nouns, the English philosopher Jeremy Bentham conceived his panopticon: the prison in which the prisoners behave because they all see the tower from which they can be seen (even though no one may be in there watching). This is a secularised form of eternal judgement from which later emerged the architectures of the gulags and the death camps. Planned, patrolled and surveilled landscapes.

This is the forensic gaze Foucault excavated and critiqued, the ocularcentrism that Derrida problematised. Michel de Certeau called this call for transparency a 'white ecstasy'. It was as engulfing as the mystic's silence or death's oblivion: the unendurable lightness of certainty. It is the product of the domination by the left hemisphere of the brain over right-hemisphere ambivalence, in McGilchrist's neurophysiological typology.

And postmodernity challenged it with its ironies and parodying surfaces, its exaltation of the kitsch and the complex.

At the conclusion of Chapter 12 in McGilchrist's potted cultural history of the shifts between left- and right-hemisphere dominance, he teases out a change in the value according to belief in postmodernism:

> Post-modern indeterminacy affirms not that there is a reality, towards which we must carefully, tentatively, patiently struggle; it does not posit a truth which is nonetheless real because it defies the determinacy imposed upon it by the self-conscious left-hemisphere interpreter [...] On the contrary, it affirms that there *is* no reality, no truth to interpret or determine. The contrast here is like the difference between the 'unknowing' of a believer and the 'unknowing' of an atheist. Both believer and atheist may quite coherently hold the position that any assertion about God will be untrue; but their reasons are diametrically opposed [...] One says 'I do not know', the other 'I know... that there is nothing to know'. One believes that one cannot know: the other 'knows' that one cannot believe.

My suggestion here is that McGilchrist is observing what contemporary Western culture is evidencing: two dominant forms of believing. The first form of believing ('I do not know') is conducive to an acceptance of unknowing or half-knowing and creative ambiguity (right-hemisphere activity) and the other form of believing ('I know... that there is nothing to know') is what emerges when the epistemological conditions generated with left-brain hegemony are such that there is neither truth nor reality, only simulacrum. The latter condition is Locke's understanding of believing as a weak mode of knowledge taken to its extreme, where knowledge itself implodes and scepticism stalks all the way down a hall of broken mirrors. The first form of believing is possible on the basis of transcending truth, empathy and belonging to a context that far exceeds the limitations of the atomised individual. The latter form of believing is the product of fragmentation, lack of trust and over-reliance on the convictions of an isolated subject afloat upon a world where certainty is no longer possible, or unendurable. Such certainty becomes, to return to Taylor's thesis, 'no longer intelligible'. The first form is a believing *in* – in an object, a relation, and an active commitment – but it cannot be grasped, only lived and participated in. The second form lacks an object, relation or commitment. These are all consoling illusions. It is a passive residual state when the gods have fled and in their place is a profound distrust of what one is told was certain.

Hope lies in the modulations between the invisible and the visible and the possibility of the epistemological conditions of this last understanding of believing providing some basis for conversion to the first form of believing. To articulate the ground for this hope is paramount in an enquiry into what makes a belief believable; for only by attempting to distinguish different forms of making a belief believable can we begin to disentangle the two forms of believing prevalent in our contemporary culture and recognise how the first (right-hemisphere form) might be encouraged and educated in its self-understanding in the left hemisphere. Such an encouragement and education would mean, in McGilchrist's terms, a rebalancing of the activity of the left- and right-hemispherical activity. That rebalancing, I would contend, is at the very core of poetic and religious faith. And that's where our examination has to go next.

VI

The Poetics of Believing: Practising Hope

No one has ever been to Minas Tirith, with its thick walls and its tall towers. No one has ever strolled down its arched streets, climbed its steep cobbled alleys or sketched its pillared porches of grey and weathered stone. No tourists have rested their arms on the moss-flecked battlements and balustrades looking east across the plains of Gondor or west towards Rohan and the distant forest of Fangorn. But the reader's ability to understand 'alleys', 'battlements' and 'plains' requires knowing what these words refer to, and either a prior exposure to such objects or to descriptions and definitions of such objects.

No one has wandered down the dusty lane of the Méséglise Way, observing its borders of nasturtiums, breathing in the scent of the hawthorn blossoms and the lilac trees, and peering over the fence into Monsieur Swann's park. But a number of Proust scholars and biographers have located the village of Combray and observed the rustic spires upon which the account of those in Saint-André-des-Champs was based. And many have walked the streets of Rheims where Swann's wife and daughter were one important day, when the first novel opens, or Paris, where Swann himself must go in a day or two.

And when, in Joyce's short story of 'The Encounter', readers walk along the North Strand Road until they arrive at the Vitriol Works and turn right to continue along the Wharf Road, they can take out a map of Dublin or make a visit to the city itself and confirm the details and the actual existence of these roads.

With these three literary creations – with *Lord of the Rings*, *À la recherche du temps perdu* and *Dubliners* – we are treating not only different modes and degrees of representation, but also the making believable of a belief. It's a poetic belief in which the three novels treat aspects of presence and absence, or, more strictly, *making present* what is absent. And that *making present* requires *making* us believe. In this chapter I want to examine that believing and what literary fiction enables us to understand about the operation of belief in which what is not seen is made to appear, and appear in ways that convince.

POETIC FAITH

In our three examples of the production of poetic believing, what is absent differs in kind and character as we move from descriptions of Minas Tirith, to the Méséglise Way, to the centre of Dublin, and we will have to consider whether this affects the nature of *making present*. Tolkien's world has no external existence, Joyce's does, and Proust's Combray has what we might call a quasi-external existence, since Combray was identified as a village near Chartres called Illiers which, after the success of Proust's novel, changed its name to Illiers-Combray. But the *making present* in each instance is a creative act, as *making* indicates. We are neither passively observing, nor discovering another world. In Chapter IV I spoke about mirror neurons, which are excited when a person engages with the active environment. They mimic the action somatically and affectively. Reading is such an engagement, and the world *presented* to us is both given (by the text) and responded to (by the reader). There is not another world, for we in part create the world we imagine and emotionally interact with as we read. This is how stories change us.

Furthermore, the language of 'another world' distinguishes the act of perceiving from the act of imagining, and these are not distinct processes if we only see *as*. Rather we create the textual world internally that expands our own being in the world externally. Imagining and perceiving are different acts – I do not perceive Minas Tirith – but the distinction between them is less than we might think. Having read and imagined this towering city state, we perceive it in visits to Sperlonga, on the Italian coast between

Rome and Naples, or Sienna. Like the positions internal and external, the boundaries between the perceived and the imagined are fluid and malleable. Each act mediates between the physico- and psychosociality of the body and the operations of the mind in which thinking is felt.

Famously, the English poet Coleridge writes in his 1817 volume *Biographia Literaria* of the 'semblance of truth' with which all acts of literature are involved and of a procuring for the imagination of 'that willing suspension of disbelief for the moment, which constitutes poetic faith.' I wish to make two points about this much discussed text that impact upon the account of believing we are examining here. There is also a certain tension evident in Coleridge's observation that we will need to explore further.

First, the verb 'to procure' becomes increasingly significant the more it surrenders its innocence. The imagination desires; it is associated with the complexly intra-associated dispositions from within which believing emerges. Recall the etymology of the English word 'belief' noted earlier – it is associated with desire. Literature panders to desire. And what is desired is the 'suspension of disbelief' – letting go of the anxieties of doubt and scepticism. For Coleridge, as for Aristotle, desire and willing are inseparable, optative modes of existence related to hope. I'm going to return to the dynamics and erotics of the imagination shortly. But the metaphor of procuring also suggests a certain guilt – the guilt of seduction or wanting to be seduced. That guilt, and the indulgence granted to the imagination, is made clearer by the opposition Coleridge sets up between 'disbelief' and 'faith'.

I suggest that there is no such thing as 'disbelief', only a displaced object of another belief. There has been some work done in Oxford by Miguel Farias, which demonstrates that, according to various forms of psychometric testing, there is nothing experiential distinguishing an atheist from a religious believer. It is just a matter of the objects of their belief – which, psychologically, doesn't add up to much.

Here, with Coleridge, the word 'disbelief' is the suggested antithesis of 'belief' and a correlate of something like rationalism. Locke's epistemology still holds cultural sway. In his note on 'Negative Capability' to his brothers George and Thomas, written on 21 December 1817, John Keats upbraids Coleridge for his lack of a commitment to 'being in uncertainties, Mysteries [*sic*], doubts, without any irritable reaching after fact &

reason'. The rational mind is not open to the possibilities of miracle. Nor would it be open to the disclosure of what Coleridge himself describes as 'the wonders of the world before us'. The rational mind cannot transcend the natural, the everyday, and respond to the transcendent. And yet to suspend disbelief, not as an act of the deliberate will, but as a giving-in to the erotic solicitations of the poetic, is morally ambiguous. A shadow crosses the relationship between the affective (desiring), imagining, believing and knowing. It is the shadow of seduction, the eclipse of reason by the libidinous passions, and the overwhelming of the will.

Secondly, we nevertheless have to note that Coleridge makes this observation in the context of his account of how he and his friend William Wordsworth set about composing the *Lyrical Ballads*. In particular, Coleridge wishes to distinguish between his own poetic endeavours ('directed to persons and characters supernatural') and Wordsworth's ('to give the charm of novelty to things of every day, and to excite a feeling analogous to the supernatural'). The excitation of feeling is directly associated with 'awakening the mind's attention', the emotional inseparable from the intellectual, through the imagination. The result is therapeutic, or even, given Coleridge's language, salvific: in fact, the announcement of a new gospel. For Coleridge views the effects of this emotional, intellectual, imaginative and erotic activity as revoking a situation in which 'we have eyes yet see not, ears that hear not'. In the poetic faith solicited there is a transcendence that, the language suggests, has both theological and ethical significance; we will be shaken from our 'selfish solitude'. The constitution of this poetic faith is transformative. Belief is not only given expression, it is created.

The very structures of believing that we mapped out in the last chapter are galvanised and affected by literature as one transcends the location and the perceptions (geographical, moral and spiritual) of the individual ego. The natural or everyday is transfigured and defamiliarised. Neither Normandy nor Dublin remain the same after reading Proust and Joyce, just as walking up the twisting alleys of Mont-Saint-Michel and walking through an English woodland both take on different semantic colouring after reading Tolkien. We see *as* differently. It is with the attempt to understand something of the nature and operation of these transfigurations affected through the working of the imagination upon the archaeology, architecture and structures of believing – the making of the believable – and its ethical consequences, that this chapter is concerned.

IMAGINATION AND PERCEPTION

Attempting to investigate the nature of the transfiguration in poetic believing requires a different philosophical approach, a phenomenological approach. As I said with reference to Edmund Husserl in Chapter II, the phenomenological approach enquires into that seeing *as* and the inseparability of perception from the interpretation of the meaningful. It asks: what are we seeing when we see, and why? The phenomenological approach to literature asks an analogous but different question: what are we reading when we read, and why? In other words, what are the affective and cognitive processes within consciousness whereby I tour Minas Tirith, the Méséglise Way or Joyce's Dublin? In turn, the answer to this question requires an examination of the work of the imagination. But since imagination cannot be divorced from the wider operations of the mind and its mental mapping, we need to pay attention to distinctions and differences with respect to perception and the making of what is meaning: seeing *as*.

The French existentialist Jean-Paul Sartre, in his own excellent phenomenology of the imagination, notes:

> To read a novel is to take a general attitude of consciousness [...] It is preparing to discover a whole world, which is not that of perception, but neither is it that of mental images [...] To read is to realise contact with the irreal world *on* the signs.

The irreal is Sartre's word for that which is 'without doubt present' but simultaneously 'cannot be seen, touched, smelled'. What we are treating then in the believability of poetic faith is this 'realised contact' with the 'irreal' world, a world that is *made present* for us, by us, through the writer's text.

In our three examples, as I said, the *making present* differs in so far as Normandy and Dublin have a concrete existence outside the text. But even if a reader stood on the North Strand Road (to reduce a situation to its absurdity) reading Joyce's autobiographical story, Leo Dillon and Mahoney would still transcend its topographical details and continue to require a making present of what was not empirically there. Reading is not then a mode of perception, and yet there is a seeing, a hearing, and even sometimes a smelling, tasting and touching, perhaps more acutely focused than in ordinary perception, that takes place in this making present, which we associate with the work of the imagination. And imagination, like perception, is a form of consciousness. It is a consciousness informed by (in the act of reading) words rather than the qualia of things (to use a philosophical term). But words are not images; they are lexical signs or signifiers pointing to and standing in for what is absent, the signified. Different forms of reading practice suggested by any text's register dictate the orchestration of these signifiers. For example, in a philosophical book or a scientific article, the orchestration is orientated towards the acquisition of understanding and knowledge. The signifiers are then related to conceptual schemas and ordered according to a specific discursive logic. Training and practice in this kind of reading of philosophical or scientific texts, being proficient in their technical languages, is necessary for the orchestration to be competent. There are better and poorer readings strongly related to this training, practice and proficiency.

But consider the following description of Weathertop by Strider in the first volume of *Lord of the Rings: The Fellowship of the Ring*:

> long before, in the first days of the North Kingdom, they built a great watch-tower at Weathertop, Amon Sûl they called it. It was burned and broke, and nothing remains of it now but a tumbled ring, like a rough crown on the old hill's head. Yet once it was tall and fair.

The orchestration for a competent reading of this text clearly differs from that governing the reading of a philosophical or scientific text. No doubt we need to have a memory of what is signified by each of these words – verbs like 'to build' and 'to burn'; nouns like 'day', 'ring' and 'head'; adjectives like 'fair' and 'tall'. This knowledge has come through language acquisition and application. This acquisition may enable some to pick up the biblical tonality of 'North Kingdom' and 'watch-tower', though there are some words for which there is no direct association with a signified object – Amon Sûl, for example. Yet their very sound relates to and recalls sounds a practised reader may have heard before, generating not meaning but connotations (of ancient Egypt, say, and its worship of the sun god). The textual orchestration goes beyond knowledge and the ability to identify in order to create a scene that does not dissolve into a mere pattern of sounds, but plays with them. The words insist there are places, peoples, histories and cultures that we know nothing about within which the present narration is situated. We suspend our disbelief that these things are not really there as the sounds (alliterative and assonant) and the rhythms (the rise and fall of each sentence) generate a sense and a seeing.

Nevertheless Sartre is correct: we are not dealing here with mental images as mental images are understood as perceptions or memories of perceptions. In fact, as Sartre explains:

> when the reader is engrossed, there is no mental image [...] A multitude of images is the characteristic of inattentive and frequently interrupted reading [...] [I]n reading as in the theatre, we are in the presence of a world and we attribute to that world as much existence as we do to that of the theatre; that is to say, a complete existence in the irreal.

I would suggest we can go even further with reading: to be 'engrossed' is to be absorbed into the world presented; its world co-evolves with our participation. There is no distance, as there is in the theatre or in watching a film. The perceiving is of another order than image-making. The *making present* is not imaging as such – not in the way we might daydream or anticipate a future encounter with a friend – but imagining.

IMAGING AND IMAGINING

Some synthetic process takes place in our reading that enables us to believe poetically. We need to examine that process. Located in the fixtures and furniture of the place in which we are reading – the chair in a study, lying on the beach – our capacity to believe is engaged in an invisible somewhere that we, in part, create. This engagement is not just a cognitive event, for the act of reading involves the body (excited, the heart beats more quickly; the eyes are always moving across and down the page), and there is an inner hearing, a certain synchrony with the cadences of the prose, and an emotional affectivity. Phenomenology would have to call this engagement transcendence, and I will say more about this in the final chapter, but it is not purely intentional because there is more than 'I' involved here; there is the author's writing. It is a transcendence beyond the consciousness of our physical location, constituted by an imaginative experience. We enter an interaction that resituates us, not topographically, but in terms of what we are receiving and responding to in our substituted locality. That receiving and responding acts upon and within our structures of believing. We could not read at all if we did not have the capacity to believe; to *make believe*, which is the first principle of play. We saw this earlier in the relation between believing and evolving into a symbolic species. Suspension of disbelief makes possible alternative states of believing; and, as a corollary, the suspension of belief itself is impossible. *Cum spiro credo*. The sceptic does not suspend belief; he or she suspends assumed knowledge.

If a phenomenology of the imagination can establish a difference between imagining and perceiving, then a comparison between different forms of reception and response may enable us to discover the distinctive nature of the synthetic activity engaged in by reading. As a thought experiment, then, we might ask what the difference is between encountering a person you have never met before and encountering a character for the first time in a novel. In Proust's own famous phenomenology of reading, Marcel observes the following:

> It is true that the people concerned in them [the book] were not what Françoise would have called 'real people'. But none of the feelings which the joys or misfortunes of a real person arouse in us can be awakened except through a mental picture [*par l'intermediarie d'une image*] of those joys and misfortunes; and the ingenuity of the first novelist lay in his understanding that, as an image was one of the essential elements in the complicated structure of our emotions, so that simplification of it which consisted in the suppression, pure and simple, of real people would be a decided improvement [*un perfectionnement decisive*]. A real person, profoundly as we may

sympathise with him, is in a great measure perceptible only through our senses, that is to say, remains opaque, presents a dead weight which our sensibilities have not the strength to lift [...] The novelist's happy discovery was to think of substituting for these opaque sections, impenetrable to the human soul, their equivalent in immaterial sections, things, that is, which one's soul can assimilate.

Marcel's snobbery towards, and yet affectionate criticism of, Françoise surfaces here in making the judgement between 'real' and novelistic people hers. The irony, of course, is that Françoise too is not a 'real' person, but the creation of Proust. Nevertheless, the inverted commas around the use of 'real people' betray Marcel's own evaluation that in encounters with both 'real' and fictional people we are treating images or 'mental pictures'.

We can take this further. Both types of encounter, I would contend, involve acts of reading. It is not simply a matter of registering details, but also of coming to a judgement about what this choice of tie, that inflection of the voice, this opinion or gesture signifies. There is then a reception, an interpretive, interpreted response and, as in any act of reading, there is a projection of meaning followed by a series of modifications. The projection is an index of desire and belief with respect to the constitution of the other person or character. The projection might take the form of an identification or Proust's 'profound sympathy'. The projection might take the form of a caricature – fitting the other into a pre-held format, a stereotype: people who wear hats are these kinds of people. There is something of a caricature about Marcel's Françoise. The projection might take the form of a fantasy, where desire is strongest and most clearly evident. Later in the passage, Proust describes how in the act of reading 'there was always lurking in my mind the dream of a woman who would enrich me with her love [*qui m'aurait aimé*].'

Nevertheless, though the modes of projection may be multiple, in all projection (as we saw in Chapter II) there is an anticipation. Beginning in a state of ignorance, there is a slow coming to a certain (never complete) understanding, which Proust traces both in Swann's self-destructive love for Odette and Marcel's own obsessions with Albertine. Anticipation and the projecting of a judgement that will subsequently be modified are inseparable from that coming to an understanding of what the Belgian poststructuralist

Paul de Man, in his deconstructive reading of the passage in Proust cited above, describes as 'the flight of meaning' that the reader must pursue. This projection establishes reciprocal relations in which something has been given, something received and something awaited.

At this point I am establishing that there are strong similarities between relating to another person and relating to a fictional character. That similarity lies in the operations of belief and desire as they interpret signs, whether they are from a perceived image or an imagined representation. Proust, in his immersion and participation in what he is imagining, describes his 'belief [later 'central belief'] in the philosophic richness and beauty of the book I was reading, and the desire to appropriate them for myself.' Let us examine *that* believing.

This experience of believing is given an extended metaphorical scenario in which Proust describes first viewing the book in Borange's bookshop:

> tied with string to keep it in place in the mosaic of monthly serials and pamphlets which adorned either the side of the doorway, a doorway more mysterious, more teeming with suggestion [*plus semée de pensées*] than that of a cathedral.

A little further in the novel we return to this operation of the imagination in a way that opens up a deeper analogy between aesthetic and theological modes of believing: 'the spirit of faith [*foi*] in which my mind would exceed and anticipate his [the author's] printed word, as it might be interpreting a revelation.' Commentators have written much on Proust's reference to Roman Catholicism: the iconography, liturgy and architecture of Christianity. I will not rehearse their conclusions, though what they indicate is significant for what we will have to say about believing and religious faith in the final chapter. What is significant for the argument now is the way an imagined projection operates as distinct from a perceived image: there is an excess, *plus semée de pensées*, of suggestion, a deeper excitation of that synergy between believing and desiring. It is for this reason that Françoise's reflections, Marcel's reflections, point to a more profound appreciation of the fictional character rather than the 'real' person. What is being appreciated is the excess of suggestiveness in the character from the novel over the excess of perceptual detail about a 'real' person who 'presents a dead weight which our sensibilities have not the strength to lift.' The image multiplies; the imagined synthesises, unifies, concentrates. Let's now take this further.

In meeting another person or a character in a novel, we have set before us a set of appearances, and as the encounter develops (either in real time or narrative time) these appearances will either gain or lose credibility; that is, further appearances link up to past appearances and there is a unity that binds them to form one subject. We will either continue to believe in, become sceptical of, or discredit what is being given to us and which we are being solicited to receive. When a radical discontinuity opens between appearance and the repertoire of our previous experiences that constitute our appreciation of the believable, we start distrusting the other person or disbelieving in the character. If the person before us claims intimate knowledge of a supermodel or our favourite film director, and all we have been given previously belies such knowledge, and all supporting evidence seems lacking, then what we believe about that person or character becomes discredited.

Take, for example, Joyce's 'I' in the story 'The Encounter'. We are caught up in the experiences of a child, but much of the effectiveness of the story comes from a difference that opens up between the reader's recognition of the sexual nature of the encounter of the adult with the two boys and the children's own ambivalent awareness of what the man is doing when he retreats from them to masturbate. The 'I' cannot connect Mahoney's 'Look what he's doing' – though he keeps himself from looking at what the man is doing – and the talk with the man about little girls beforehand. The character of the 'I' is constructed around a nascent but still unconscious understanding of the sexual. Had then Joyce given us some explicit detail about the 'I's' previous sexual experiences with girls, the characterisation of the 'I' and most of the subtle complexity of the experience being described would have been radically disturbed. The ability to continue believing in the 'I' is related to the ways in which the reader can synthesise and respond to what is being given as the writing develops. Experienced readers become adept at identifying unbelievable characters.

One further point: desire. Both Proust's accounts of Marcel and Joyce's story are narratives of desire. The desire operates on two levels. First, the plots are consciously concerned with desire; secondly, the writing itself desires to inform us about this desire. But what is the desire for? What orientates it? Proust appeals to two metaphors, one related to travel and the anticipation of discovery, the other related to love and 'the woman I love in the setting I most longed at the time to visit'. Both metaphors figure a constant and fundamental 'reaching out from my inner self to the outer world [*incessants mouvements du dedans au dehors*], towards the discovery of truth,' and later, 'the perpetual struggling to transcend it [the sensation of always being enveloped in, surrounded by, our soul], to break out into the world'. In the encounter with both the stranger and the fictional character, in the projection, the anticipation and all the affectivity that the operation of the imagination excites, there is a desire to understand ('truth'); a desire for the immediacy of relation (breaking out into the world); and, recalling the earlier passage about the opacity of the 'real' person, a desire for transparency. There is in the relays of sensation, belief and imagination that any encounter instigates a play of the transcendent, where the transcendent is called forth by the enigma of the other. Desire, and belief – both dispositions as we have seen that are also and simultaneously forward-looking drives related to what the German critical theorist Ernst Bloch termed 'positive expectant emotions' – are implicated in this play of the transcendent.

BETWEEN THE REAL AND THE FICTIONAL

We can sum up three places where the encounters between a 'real' person and a fictional character diverge, but each will still necessarily engage believing, desiring and imagining. First, in encountering an unknown person, the relation established is two-way in a manner not possible with a character. The other person is also making judgements about me and the other makes me conscious of the details of how I might be appearing. A certain look can affect the manner or even the possibility of my reception and response. A character, on the other hand, cannot reciprocate, and so any modifications of my judgement occur in and through the text's own characterisation process and my participation in it.

The two-way nature of the relationship with another person has a further consequence. Namely, there is room for deception and manipulation.

I can mislead; I can be misled. But there is no scope for my manipulation with what Proust describes as 'this new order of creatures [*un nouveau genre*] [...] since we have made them our own, since it is in ourselves that they are happening, that they are holding thrall'.

Secondly, there are differences with respect to projection and anticipation. For what is anticipated with a character is a narrative – a future development related to the direction taken by the plot. If we are not in Kindle mode, then we hold in our hands the thickness of the pages yet to come; there is the presence of that which is not yet realised, a textual terrain to travel, an unknown. Of course, we can imagine a possible narrative for the person we have encountered. But that is our story, not theirs. The character in the narrative is already there; the curiosity to know that informs our reception and response cannot be divorced from an expectation that something is certain to follow.

Thirdly, poetic faith differs from beliefs about another person in so far as what we are treating in our reception of and response to the fictional character is a fundamental absence, a more profound and affective invisibility. That calls for a deeper commitment to and engagement in the processes of believing. With the stranger before us, we are not asking whether or not they exist. With a character we are co-creating, we are making them present within us, not before us; and whilst believing in them, we know they are not there at all. Poetic faith exactly concerns the ability to *make present* and *be present with*. *Making present* and *being present with* are experiences, and our absorption is an index of the intensity of our 'willing suspension of disbelief'.

What is significant for our concerns here is that an ontology announces itself with this presencing of what is invisible. It is an ontology whose distinctiveness lies in that *making* believable of the belief. For the stranger I am also present as he or she is present to me. But I am not charged to make him or her present as I am with a fictional character. Nevertheless, that *making present* cannot be dismissed as a mode of non-existence, as just illusion or a mode of falsehood. That which is *made present* bears ontological weight: it changes us, it impacts upon the cultures in which we live; it transforms values and ideas; it informs behaviour.

POIESIS

The ontological investment in this making becomes clearer if we look back at Aristotle's understanding of *poiesis*, for *poiesis* is the name he gives to 'making' as in 'creating'. The noun relates to the verb *poieo* – to produce, perform, execute, compose or, more generally, be active. *Poiesis* is an historically specific operation concerned with creative action. As such, it would constitute one aspect of a theory of action – cultural and moral action – and in this way it is associated with *praxis*, from the Greek *prasso*, meaning to act, manage, do or accomplish. For Aristotle there appears to have been a distinction between a specific form of making (*poiesis*) and the more general notion of doing and being involved in an activity (*praxis* or *pragma*). *Praxis* would be associated with ethics, politics, and the formation of character. But the distinction between *poiesis* and *praxis* cannot hold strictly; not if we accept what I have outlined about the psychobiology of believing and desiring. So I wish to take *poiesis* in a complex sense that would not isolate aesthetic production from political and ethical activity. Neither can *poiesis* be reduced to *techne*, because it does not simply reproduce; it draws into visibility that which is invisible and in this way creates anew. The Italian philosopher Giorgio Agamben relates the creative act of *poiesis* to 'truth-making' or *aletheia* – the truth that emerges only in and through the act of creation.

All this was familiar to Coleridge. Aristotle's term came to be translated in the Renaissance as 'poesy' – as in Sir Philip Sidney's *An Apology for Poetry (or The Defence of Poesy)* (written in *c.*1579). Sidney is clear that 'poesy' is not about mirroring or representing, but rather *making present*; that is, given the sin-ridden fallenness of the world (as emphasised by Sidney's Protestant background), an act of poesy refashioned the world in a way that reorientated it towards the paradise that had been lost.

For Aristotle, *poiesis* was profoundly indebted to modes of affectivity. In his treatise 'On the Soul', neither desire, thought nor imagination can be separated out from sensation. In fact, all three are actualised by sensation and its emotional correlates. He observes that if there is '[sense] perception [*aesthesis*], then also [there is] imagination and desire [*orexis*]. For where there is perception, there is also both pain and pleasure, and where these, there is of necessity also appetite [*epithumia*].' *Orexis* is a general word for longing in which there are three forms of desires: passion (*thumia*), wishing (*boulesis*) and wanting (*epithumia*) – each of them primordially dispositional. And that which actualises what desire desires, what believing believes and imagination imagines is *poiesis*.

Exactly what is at stake here ontologically can be understood with reference back to Sartre and what his own phenomenology attempts to establish contrary to those followers of David Hume – the positivists, behaviourists or material reductionists. He writes: 'I do not make of it [the image] a reborn sensation, but on the contrary an essential structure of consciousness, better still a psychic function.' The image is only the beginning for the imaginary. This mental operation is also fully corporeal: 'the image is not a simple content of consciousness among others, but it is a psychic form. As a result, the whole body collaborates in the constitution of the image.' The seeing *as* of perception becomes a form shaped by the dispositions and laden with corporeal affect. In this way believing cooperates with imagination. For the Humeans, positivists, behaviourists and material reductionists, if the image is not simply an illusion, an epiphenomenon (Dennett et al.), if it has any ontological purchase whatsoever, then its truth is measured by the sensations that have delivered it – sensations stimulated by an object 'out there'. If there is no object corresponding to the image, then we are dealing with fantasy. But, at best, if there is an object, the image is only a dilute copy of it. In such a scenario consciousness passively receives and therefore can be disregarded: what is received and how that impacts upon behaviour is more important than whatever the receptor might be. Consciousness might only be a by-product. It doesn't do anything itself. Sartre, on the other hand, returns us to Aristotle's understanding of what a soul is by emphasising the psychic operation of the imagination, its creative synthesising and its affectivity.

What I am suggesting in this chapter is that reading is a *poiesis*, a transformative existential act that both actualises and demands belief. It cannot perform the act it does without engaging our belief structures. Furthermore, because reading is not a matter of escapism but expansion, then our believing, and our investment in believing, is enlarged in reading. We are freed from certain material limitations. The structures of belief are changed, refashioned. This is significant if we return to those three differences between encountering a stranger and a fictional character. With the character, we are engaged in sustaining (and the sustainability of) that which is invisible: an imaginary externality. It is the nature of this virtual externality that extends us, transports us, because it transcends intentionality. We as subjects (a complex notion itself to which we will have to give some thought in a future chapter) do not control either the extension of ourselves or our transportation. Reading is not an analogue of autism. It is not solipsistic; imagining, desiring, and believing are not reducible to immanent activities. What we perform is a score given to us and outside us.

The examination of reading, then, investigates both a making presence and a knowing absence, both of which call upon forms of affectivity and our disposition to believe. In so far as the reading is a continual relational activity with respect to these affections and this believing, orientating us towards maintaining an imaginary externality that nevertheless transcends and reorders us, then there is an ethics of narration. And so the disposition to believe can have, might have, an ethical teleology.

THE THREE AXIOMS OF ETHICS

That last statement is controversial and will need further substantiation, although we have already explored the possibility of teleology in Chapter IV and being target-driven in Chapter V. I am still mid-argument, but let's see if we can flesh out the idea of believing as ethically orientated. What do I mean by ethics here? I am not speaking of specific moral principles or norms. Of course, certain literatures do adopt explicit moral positions. Robert Browning's *Pied Piper* concludes with a four-line moral adage about always keeping promises. But the sheer musicality of the language, the narrative wit and the magical content explode the tight constraints of this terse maxim. The reader's imagination has travelled too far among too many colours, fabrics, sounds and emotions to be brought to a halt so abruptly and solemnly. The forced ending, in the light of this, sounds ironic. Whilst being aware of the author's presumed moral purposes, I am not discussing seemingly moral or immoral content by the 'ethics of reading' here. Nor am I referring to the vague 'morality' of literature that treats life seriously and constitutes what the English literary critic F. R. Leavis described as the 'great tradition'.

The critic Paul de Man once claimed that 'any narrative is primarily the allegory of its own reading.' That may sound very postmodern. But what I am claiming throughout this chapter is that any reading is primarily an allegory of poetic faith – the operation of our dispositions to believe, to imagine and to desire; that is, there is an intention signified that is more profound than what is given to us at the level of character, plot, landscape and themes. In the *making present* there is always something else, something other (hence *allegoria* from the Greek word for 'other'): a journeying, a believing, a desiring, an encountering, a discovering, and an expansion of our horizons that subtly changes the structures of sensibility and possibility. The ethics I am speaking of therefore are intrinsic to this journeying, believing, desiring, encountering and discovering in narrativity itself, and its orchestration in the act of reading.

Frodo Baggins and Gandalf express this well at the beginning of their adventures:

> 'As for *where* I am going,' said Frodo, 'it would be difficult to give that away, for I have no clear idea myself, yet [...] For where am I to go? And by what shall I steer? What is to be my quest?' [...]
>
> '[Y]ou cannot see very far,' said Gandalf. 'Neither can I. It may be your task to find the Cracks of Doom, but that question may be for others: I do not know.'

As Bilbo remarks, once you step on the road outside your door, there is no knowing where it will take you. Tolkien's novel is structured around various degrees of knowledge that depend upon where the character is situated in a story far larger than all of them. The reader sets out on the narrative journey at Frodo's naive level, with fragments of knowledge culled from Bilbo's story and Gandalf's allusions. But Gandalf has to set off in his own attempts to find other threads of the narrative. The four hobbit ring-bearers' encounters with Strider (Aragorn), Elrond and Galadriel are encounters with characters embedded within their own narratives who are only able to see so far. Even the wizard cannot discern what will happen once the road has been taken, for there is something of the workings of providence in the very setting out and in all the encounters that Tolkien makes us aware of: a providence beyond the projections and anticipations, receptions and responses of reader/listener and author/storyteller, the traveller or the one who sets the traveller on the road. Marcel reflects on 'things, half-felt by me, half-comprehensible [*à demi pressenties, à demi incompréhensibles*], the full understanding of which was the vague but permanent object of my thoughts.' We are being led, rather than determining the road for ourselves. There is a following after that requires a submission, belief-informed, to belief formation. This is the first fundamental axiom of the ethics of believing I am sketching here. But there is something more.

Frodo recognises in the road opening up before him an invitation – 'Why was I chosen?' It is an invitation with the urgency of a summons from a source even other than the Dark Lord's. Yet he can refuse the call, just as Marcel can refuse the levels of self-reflection and personal vulnerability that will be needed if he is to pursue that 'full understanding'. The second fundamental axiom of the ethics of believing is the commitment to act, to engage, to answer the call, to surrender to what will unfold. It is a capitulation to the future, and to those future-orientated, survival-orientated dispositions: belief and desire. It is the taking-up of what Frodo calls the 'task' and Marx called 'work'.

In a fascinating passage from the opening volume of *Das Kapital*, Marx outlines how, without imagination, there is no action; nothing can be undertaken. Distinguishing human labour from a spider's weaving or a bee building a cell, Marx explains that for human beings,

> at the end of the work process there is a result which already existed in the *imagination of the worker* at the beginning of the process, i.e. already existed *ideally*. Not that he only *effects* a formal change in the real; he also *realises his purpose* in the natural world.

You can see from this why the making of the first hominid (Oldowan) tools, between 2.2 and 1.7 million years ago, is so important for an archaeology of belief (see Chapter I). Imagination is belief in action, projecting and anticipating, receiving and responding.

We embark upon a specific human practice – not weaving or building, but reading. In a beautiful simile Proust recognises that reading is 'like a hand reposing motionless in a stream of running water, the shock and animation of a torrent of activity'. In this, as in all human activity, imagination and desire are not free to wander anywhere. In reading, the structures of belief and affect involved are disciplined by the narrative. We can take this further by referring to an important work by Paul Ricoeur on the imagination, especially because Ricoeur takes us beyond the individual reader by recognising how the operations of the imagination and belief are implicated in social praxis. I will develop this more in the next chapter with respect to the political, but here in an examination of freedom and its limits I offer a preview. Where Marx valorises the imagination in acts of transformation, Ricoeur explicitly relates the ethics of the imagination to freedom. Without some notion of freedom there can be no ethics – which is why the reductive materialists commit themselves to a radical determinism with both the self and moral choice as illusions. The notion of freedom is the third fundamental axiom of the ethics of believing.

In his seminal essay 'The Imagination and Discourse', Ricoeur gives the imagination a central role in the critique and transformation of the social status quo. He relates its projective aspect to 'the very dynamics of acting' and 'the very process of motivation'. Action for Ricoeur is rooted in imaginative possibility. It empowers us to act for and engender alternative belief-possibilities, variations on the conditional mood of 'I can'. There is then in its operation a utopic moment (the political equivalent of a conception of well-being and flourishing found at the evolutionary level of biology), and this moment is inseparable from – even from the condition for the possibility of – the imagination's own free movement. It is in this context that Ricoeur offers a gnomic but highly suggestive observation: 'There remains to be discerned, in the freedom of the imagination, what could be termed the imagination of freedom.'

Freedom is never unbounded in our reading practices, as we have noted. But neither is it entirely circumscribed by the writer or the writing. The spontaneous play of the imagination not only opens belief up to other horizons, but is itself an expression and realisation of our freedom, our freedom to go beyond the visible and the concrete. Freedom, at least throughout modernity, has always been figured spatially; and so the freedom of the imagination opens the possibility for alternative freedoms, future freedoms, in which desire longs for and belief shapes new forms of physiological and cultural flourishing. But the exercise of the imagination is itself an experience and anticipation of this future freedom, a freedom both realised and projected. In this way imagining has the same structure as hope; for hope too is both a realised and a projected state.

THE PRACTICE OF HOPE

In his sprawling but often incandescent masterpiece, *The Principle of Hope*, Bloch situates hope among the expectant emotions:

> *Expectant emotions* (like anxiety, fear, hope, belief) […] are those whose drive-intention is long-term, whose drive-object does not lie ready, not just in respective individual attainability, but also in the already available world, and therefore still occurs in the doubt about exit and entrance. Thus the *expectant emotions* are distinguished […] by the *incomparatively greater anticipatory character* in their intentions, their substance, and their object […] [T]he expectant emotions open out entirely into this horizon [of time][…] [T]he most important expectant emotion, the most authentic emotion of longing and thus of self, always remains in all of this – hope.

Hope is inseparable from belief and longing or desire.

The kind of action brought forth in imaginative freedom and by hope returns us to *poiesis*: it is not an action that has an end in itself. For Aristotle, such actions are characteristic of *praxis*. But *poiesis* goes beyond what is available, its 'drive-object does not lie ready': it is not visible. The teleology of a practice of hope exceeds the finitudes of individual intending, opening out every horizon. It imbues the sense of an ending with a certain apocalyptic quality: where *apokalupto* defines an unveiling, a bringing out of concealment, a reversal of the Greek *apokrupto* (to hide from). In this apocalyptic quality lies the allure of metaphysics, and literature borders on both the philosophical and the theological. So the reader moves through the story with the expectation of an end that lies in the future. The imaginative processes of reading are interwoven with other imaginings in which the ending of the story is continually being guessed at. There is a *making present* and a projected anticipation, the play of presence and absence that characterises believing. The practice of a narrative hope leads us towards a transcendental condition that is absolutely intrinsic both to all symbolic practices and being human. More specifically, the practice of hope engages with a promise, what the French philosopher Jacques Derrida will call, in writings following *Specters of Marx*, a messianism without the messiah. Not only is the *nature* of this promise indefinable, so is its *province*. From where does this promise issue? Whose promise is it? But hoping and believing are predicated on this promise that opens up the allure of the metaphysical and the theological.

We arrive at the ethical core of the narrative practice. But let me again emphasise that this is not just a mental or even affective practice. Narrative, as the activity of believing, goes all the way to the physiological. The neuroscientist Antonio Damasio writes:

> Wordless storytelling is natural. The imagetic representation of sequences of brain events, which occurs in brains simpler than ours, is the stuff of which stories are made. A natural preverbal occurrence of storytelling may well be the reason why we ended up creating drama and eventually books [...] Telling stories, in the sense of registering what happens in the form of brain maps, is probably a brain obsession and probably begins relatively early in terms of evolution and in terms of the complexity of the neural structures required to create narratives. Telling stories precedes language, since it is, in fact, a condition for language, and it is based not just in the cerebral cortex but elsewhere in the brain, and in the right hemisphere as well as the left.

The practice of imagination, belief and desire cohere to the expectant emotion par excellence of hope. As we have observed, reading is a following after, a submission to, a living and experiencing beyond oneself and the visible; and it is both fundamentally human and fundamentally ethical. The three axioms of the ethical I sketched can be summed up in the promise that meets and is intrinsic to the hope. This promise that arrives with hope is not ours to fulfil. It is only given to us to await an arrival, a fulfilment. Because while intrinsic to our dispositional nature but also external and other to us, we enter what we might call an economy of response – where 'economy' means a managed unfolding of a certain logic. Our reading participation is an economy of reception, but our imagining, believing, desiring and hoping is an engagement responding to our reception. What is hoped for and what is promised provide the dynamics for the projective operation of the imagination and belief. The ethical lies in the immersion in this affective economy that impacts on the very structures of our sensibility, modifying belief, desire and hope.

The practice of hope, this exercise of freedom, this encounter with the other that is the core of the ethical, is intrinsic to imagining and constitutes poetic faith. Imagining is a relational and synthetic activity that opens towards the metaphysical and the theological, but need not embrace either. Imagination can simply expose the horizons of possibility, point towards a transcending ambivalence in an interrogative mood. Sartre, the atheist, the one who rejects traditional metaphysics in favour of the immanent alone, can still write: 'The act of imagination […] is a magical act. It is an incantation destined to make the object of one's thought, the thing one desires, appear in such a way that one can take possession of it.'

If language is not simply an instrumental means for the imaginative process, but rather constitutive of the imaginative, then Sartre's rhetoric cannot be dismissed as accidental. Rather, the religious language of 'magic' and 'incantation' is inseparable from what is being described. I would also qualify his use of the words 'one can take possession of it' as being too ego-centred an appropriation. We are opened to what is other and beyond us by imagination. It is not a form of autism. We are also open to being *taken possession of*. Nevertheless, the atheist Sartre bears witness to the allure of the metaphysical and the theological that pertains to the operations of imagination and belief.

With Tolkien, these magical operations of the imagination are inscribed within the very landscape, characters, themes and plot. In fact, the apocalyptic structure of the narrative itself climaxes twice. There are the culminating events on Mount Doom, but the second climax is the recognition of Aragorn as a messianic figure.

[W]hen Aragorn arose all that beheld him gazed in silence, for it seemed to them that he was revealed to them now for the first time.

154

> Tall as the sea-kings of old, he stood [...] yet in the flower of man-
> hood; and wisdom sat upon his brow, and strength and healing were
> in his hands, and a light was about him. And then Faramir cried:
> 'Behold the King!'

The textuality of *Lord of the Rings* is soaked in the metaphysical and theological. With Proust, aesthetic sensibility treats the metaphysical and the theological as resources for metaphors and symbols: Elstir's maritime paintings are attempts to express the sublime, the unbounded, the unpresentable; Berma's performance of *Phaedre* reveals the divine face of an implacable God; the beauty of the church at Balbec cannot be compared to the jewels of the cathedrals at Rheims or Chartres or the pearl of Sainte-Chapelle de Paris.

CONCLUSION

I think we can make an important observation about the ethical axioms governing the activity of imagination and believing: there appears to be no difference – at the level of the operations of imagination, believing, desire and the expectant emotion of hope – between 'visiting' places that are totally fictional (as in *Lord of the Rings*), quasi-fictional (as in *À la recherche du temps perdu*) or non-fictional (as in *Dubliners*). Style creates verisimilitude and so invents characters and places that are believable. Belief in them constitutes poetic faith, as Coleridge understood, but it is the extent to which that belief is made believable (and sustained in its believability) that guarantees the strength of the emotional engagement with narratives. This engagement not only embodies and operates through structures of desire, expectation and hope, but it also forms, re-forms and transforms our own structures of believing.

With Joyce, we have a story in *Dubliners* that expresses all and more than this chapter has been attempting to explore. 'Grace' is a story about five Irish men who agree to attend confession and receive absolution. They are brought together through the ignominious situation of one of the men, Mr Kernan, who, at the opening of the narrative, is found lying drunk and bleeding in 'the filth and ooze of the floor' outside the lavatory in a Dublin pub. He has fallen down the stairs, and Joyce plays out that fall on topographical, moral and theological levels throughout the story that ensues. The scenes we enter as readers and interlopers do not speak of hope. A rich, earthy complexity is uncovered by Joyce in which politeness masks a feral opportunism criss-crossed by contending forces – law and disorder, middle and working classes, Protestants and Catholics, snobbery and humiliation. These five men, and Mrs Kernan, are situated in a tenuous web of human relations, 'impregnated with a personal odour' of a dank unhappiness, like that in Mr Kernan's bedroom. If there is hope, an aim, it is in a lackadaisical longing for a redemption that not one of them is sure is available. Even going to confession is understood as a 'scheme [that] might do good and, at least, could do no harm'. The story concludes in a church, with the five men sitting in a quincunx (a symbol of the five wounds of Christ) listening to a sermon by Father Purdon (a play on the Irish pronunciation of 'pardon') about businessmen living in the world needing to set right their accounts.

It is in the silence that follows this ending that the hope announces itself. The reader, like the five men, sits and waits for the possibility of a coming, a gift, the operation of grace. No epiphany is offered, and even the expectation is fretted with doubts. And yet, nevertheless, we are brought to a certain threshold in which we, the readers – like the characters – have submitted ourselves into recognising something about the pettiness and possibilities of being human. The act of going to confession, like the act of reading, is a practice of hope, a solicitation and expression of a belief, however inchoate, in which there is a certain reordering of human relations. The hope lies only in the action. The human situation in the story is without hope; despair is held at bay with alcohol, social aspiration and the maintenance of civil law. We are led in this practice of hope to the portico of a transcendence that is not only ethical, but also metaphysical and theological. A transubstantiation *might* take place. Imagination has brought us to a point where our poetic faith in these five men before the pulpit of Father Purdon *might* itself translate into another mode of believing – in the grace that comes, in the redemption and cleansing that might follow. The power of Joyce's writing lies in the subjunctive, but the very operations of the practice of hope also lie in that subjunctive. The subjunctive is the verbal mood of imagination and belief itself. Fact, fiction, real and irreal swirl like the magpies around the steeple of Saint-Hilaire or even the raven spies of Mordor – and new configurations of the world emerge, new possibilities that inhabit the manners of our perceiving.

No one has been to Minas Tirith with its great walls and its tall towers, and yet anyone who has read of the battles fought over Minas Tirith, of the tragedy and the victory experienced by its people, finds intimations of Minas Tirith in every reference to a mediaeval citadel. And every forest entered will tremble with the elfin light of Lothlórien. For poetic faith, at the heart of imagination and making belief believable, inhabits the very possibility of apprehending the irreducibility of the real. Sartre: 'all apprehension of the real as world implies a hidden surpassing towards the imaginary [...] Thus imagination, far from appearing as an accidental characteristic of consciousness, is disclosed as an essential and transcendental condition of consciousness.'

PART THREE

The *Making* of Belief

VII

Myths, Lies and Ideology: The Politics of Belief

t's often called the 'noble lie'. It's the founding myth of Plato's ideal city, a myth that is told to the Guardians and passed down through them to the Auxiliaries and then the 'farmers and the other workers'. But it has to be told to them in such a way that they forget that it is a just a 'story like those the poets tell and have persuaded people to believe' and accept it as the truth. The lie is this: that everyone in the city is a brother, created from the depths of the earth by their mother, Earth, who brought them up and provided them with arms and equipment so that while they live they are to protect her. And that each person was created with a mixture of certain metals: the Guardians are qualified to be Guardians because of the gold in their composition; the Auxiliaries are qualified to be Auxiliaries because they have silver in their composition; and the workers are qualified to be workers because there are mixtures of bronze and iron in their composition. Not that there is no upward mobility: people can be created with gold in them though their parents were of bronze or iron; people with gold and silver in them can create children of bronze and iron. The important task is always to watch over the children carefully in order to see the quality of their metal and ensure they take their rightful place in the order of things.

The social classes relate closely to the hierarchical levels we have already outlined in the allegory of the cave, which appears much later in *The Republic*. Any number of scholars have accused Plato of fascism on this matter; others have defended him. Certainly, whatever the upward mobility and attention to caring for the community at the cost of individual

161

interests, Plato was no liberal democrat. He thought democracy left too much room for the lies and the demagogic abilities of individual politicians to mislead the people. Such politicians were more interested in the power of having office, rather than the good administration of the State on behalf of all the people. As if things have changed! But the 'noble lie' or, in Socrates' words, the 'magnificent myth', allows us to explore the ways in which 'poetic faith' can be manipulated. Aesthetics to one side, there is a politics of belief. The more we engage with one another in and through the symbolic realm, the more we are prey to the politics of persuasion and the hidden persuaders and, in some cases, the paranoia of conspiracy theories.

What remains controversial, for Plato and political theorists since, is the founding fable. And what remains significant for this study is the recognition believing plays in its gaining acceptance and credibility. *Making* belief believable is, for Plato, the second principle of politics. The first principle is his conception of the Good and its translation into what is Just. But it is all too easy to get the principles confused or to conflate them. Having defined the nature of the abuse of belief – the way belief can be displaced either voluntarily or involuntarily ('[v]oluntarily when the belief is false and we learn better', and involuntarily through 'people being persuaded to relinquish' what they have believed in as true, or forced 'under the influence of pain and suffering') – Socrates ends this part of his dialogue with the question: 'Do you know of any way of *making* them believe' (italics mine) the founding fable? The irony is not lost – though it isn't commented upon, either.

The irony strikes at the heart of a paradox in Plato's *Republic*: the banishing of the poets, the myth-makers, from the ideal city, on the one hand, and his concern that children should be brought up on the right kind of myths that will mould their souls, on the other. Plato is himself a myth-maker: the ideal city is never to be identified with an historical reality; it is the aspirational goal of an educational programme orientated towards the Good and the Just. But the mythic representation of what is the ultimate truth, the Form of the Good, is simultaneously a 'lie' (*pseudos* – a falsehood). And in that lies the danger of myth: the aesthetic can also be, will also be, an anaesthetic. The seductions and soteriologies of poetic faith are both exposed.

But we need not linger on the contents of Plato's particular myth. My concern here is with the way in which symbolic form (myth like literature and cave art) organises the political, social and cultural life of human beings. We are concerned then with the function of myth, the circulations of its symbolic form and its infiltrations into other symbolic forms, and the relation of those circulations and infiltrations of belief. For Plato puts myth at the beginning of his educational programme because it has the ability to mould souls. The tripartite city – with its three classes of citizens as a macrocosm of the tripartite soul; the individual is an analogical part of the corporate – is more than a system of expressed beliefs, and to that extent myth is irreducible to ideology as a set of interrelated ideas. It is composed of beliefs, beliefs that it is hoped (by Socrates) will be believed. But it is the fashioner of beliefs. It is not only to be believed, but its power also lies in *making* believable the beliefs. So, beyond understanding the social and political function of myth, we need to explore both why and how it is so powerful.

MYTHOS AND PATHOS

The influence of Plato's mythic State has been profound, and the reason for this is in part the way it expresses a vision of the collective; a collective ruled by the law of the Good and the Just as it is written into the very fabric of the cosmos. There is an eternal Reason (Logos) that establishes an eternal order (Nomos) that constitutes the world as we know it (Cosmos). The collective gathers the microcosm of each embodied soul and the macrocosm of the State into one. The Roman architect Vitruvius pictured this oneness as the body of a man; St Paul used the body of a particular man (Jesus Christ) as a depiction of the Kingdom of God.

As the Irish scholar of international studies Benedict Anderson famously elaborated, these mythic collectives are 'imaginary communities'. He was talking about the modern nation state in which there are various instruments – like the map, the daily newspaper, the museum and the census – that facilitate the sense of national belonging. But the community of face-to-face individuals does not exist as such. It is a symbolic construction, and a necessary symbolic construction that we might be governed (rather than become tribal and anarchic). The state has the power to raise money through our productivity and exclude us when we step too far out of line. In part, then, the power of myth lies in its imaginative reach – its ability to make us believe this is the society in which we live or in which we should aspire to live. And the myths may not be written as such, like Plato's *Republic* or Thomas More's *Utopia* and Francis Bacon's *New Atlantis*. They might be dreamt, designed and planned like the urban landscapes of Ebenezer Howard. They might be drawn and built, as with the French architect Le Corbusier and his conception of the Radiant City. They might be filmed, like Woody Allen's New York (*Annie Hall*), Danny Boyle's Mumbai (*Slumdog Millionaire*), Peter Cattaneo's post-industrial Sheffield (*The Full Monty*) or Sophia Coppola's Tokyo seen through the eyes of two American visitors (*Lost in Translation*). They might be sung, like 'Ethiopia' by the Red Hot Chili Peppers or Bruce Springsteen's 'Incident on 57th Street'. They might be danced, like Gene Kelly's 1927 Hollywood (*Singin' in the Rain*), Liza Minnelli's 1930s Berlin (*Cabaret*) or Baz Luhrmann's Sydney (*Strictly Ballroom*). They might be composed, like the sonic landscapes of Stravinsky's *Dumbarton Oaks,* Mendelssohn's *The Hebrides*, and any number of musical tropes that can conjure Spain (Rodrigo de Aranjuez's *Guitar Concerto*), a Buenos Aires tango or the Arabic sounds of Sami Yusuf.

The power of the myth lies in the way what has been imagined and put into symbolic form *can be* collectively imagined or represent what *is* collectively imagined. The Canadian social theorist Charles Taylor and the Greek-French social theorist Cornelius Castoriadis both call this activity of collectively imagining our social life the 'social imaginary' (Ward). Two structural features of such myth-making and the belief it can conjure are most evident. The first is epistemological: the ability to recognise (New York, say, in U2's song of that name), and the second is affective: the ability to empathise or attune oneself (with the depiction of London in the 1990s, say, in Zadie Smith's *White Teeth*). Recognition and empathy (we have seen the work of these two aspects of believing when we examined the archaeology of belief) enable the imagined to be shared, communicated, transposed from one to the other, circulated and participated in. Myth as symbolic form is not simply an objectification or condensation of our common beliefs; myth is immersive. We are immersed in the symbolic orders it orchestrates around us. That's why, as Plato saw, the poetic faith solicited can either be ethically beneficial, forming furrows for virtuous action, or a dangerous form of what Friedrich Engels called 'false consciousness'.

POLITICAL MYTHOLOGIES

In the opening pages of his last book, *The Myth of the State*, the philosopher Ernst Cassirer, who wrote much about the nature and effectiveness of myth, says: 'The preponderance of mythical thought over rational thought in some of our modern political systems is obvious. After a short and violent struggle mythical thought seemed to win a clear and definitive victory.' The book arose from a series of lectures he gave at Yale and Columbia in the 1940s, having escaped Nazi Germany through Gothenburg in Sweden. The reference is to the fascist myths of Hitler and Mussolini that were both nationalist and racist. His lectures were aimed at trying to elucidate how this 'clear and definitive victory' over the imaginations of millions of subjects was possible.

> The question necessarily arises why men cling so obstinately and forcibly to such phantasmagoria. Why do they not directly approach the reality of things and see it face to face; why do they prefer to live in a world of illusions, of hallucinations and dreams?

In part we know the answer to that question: because we never can 'approach the reality of things and see'; we only see *as*. That seeing *as* does not necessarily assign all we see to the status of hallucinations, phantasmagoria and illusions, but it does necessarily require that we examine the nature and operations of why we believe what we believe. What Cassirer's lectures charted was a diachronic axis in the changing nature of the political mythology of the State from Plato's *Republic*, to Augustine's earthly and heavenly cities, to the theory of the 'totalitarian race' and the influence of the political thinking of Hegel.

There are some notable exceptions from his chronology of political myth-making: the Divine Right of Kings, Hobbes' *Leviathan*, Rousseau's social contract, Kant's ethical commonwealth, Thomas Paine's Federalism, the communism of Marx and Engels, and the various nationalisms that dominated early-twentieth-century thinking – to name just a few. Each of these attempts to conceive a social imaginary, to expound a theory of the State, is an exercise in political myth-making and the art of *making* a belief believable. And while some invoke liberation from false ideological consciousness and oppressive hegemony (like Rousseau, Marx and Hegel, in their different ways), in each political myth, as Cassirer tells us, we 'begin[s] to learn a new and strange art: the art of expressing, and that means organizing, [our] most deeply rooted instincts, [our] hopes and fears.' And the myth of liberal democracy has to be included here. Its foundations are shaky, as the number of 'crises' of democracy from the 1920s to the 1970s and the more recent appeal to the language of 'post-democracy' testify. In an era of fast-tracked transnational relations, global markets and international finance, new political myths are being hatched. Two current myths are prominent, and contradictory. The first is of an internationalism that emphasises inter- and intradependence – the theoretical dream preoccupying departments of International Relations in a new cosmopolis. The other is the clash of civilisations – an apocalyptic vision of competing tribal, transnational identities, both ethnic and religious.

To recognise further what is at stake in political myth-making and the politics of belief it mobilises, we need to go back prior to Cassirer, to the French philosopher and political reactionary Georges Sorel. Sorel's late-nineteenth- and early-twentieth-century reflections on political myth grew out of his own acquaintance with Marxism, fascism and the bourgeois *fin de siècle* Third Republic. Champion of Lenin's revolution and one-time member of the right-wing nationalist party *Action française*, Sorel's account of the relationship between myth and politics is announced most clearly in his *Réflexions sur la violence* (1908).

Sorel views myth as collections of images and narratives of heroes, invoking ideals to die for, revolutions in living, missions for utopian kingdoms of eternal peace, homogeneities (national or ethnic), Gnostic battles between good and evil, apocalyptic struggles between civilisations, and, perhaps most terrifying and fascinating of all, war, conquest, expansion or, its obverse, holocaust and infinite, inconceivable suffering. Myth is rooted, for Sorel, in the three dispositions we have been treating throughout this essay: desire, belief and imagination. It arises from a human need for mutual recognition and vivid objects that feed that imagination. Human beings want to belong, they want a homeland (as in the German *Heimat*), and they want to commit themselves to great collective causes. These human needs are also human weaknesses. They see and even (at some level) enjoy the potential for personal sacrifice. In a way that returns to the diachronic axis of belief, Sorel understood myth as an historical force whose power lay partly in the nature of human weakness and the emotional substrate that underpins all acts of reason.

It's as if he had in mind the band of young revolutionaries in Victor Hugo's novel, *Les Misérables*, the so-called Friends of the ABC, led by Enjolras. Hugo ironises their heroics and their bombast as they prepare, following the death of General Lamarque, to mount the barricades and defend the rights of the impoverished. But for all their bravery and cama-raderie they are slaughtered, mercilessly, in the ensuing Paris uprising of 5–6 June 1832. Their convictions, nevertheless, are strong, even noble, which makes the waste of their youthful vigour and ambitions all the more poignant. The myth of liberation they espouse, a direct descendant of Revolutionary fervour, portrays what Sorel viewed as the mythic power to deeply move the masses. Its believability was emotional. 'As long as there are no myths accepted by the masses, one may go on talking of revolts indefinitely without ever provoking any revolutionary movement,' he wrote.

Myth, then, frames action: in this case political action. It inspires and gives it a meaning that is not simply arbitrary or pragmatic. It commits people to 'combat that will destroy the existing state of things'. While a utopian element pertains to such political myths (for as theories of the State they seek its comprehensive organisation), they have a life of their own and survive while belief in them remains. This life is also rooted in their emotional and imaginative power. It is for this reason that Sorel saw '[a] myth cannot be refuted since it is, at bottom, identical to the convic-tions of a group, being the expression of these convictions in the language of movement.'

The appeal to the imagination renders myths aesthetic. Sorel describes the way the power of their ideology lies in the 'idolatry of words'. Speech-making and demagogy are the natural surfeit of mythic thinking. Symbolic form themselves, they galvanise and energise the further production of symbolic forms and its variety. For myths do not just trade in words. One thinks of the uniforms and flags of Hugo's insurgents. One thinks also of much grander political and mythic visions in the architecture of Albert Speer for the Third Reich, Goebbels' rejuvenation of the German film industry as key to his Ministry of Propaganda and Chamber of Culture, Frederick the Great's *Unter den Linden* development in Berlin, crowned by the Brandenburg Gate, and Mussolini's urban restructuring of Rome. What is imagined is subsequently fashioned; the invisibility of thought becomes material culture. What might begin in an 'idolatry of words' may become mausoleums for national heroes (the Panthéon), monuments to democratic ideals (the Lincoln Memorial in Washington), and sites for the veneration of monarchs (the Banqueting House in Whitehall Palace). It is through this generation of symbolic form that belief in myths can foster an immersive and environmental appeal: to an imagined glory, an imagined heroism or martyrdom, and an imagined sociality. As Sorel observes, the power of such mythic thinking, when culturally pervasive, 'cannot be refuted by syllogisms'. Politically, the only way a myth is overturned is by a revolution, not a reformation. A revolution is a total reimagining of a social and cultural landscape.

CIVIL WAR: THE CLASH OF POLITICAL MYTHOLOGIES

We have come across cognitive dissonance before – where two sets of antithetical or incommensurate logics clash. It's a disturbing condition, with strong somatic effects, from sweating, nausea, palpitations, indigestion and sleeplessness to anxiety and even panic attacks. As human beings are biologically orientated towards homeostasis, in which the body regulates itself internally to achieve maximum stability and establish optimum conditions for survival, cognitive dissonance (which we can see is not simply cognitive at all) is not something we seek. We are creatures of habit. Adaptation and co-evolution is a slow process of acclimatisation to new sets of circumstances, but dissonance is interruptive. It is the individual's own experience of what, in the body politic, is impending revolution. On a day-to-day basis, most of us cope with such dissonance through repression and denial, refusing to see the world in any way that departs from the customary. Hence most of us see very little. The seeing *as* has become a seeing *as we want to see it*. What we don't attend to, we don't see. Repression and denial is only the internalising flip side of projection and anticipation. Freud has taught us all about this.

In detailing the diachronic axis of belief, we have also briefly examined cultural forms of cognitive dissonance, such as the complex situation in seventeenth-century Loudun that Michel de Certeau investigated. The cry of the mystic or the possessed gave animal expression to a cultural pain that was being experienced in the transition from one world view (the embedded, enchanted world of Christendom) to another (the disembedded, disenchanted world of instrumental scientific reasoning). But cognitive dissonance can also be social. Two dominant and incommensurate mythic systems can collide, each seeking and winning its own adherents, who then socialise and internationalise aspects of the mythology in a process of self-identification. When this happens politically, revolution and civil war are difficult to distinguish.

Oxford today, even with the influx of tourists, is a quiet, well-ordered polis; still a topography of dreaming spires. Not so between the winter of 1642–43 and the summer of 1646, when it became the new centre for Charles I's Royalist party at the outset of what is known as the First Civil War (there were three of them). Political loyalties were savagely divided between the Royalist Cavaliers and the Roundhead Parliamentarians, each developing its own political mythology espousing a logic of legitimation. The Royalist cause was based on the sacramental notion of the Divine Right of Kings; the sense of Royal protection and order that two centuries of relatively stable monarchic government had achieved; and religious convictions that were deeply troubled by radical forms of Puritanism. The Roundhead cause was based upon an evolving notion of democratic republicanism and later theocracy; Parliament as the legitimate organ for government, with a constitution guaranteeing rights and a balance of power; and Puritan sympathies for the priesthood of all believers and the freedom of the individual conscience. Loyalties shifted, the political myths had their soft and interpretable edges, but these two political world views could not be reconciled, and only hardened as the Parliamentarians gained confidence. Civil war ensued throughout the country, from Newcastle in the north to Taunton in the south. Charles I was captured and later executed at the end of the Second Civil War on 30 January 1649, and is claimed even today by some as a saint and martyr. Oliver Cromwell came to power. And for a time the Parliamentarians governed.

Civil wars are complex, but marked by strong loyalties divided by different political ideologies and their mythic shaping. Myth here does not mean lacking in historical and concrete reality. As Mary Midgley has more recently written: 'Myths are not lies [...] They are imaginative patterns, networks of powerful symbols that suggest particular ways of interpreting the world. They shape its meaning.' They also shape our beliefs, thoughts and actions because they are 'based on an imaginative vision fired by a particular set of ideals, a dream which can help to shape our enterprises, but will mislead us if we trust it on its own.' As a help in shaping our enterprises, myths have their use. Midgley cites Rousseau's social contract as one such 'useful' myth. But she concludes: 'some myths are much more useful and reliable than others.'

The clash of political mythologies, often hardwired with religious conviction, remains a permanent feature in civil wars as different as the American Civil War, between the Union North and the Confederate South; the African civil wars in Uganda and Angola; and the civil wars that followed the break-up of the former Yugoslavia, in which Slovenians, Bosnian Serbs and Bosnian Croatians battled. Here, as with the English and American Civil Wars, religion gave further depth to the imaginative visions, intensifying the political mythologies, as the tensions mounted between the Muslim Bosnians, the Orthodox Serbs and the Catholic Croatians, and neighbour betrayed neighbour.

Politics may certainly be an art (a *techni*, Machiavelli said) but their mythic element issues from some transcendent or universal principle, a truth demanding allegiance: a sovereign, fortune, the people, a pope, nature, history, necessity, a destiny, and even Jefferson's 'common sense' that commands consent because it is 'an expression of the American mind'. The bodies of women and children lying in lines with their throats slit in the dusty streets of Syria is a telling testimony to the victims caught up in the complexities of clashing political mythologies. Cognitive dissonance is not all – probably not ever – in the mind.

MYTH AND CULTURAL POLITICS

We begin to see that what may start as an examination of governmental myths, elaborate theories of the State, may finish as an examination of the cultures and socialities promoted by and supporting governmental myths. The political, as the organisation, distribution and circulation of power within any polis, is a cultural phenomenon, not just statecraft. Sorel, riding the tide of rampant European nationalism and in the wake of imperial dreams of colonialisation, recognised that it is at the cultural level that the 'idolatry' can become so profound. In particular, mythic thinking for him (as for the English writer Thomas Carlyle) frequently focused on hero worship and the modern celebrity of leadership that began, probably, with Napoleon and continued with the likes of Lincoln and Lee, Mussolini and Hitler. Oliver Cromwell was one of Carlyle's particular political heroes. When Ernst Cassirer fashioned his genealogy of the myth of the modern political state, he viewed the nineteenth-century cult of the public hero as key to twentieth-century political mythologies. The historical person and the events he initiates – battles, reforms, an entry into a city as its conqueror, a display of temper and contempt in Parliament – became wrapped in the iconographic and the spectacular.

In the years following the publication of Cassirer's last book, one of the few to have bettered his analysis of ideology and its relationship to culture is the French cultural theorist Roland Barthes (although credit is due to those two bastions of the Frankfurt School, Max Horkheimer and Theodor Adorno, for their own pioneering investigations into cultural studies). Interestingly, and significantly, the work of the Frankfurt School was not known in post-World War II France, even though Barthes opens his celebrated 1957 volume *Mythologies* with the recognition that the analysis he undertakes constitutes 'an ideological critique bearing on the language of so-called mass-culture'. This could have come straight from the writings of Horkheimer and Adorno. Michel Foucault, after the success of his own early studies, comments upon this astonishing lack of acquaintance with the examinations of ideology and the culture industry by the Frankfurt School. Barthes, like Adorno and Horkheimer, makes myth-making the centrepiece of his cultural criticism.

Roland Barthes' analyses begin where Sorel and Cassirer left off. Take the mythical 'superhuman essence' of a hero or a king in his piece 'The Blue-Blood Cruise', in which he submits a collection of royals on the Greek yacht *Agamemnon* to a critique that is thin-sliced with irony. While the trivia of their daily existence brings these celebrities down among us, the 'mythical character of our kings is nowadays secularised, though not in the least exorcised.' The divine right remains a divine right, and it is through this right that they are pictured among us in the tabloids and on the television.

Barthes' work begins with such subjects but, more incisively than Mary Midgley's examinations of the myths that haunt contemporary science, Barthes has his eye on the everyday. Years before Slavoj Žižek made us laugh at the advertising myths behind chocolate laxatives or Coke Zero, Roland Barthes was exploding the mythic fallacies behind margarine and *Omo* detergent.

His attention to mass culture is intentional and significant; for it is in mass culture that the 'collective representations' defining myth operate most effectively; that is, invisibly on our beliefs. Such mythic significations operate fundamentally 'for the mystification which transforms petit-bourgeois culture into a universal nature'. They are inseparable from the circulation of signs that constitute social discourse. Barthes lists the newspaper article, a photograph in a weekly magazine, an advertisement, a film, and a staged event like a wrestling match and exhibitions. Today we would have to add television, the internet, cyber gaming and social media, because we have become increasingly immersed within and dependent upon the circulation of signs. Indebted to the attention to semiotics following the discovery of de Saussure's work and the various French structuralisms, Barthes recognises that elements of the mythic imagination cannot be expunged from any form of communication. But when a sign is used mythically it is used as a token for something else; a token of a much more abstract value. We can see the formation of the sign as myth in the establishment of brand names and logos. A trainer is not just a trainer when it carries the Adidas triple stripes; a cup of coffee is not a cup of coffee when it comes from Caffè Nero; a motor car is not a motor car when it carries the insignia of a Mercedes-Benz, or a Rolls or a Bentley; a watch doesn't just give you the time when it's a Rolex or a Breitling. This is the 'mystification' that Barthes is pointing to. It issues from the collapse of the signified object into the sign itself, an 'emptying out of interiority to the benefit of its exterior signs, this exhaustion of the content by the form'.

'Mystification' is Barthes' rebranding of Engels' 'false consciousness', but it is not inappropriate because Marx's own descriptions of the power of money in the first part of *Das Kapital* employ a similar vocabulary. 'Not an atom of matter enters into the objectivity of commodities as value', such that 'the characters who appear on the economic stage are merely personifications of economic relations,' Marx wrote. And in this way the material and social order is overlaid by a cultural order that is pure allegory. The material and the embodied are consumed in the conceptual. People and relations carry price tags: valuable, not very valuable, reduced for a quick sale, cheap, worthless. They become objects in networked connection with other objects, and they are either alienated or fetishised as capitalism generates what Marx calls the 'mystical', 'mysterious', 'enigmatic' or 'fantastic' forms of relations, whose only analogy 'is the misty realm [*Nebelregion*] or religion [*die religiöse Welt*].' The religious in both Marx's account of the commodity and Barthes' account of myth as mystification is not at all irrelevant. But it is an empty religion, a secularised religion: what Jacques Derrida called a religion without religion.

We are encompassed by the mythic as such because it is the common currency of all communicative acts of persuasion: from sermons to the meetings between avatars in Second Life and Facebook profiles. As such, Barthes writes, myths 'are not content with meeting the facts: they define and explore them as tokens for something else' – tokens of values. This makes them hard to pin down – hence the mystification they engender – because 'the knowledge contained in a mythical concept is confused, made of yielding, shapeless associations' that are 'formless, unstable, nebulous condensation[s]'. Sorel recognised this: that is why for him myth cannot be refuted. What things mean is constantly coming into and going out of focus.

Barthes comments upon two of the most important functions of myth. First, its universalising function and its effects of transcendence: material objects become ideas that bear a suggestion of aura. Plato's world of the Forms becomes a 3D interactive fantasy. And second is myth's ability to transform 'history into nature'. Both the immediate impression the mythological delivers and the convictions it can call forth are inseparable from the naturalisation of its objects and ideas that myth performs. It

173

announces: 'this is the norm'. Barthes: '[M]yth has the task of giving historical intention a natural justification, and making contingency appear eternal.' Hence the utopian colouring of liberation, even eschatology, governing the operation of the mythic. Myth, Barthes insists, is 'not a symbol' because nothing is symbolised. It is the symbolisation of symbol; where symbolic action is preoccupied with itself. Beliefs float, form, dissolve, shape-shift and freely associate like the melding of images in daydreams and hypnagogic states. A toaster or a four-wheel drive can transform itself into a killing machine or a saviour; we have seen the films. We will return to this in our conclusion.

THE MYTH OF SECULARISM

This *making* beliefs believable – where believing itself is an object to be fashioned – finds its most dominant form, its deepest, invisible and normative ideology in the myth of secularism. And with the new visibility of religion in the public realm (and evangelistic, crusading atheism is only another form of the visibility of religion) this is becoming increasingly apparent. Let's have a look at its operations.

On 11 April 2011, following two years of intense debate by the President of the UMP in the French National Assembly, the French government passed a law that made it illegal, in effect, for Muslim women in France to wear the hijab or burqa publicly. The UMP (*Union pour un Mouvement Populaire*) was the conservative party in office at the time. The law was not that explicit. It was described as a law to prevent the concealment of the face in the public realm. But the effect was the same. The grounds for the passing of the law were stated in terms of domestic security.

The law was the last in a number of government moves under the banner of *laïcité* in France that began in 1989 and intensified in the post-9/11 climate. But *laïcité* itself – a complex and evolving idea that came to be understood in terms of state-monitored secularism – goes back to prior laws preceding, including and succeeding the 1905 *Law on the Separation of Church and State*. The fight here was State control of Roman Catholicism following years of conflict in France between republican anti-clericalism (with roots in the Revolution) and Catholic anti-republicanism (at the heart of the Counter-Revolution), with a review of its 1905 legislation separating Church and State. The 1905 law became the legal basis for *laïcité*, but it has to be understood in terms of what it did *not* do. It did not, for example, separate Church from State, despite its title. In fact, there is only one mention of the word 'separation' in the law, and that is in the title itself. It was therefore *not* state legislation for either the absence of religious affairs in public debate or the absence of government involvement in religious affairs. It declared the government's neutrality and its capacity to act as an arbitrator in religious matters. Whether the government had any competence in playing the part of the umpire was a moot point, to which we will return. As the legal theorist Raphaël Liogier observes:

> *laïcité* is not the separation of the religious from the political, but a highly singular mode of political interference in the religious field [...] But *laïcité* is no mere methodology of management; on a deeper level it is also the culture socially constructed by a segment of the population in order to legitimise just such a mode of management.

The law appeared to announce the separation of private life from the public sphere. But still today French public holidays remain closely tied to the Christian calendar; the French government reserves the right to supervise the appointment of important French bishops; Catholic places of worship predating 1905 are maintained by the State because they are regarded as public property; Catholic dioceses benefit from certain tax exemptions; and the majority of state-funded private schools are Catholic. Only one is Muslim.

On 10 September 1994, the Minister for Education, François Bayrou, instructed the French public school system that students had the right to wear discreet religious symbols, although the veil was not among them. The instruction caused confusion as it was not legally binding. The instruction reflected, in part, two national beliefs: first, that France was a country that tolerated religious freedom, a country committed to *communautarisme* – a non-technical word for 'multiculturalism'; and secondly, that Muslims coming from ex-colonial territories were 'not treated as a domestic problem but as a foreign policy concern' (Liogier). The Muslims were considered to be people who were passing through. So Islam had to be constructed as a

175

domestic social problem – and such a construction focused on the wearing of the veil. This construction followed the resurgence of terrorist attacks in both Algeria and France in the 1990s.

Following 9/11 there was much discussion in the *Conseil d'État* and reflection upon what remains the first article of the French Constitution: '*La France est une République indivisible, laïque, démocratique et sociale*' – which led to the setting-up of a commission headed by Bernard Stasi. This was an ad hoc commission established by the French prime minister at the time, Jacques Chirac, and 'erected in order to "rationally" justify already pre-existing religious prejudices and legitimise a priori decision-making' (Liogier). The commission published a report in December 2003 that recommended a number of far-reaching measures concerning both religious symbols in public places and the importance of religious minority feasts as public holidays. It recommended the banning of the veil on the grounds that it was 'enforced' (though there was no sociological evidence brought forward to support the view that Muslim women were being made to wear the veil outside the private sphere of the household). Such enforcement was an infringement of civil liberties for women and the human right to the equality of the sexes. Technically, the veil as such would not be banned, only its imposition.

In 2004 came the first law banning religious symbols in public. The law does not name any particular symbols and it covers large Christian crosses, the Jewish Star of David, the Muslim hijab and the Sikh turban. Much discussion in the public sphere ensued, with objections that this development in the policy of *laïcité* curtailed civil rights. Evidence was now collected that demonstrated the wearing of the veil in public was not forced but voluntary. The question also arose regarding 'competence'. In Islam only an imam can pass such a judgement, and a ban of this kind amounted to a *fatwa*. In turn these debates raised the spectre of State secularism as an ideology that was not being advanced on the grounds of sexual equality but rather for the purposes of cultural assimilation – Gallicisation. And assimilationism is just a modern form of racism (Yolande Jansen). As Liogier writes: 'those who had taken it upon themselves to be agents of the dominant culture had a vested interest in maintaining such a disregard for their [religious] object, a vested interest in […] not understanding [how girls and women themselves saw the wearing of the veil].'

In the midst of these discussions, the former French President, Nicolas Sarkozy, himself a Catholic, met Pope Benedict XVI in September 2008. At the meeting the Pope spoke of the need for a 'healthy' form of secularism – what others, like the former Archbishop of Canterbury Rowan Williams, have termed a 'procedural secularism', in which the difference between religious matters and state matters is maintained in order to ensure the maximal freedom of individual citizens. The Pope did not elaborate on what he meant by 'healthy', but he did observe that people were becoming 'more aware of the irreplaceable role of religion for the formation of consciences and the contribution it can bring to – among other things – the creation of a basic ethical consensus within society.'

Nevertheless, if the law of 2004 announced a new tightening of the policy of *laïcité*, and therefore State control of religious matters, then the law of 2011 went further: there was a reinforcement of *laïcité* in hospitals and places of public service generally, advocated by Claude Guéant, the Minister of the Interior.

Now why rehearse this recent history? In part, I rehearse the history because the state legislation has greatly contributed to the new visibility of religion in France, and its endemic presence in French culture. In doing this it foregrounds the constructed nature of secularism and what the French Marxist thinker Louis Althusser called the 'state apparatus' and Michel Foucault the 'governmentality' behind such a construction. It draws attention to the modes of state practices that furnish and foster specific behaviours and habits of thinking, *dispositifs*, which, in turn, create interpellated or even split identities (where to be French and a Sikh male is in conflict). In part, I also rehearse this history because the legislation shows both the fragility and incoherence of secularism as a state-sponsored ideology wedded to a liberal democratic polity. It is fragile because private interests are always leaking into public space. It is incoherent because as an enforced ideology it is at odds with liberal freedoms and the democracy of human rights. A separation of human interests from public discourse is heuristic at best and downright deceptive at worst; deceptive, that is, of the cultural situation as such. Secularism as a kind of default human position, as the norm upon the basis of which one can simply choose one's life's options – the naturalism of secularism, in Barthes' language – is a myth.

SECULARISM AND SECULARISATION

To be clear, I am discussing here 'secularism' and not strictly 'secularisation'. The first is an ideology that emerged from the Enlightenment and modernity's commitment to progress, and the second is a socio-historical concept. Much historical work has been done recently to divorce secularisation from modernisation (by Grace Davie, Callum G. Brown and Peter Berger, for example), but secularism and secularisation are evidently not entirely separate enterprises: the more naturalised the ideology, the more it will constitute the social 'habitus' – those habits of sensibility that inform beliefs, thoughts and actions in any historical period. But three points are worth observing.

First, no one is questioning that a process of secularisation has been under way from at least the late eighteenth century and the rise of scientific explanation. No one is questioning an erosion of Christian faith in Europe – although it has taken place in different ways and at different speeds depending on whether a country's culture was Protestant in its orientation or Roman Catholic. What is being questioned is the rate of this process and the establishment of secularism as a way of perceiving the world *as* and governing a state in a particular way.

Today the view that there was an accelerated decline in belief in a personal and transcendent God – encouraged by industrialisation and urbanisation, and deepened by the impact of two world wars – is being radically questioned. The rapid decline in attendance at Christian churches is also being questioned. In the UK, for example, there was no steep decline in church attendance figures until the early 1960s. Roman Catholic adherence peaked in 1966 in the UK, and although Church of England figures peaked in 1956, the Presbyterian Church of England peaked in 1960. Other European countries such as Holland and Belgium show the same trend. This would indicate that secularism only gained cultural ground at that point. And it is the cultural ground that is significant. As Brown has argued: 'Secularisation could not happen until discursive Christianity lost its power.' And 'discursive' Christianity is a cultural phenomenon to do with the circulation of those signs to which Roland Barthes paid attention. Secularism is a set of ideas that emerge when those signs no longer act as indicators and expressions of belief in the authority and legitimation of those offices through which Christian discourse continues to be disseminated. '[S]ecularisation [...] is inconceivable without decay in discursive religiosity in which there is a loss of popular acceptance and recirculation of those discourses' (Brown). This did not happen until the 1960s, and so the secularising 'result was not the long inevitable decline of the conventional secularisation story, but a remarkably sudden and culturally violent event.'

Secondly, the main thrust of secularisation theory began at the same time in the 1960s among sociologists of religion. There are still some adherents to its arguments, notably Steve Bruce in the UK. But it is evident from their work that they valorise 'secularism' as a good thing that we ought to embrace, and then find the fulfilment of the secularisation project in quantitative data about church attendance and belief in a transcendent deity. Not only do they demonstrate vested interests in the case they are wishing to prove, and not only do they conflate secularism with secularisation, but they also fail to distinguish between secularity and a more general withdrawal from institutional commitment. There has been an increasing scepticism about institutional power (as evidenced by sociologists such as Robert Putnam in the US) that no doubt has impacted on ecclesial institutions, along with others like Rotary clubs, the Scouting movement and political parties. In fact, the years of decline in attendance at church exactly parallel the same years of decline in political party membership. Meanwhile, if we have to make the distinction between decline in church attendance and decline in institutional affiliation, we also have to recognise the rise of other forms of what has been called 'detraditionalised' Christianity, with much looser institutional bases: like the house churches and community churches at the forefront now of what is often called the 'emerging church' and charismatic Pentecostalism.

Callum Brown's emphasis upon the crisis of religion and the triumph of secularism as a 1960s phenomenon has drawn the attention of other historians to that decade. Recently, Hugh McLeod argued that there was no such dramatic fall in interest in religion in the 1960s. While acknowledging that this was the decade in which Britain came to terms with its multi-ethnic composition and the decline in the view that Britain was a 'Christian country'; a decade when procedural secularism for dealing with racial and religious multiplicity developed prior to the passing of

179

anti-discrimination legislation – McLeod nevertheless says that the 1960s were 'a time of intense, but also critical religious interest'. The decade was a time of public controversies in which religion played a major role: the obscenity trial for D. H. Lawrence's *Lady Chatterley's Lover*; the publication of John Robinson's book *Honest to God*; the reinvention of modern Catholicism that followed Vatican II; the Jesus Movement. So, the 1960s has been viewed by some historians as a period of 'spiritual awakening', despite a decline in institutional belonging.

In the light of a new visibility of religion (not necessarily a social resurgence, but a cultural perception), fuelled by international conflicts with terrorism and the politicisation of Islam that began in the mid-1970s with the oil crisis and was fast-forwarded by the Iranian Revolution of 1979, there has been a further change. Secularism was a Christian-based project. But the strength of belief in other religious pieties made complex any simple ideology of secularism. In fact, at a time when the Christian faith and the culture it fostered were becoming anorexic in Europe, the religious landscape was being changed by post-World War II attention to the Jewish question, following the Holocaust and the Arab–Israeli conflict, waves of immigration from Islamic Algeria, Turkey, Morocco, Pakistan and Bangladesh and Hindu immigration from India, the 1960s interest in Eastern mysticism and New Age cults. These factors greatly muddy the waters of any homogeneous secular culture. So while some sociologists of religion have called for major modifications to the secularisation thesis (Peter Berger) and others for minor modification (Jürgen Habermas), there have been others calling for acceptance that our cultural condition is best described as 'post-secular' (Jacques Derrida, Gianni Vattimo). If we are post-secular, and secularism is only an early 1960s phenomenon that was being queered the moment it emerged (as the sociologist Daniel Bell noted), then secularism as a cultural norm (as distinct from an administrative and procedural secularism) was a 'blip'. Indeed, a very minor 'blip' in the relationship between history and religion. Certainly, secularism as a grand narrative, and probably secularisation theories, have passed their sell-by date.

Thirdly, culturally, we are still awash with 'discursive religiosity', though it often refigures the traditional meanings of its ideas. The expiation of M's 'sin' through bloodletting and death in a Scottish chapel in the James Bond movie *Skyfall*, for example, recirculates and continues a certain Christian discourse. But it is difficult to see its direct relevance to the practice of the Christian faith in anything but the tritest of terms. Brown observes the strong continuation of what he calls the 'evangelical narrative of the life story' until the 1960s, noting that people shaped their life stories less and less around such a narrative after that date. But the cinema (particularly the American cinema, which may well be an exception) produces blockbusters with mutated evangelical narratives continually: *I Am Legend*, *Avatar*, the recent *Batman*, *Spiderman* and *Superman* series, for example. The plot structure of innocence or naivety, encountering drama and wickedness only to be saved at the last moment – often by some superhuman or superhero messianic figure – is very much a Hollywood staple. And let us say nothing of the endless variations on vampires, werewolves, witches, warlocks and sorcerers spawned by bestselling novels like the *Twilight* and *Harry Potter* series.

It is important to understand that this is not just entertainment. We do not just passively watch these spectacles in ways that have no effect upon our emotional and imaginative lives. Go back to the biology of believing and mirror neurons. We enact these spectacles within ourselves. We live them virtually. In the Cathedral shop in Christ Church, Oxford, they sell *Harry Potter* magic wands. When the Dean was questioned why a Christian institution should stock such items in its shop, he replied, 'They don't work!' And it's true. Young teenage girls do not flock to watch Bella Swan fall for Edward Cullen because they believe they too may encounter a vampire in the school car park, but it feeds their desires and hopes and orientates those primordial dispositions in some direction. They are fashioned by such orientations in some way – and we cannot calculate fully the ways such fashioning might take. Our 'habituses', or 'habiti', shape the way we believe, think and act, and they operate in and through the symbolic realms we, as hominid and human creatures, have been cultivating for 2.2 million years.

THE TRIUMPH OF THE MYTHIC IMAGINATION

Evidently, I am not using myth in the sense it has for certain anthropologists: stories of origins, archetypes and aetiologies lost in some sacred past; the origin of evil and sexual difference, for example, in the *Book of Genesis*.

Myth, in these contexts, suggests that in the age of science mythic power diminishes. Such a view of myth is itself a product of secularisation aiming at the demythologisation, or what Weber called the disenchantment, of the world. Myth is not some kind of 'primitive mentality' (the anthropological description offered by Lévy-Bruhl). Although, if the disposition towards the mythical is, as I have argued, inseparable from symbolic activity, then the anthropologists have much to offer us. To some extent I am using myth the way the early Romantics (Schelling and Novalis) understood it: as a result of the impress of the infinite upon the finite and therefore the origin of art and poetry. Yes, art, poetry – indeed language itself – is related, along with mythic imagining, to expressive symbol use, to rite and dance whose beginnings can be found in gesture. Myth is a semiotic phenomenon. But it clearly plays with levels of association more unconscious than the fashioning of signs, as Freud recognised. That is why it is associated with belief production – the formation of belief and the *making* believable of belief. Hence its powers are allusive but highly determinative. The semiotic revolution triggered by structuralism furnished new modes of analysis (of narrative, for example), a new interest in grammar and syntax, and new applications of the binary logics of *langue/parole* (Levi-Strauss) and algorithms of otherness (Lacan). But it soon deepened into examinations of the bad infinities of endless semiosis, the deferral of meaning (Lacoue-Labarthe, Nancy, Derrida), differends (Lyotard) and the play of light on the surfaces of simulations and simulacra (Baudrillard, Deleuze).

Today we inhabit the cultural world that such semiosis fostered, given strong impetus in the wake of advancing telecommunications and the proliferation of electronic and immersive virtual realities. In two 2013 surveys, one in the US and one in the UK, it was calculated that the average person in the US spends 5 hours 9 minutes a day online and a further 4 hours 31 minutes watching TV, and that 25 per cent of the British population spends 12 hours a day in such a manner. In the wake of an upsurge in cyberbullying, cyberstalking and cyber-harassment, one spokesperson for a major charity revealed that 'there is no off-line on-line mode of living for the younger generation'; the lines demarcating a difference have gone.

Certain sociologists (Bauman), cultural theorists and artists wish to talk about a re-enchantment of the world that is effected by these diachronic changes, which are diachronic changes in the structures of believing. It is not simply that the mythic imagination is dominating the box offices of cinemas – with the recent film productions of directors like Peter Jackson, Christopher Nolan, James Cameron and Guillermo del Toro – or television series like *Being Human*, *The Vampire Diaries* and *Game of Thrones*. The quotidian is being mythologised. Two brief examples from the pop video industry are illustrative.

The lyrics of Chris Brown's song 'Don't Judge Me' (2012) concern a relationship between the singer and his new girlfriend. His current girlfriend keeps hearing rumours, and has downloaded internet material about a past lover of Brown's. It is causing problems in their relationship because she is comparing herself with the ex and wanting to know more and more details about Brown's past intimacies. The song opens with Brown's current state of mind: 'I don't want to go there. We should never go there. Damn. Why you want to go there? I guess I've got to go there.' This is followed by a narrative account of the present girlfriend's situation and her jealous questions about the ex-girlfriend, leading to the chorus:

So, please, babe. Please don't judge me. And I won't judge you. 'Cos it can get ugly, before it gets beautiful. Please don't judge me. And I won't judge you. And if you love me, let it be beautiful. Let it be beautiful [repeated a number of times].

This is an ordinary enough scenario. But the video opens with Brown walking alone and vulnerable in a desert landscape only to hitch a ride on an army truck that takes him to a military base camp. In the base camp, the other soldiers greet him, and we learn he has volunteered for a lone mission into space. The song stops, and the girlfriend appears as a reporter with a TV crew, demanding to know why Brown is doing this. Brown tells the cameras he is doing this for his country, to save the people he loves and cares about. We learn now it is a suicide mission. Escorted on to some kind of spaceship, Brown is launched into space, where a gigantic alien creature sits, threatening life on earth. The ship strikes right into the heart of the flailing monster with its long, metallic tentacles, where it explodes – presumably destroying ship, threat and Brown. The video ends on a domestic scene of reconciliation between Brown and his present girlfriend, the drama over. But what is this judgement, salvation, reconciliation and beauty within such a mythic reshaping? The judgement becomes part of an apocalyptic scenario and the beauty born of it is pure jingoistic sacrifice. The domestic arguments become national and cosmic, caught up within the myths of a Gnostic battle between Good and Evil. As with all currently fashionable reality TV and fly-on-the-wall documentaries, the domestic also becomes, not insignificantly, a media event.

The second example is Lana Del Rey's song 'Born to Die' (2011). The lyrics here are of another order of subtlety, but the core is love-trouble once more. 'Don't make me sad, don't make me cry | Sometimes love is not enough and the road gets tough | I don't know why.' There is something desperate about the loving because it is played out against a background of loneliness, the need for a home and the finality of death. 'Keep making me laugh | Let's go get high | The road is long, we carry on | Try to have fun in the meantime.' The need to escape the end of all things is countered by walking on 'the wild side', drugs, and kissing 'in the pouring rain'. But the end is announced in the very opening lines: 'Feet don't fail me now | Take me to the finish line [...] But I'm hoping at the gates, | They'll tell me that you're mine.' The religious frames the mundane – life after the death one is born for, and living as a carrying on along a long road 'by mistake or design'. Life is portrayed as short, even crazy. The song is sung to someone who is told to 'Choose your last words, this is the last time | Cause you and I, we were born to die.' The video explicitly theatricalises the religious and, for reasons not at all obvious, US patriotism. It opens and closes with Del Rey and a man in a close embrace against the background of an American flag, but when the lyrics begin Del Rey is enthroned in front of the altar of an ornate baroque church, flanked on either side by a tiger. As the narrative proceeds, it flashes back to her meeting her lover on a dark and isolated road and driving with him through the rain. The church scenes cut in at this point to show Del Rey walking down corridors of the same church, or a palace it is attached to, towards some doors. The next flashback reveals her driving with the lover in the passenger seat, and then a decision to kiss as the car hurtles through a wet and foggy night. The last intercut scenes are of Del Rey walking through the opening doors towards a floodlit, indistinct other place, and a blazing fire following a car crash from which her boyfriend carries her bloody body in a limp *pietà*. Once more a Gnostic myth interprets a somewhat pathological set of love relations. It is a Christian Gnosticism only by association (with the church and the altar), but the final 'home' is in the afterlife, understood as an escape from the depressing and exhausting temporalities of ordinary life and the evasions necessary to just 'carry on'. This is the answer to the questions Del Rey has been asking herself 'like a little child'. As with the Chris Brown video, suicide (or sacrifice, when viewed in terms of the American flag and the church altar) is salvation (again apocalyptically conceived in the fires of the car crash, filmed in a way that echoes the burning of Atlanta in *Gone with the Wind*). The local inflections of a love life are situated in a mythological tension between time and eternity. But it is difficult in this video to understand the point of the sacrifice beyond winning Del Rey the freedom in which she *might* be told at the gates that her lover is hers eternally now.

The mythic imagination dominates contemporary culture, aestheticising and sometimes anaesthetising the ordinary, fashioning new possibilities for belief. I say sometimes, because, as we have seen with a writer such as James Joyce, the transfiguration of the ordinary can make us aware of profundities that are not escapist, and actually give us a sense of life's depths rather than its surfaces. Any of the stories in *Dubliners* opens the possibility of perceiving a dimension towards which myth points, particularly 'The Dead'. Or we can take Terence Davies' 1988 film *Distant Voices, Still Lives*, which wonderfully portrays the births and marriages in a Liverpool family throughout the 1950s living under the mental instability of an abusive father. Here the lingering camerawork on empty rooms and curtains blowing in an open window, and the film editing, in which voices are sometimes detached from the images, create a distance which infuses the ordinary with a reflective significance. Against the strong current of violent, male dominance, life goes on. Or there's Debra Granik's 2010 film *Winter's Bone*, about a seventeen-year-old girl looking after her mentally ill mother and two younger siblings in desperate poverty. Her father has gone missing, and the scene in which she is taken by the three matriarchs of a local crime gang to see her father's bones slips easily and simply from the rural Ozarks of the United States into Greek tragedy.

The mythic imagination need not be anaesthetising and escapist. The works of mythic imagination that I have cited disclose something of the mystery and wonder of being alive for us. They intimate that our experience (even tragic experience) of being in the world is freighted with a significance that only an appeal to the mythic can index. Mary Midgley's observation that 'some myths are much more useful and reliable than others' requires interpretative discernment, which also means interpretative, critical distance rather than immersion. We are, I suggest, living at a time when believing is reasserting its fundamental nature – and analysis of both the believability of a belief and the *making* of belief is crucial. The social and political danger lies not just in believing without belonging (the religious sociological condition of post-World War II Britain according to the sociologist Grace Davie); it lies in believing without any determinative structures at all – in which all objects and relations are relative. And this perhaps explains why religious fundamentalism (Christian, Jewish, Islamic and Hindu most prominently) is so attractive: to believe is to belong. The only 'high' that effectively competes with the fundamentalist version at the moment is an immersive escape into hybrid and ever-morphing mythologies, with the promise of a pop transcendence associated with glamour and celebrity. This promise is Marx's ultimate fetish, 'visible and dazzling to our eyes' (*Das Kapital*).

So now we begin to see what is really at stake in a study such as this one.

VIII

Faith: Following and Formation

The return of mythic thinking, the new visibility of religion in the public sphere and the myth of secularity bring us to the most historically prevalent and culturally pervasive form of *making* belief believable: religion – what many regard as believing itself.

In religion the predisposition to believe, to see *as*, is given priority status in defining what it is to be human. The peculiar condition of religious believing can be summed up in a phrase by the Christian St Paul in his *Letter to the Romans*:

> For I am not ashamed of the gospel of Christ: for it is the power of God unto salvation to every one that believeth; to the Jew first, and also to the Greek. For therein is the righteousness of God revealed from faith to faith: as it is written, The just shall live by faith. (Rom. 1: 16–17)

I am going to put aside what salvation might be (it may indeed take any number of forms) and I am going to put aside also what Paul might mean by 'the gospel of Christ' – though Christ as both fully God and fully human (to employ a latter formulation by the Christian Church) is at the very heart of Paul's account of salvation. Let me focus instead on what is most significant here for religious piety and believing more generally, and that is that such practitioners 'live' from what is unseen to what is unseen, 'from faith to faith'.

The ability to live in such a way is, according to St Paul, only partially a human condition, and that will become important. There are some divides that thoughtful, even rational believing, cannot cross. It is the power and the righteousness of God (whatever those two attributes might mean for St Paul and for Christians with respect to the divine) that enables that living. The faithful walk in the invisibility of what they believe, but what they believe is both unseen and transcendent to all such walking. Their living participates in a cosmological, transhistorical, and universal invisibility – the God no one has seen, enfolded in the ineffable, and, for Christians, a Christ who, through the historically incarnate Son of God and the icon of God's transcending invisibility, was born as a man and then ascended into heaven. As the *Letter to the Hebrews*, composed later and by an unknown writer, puts it: 'Faith is the substance of things hoped for, the evidence of things not seen' (Heb. 11: 1). And those who live such faith

> have not received the promises, but ha[ve] seen them afar off, and [are] persuaded of them, and [embrace] them, and [confess] that they [are] strangers and pilgrims on the earth. For they that say such things declare plainly that they seek a country […] an heavenly [country]: wherefore God is not ashamed to be called their God: for he hath prepared for them a city. (Heb. 11: 3–16)

Now, each religious faith takes a specific form and colouring from the tradition within which it stands. Furthermore, the practice of that faith takes on particular cultural colourings, even syncretisms (where syncretism is not a negative word but only attests to the inevitable hybridisation that occurs in the cultural and historical appropriations of religious ideas). This book is an examination into believing. It is neither Christian apologetics nor Christian evangelism – though my examples are often chosen from the Christian faith because I have some expertise in its theological traditions. But I want to draw attention to the two levels of belief being engaged in by religious believers of all faiths. First there is the believing that is, as I have been arguing throughout, endemic to the human condition itself and goes all the way down to the dispositional (or what some, like the philosophical biologists David Papineau and George McDonald, call the 'teleosemantics' of the cellular). This believing, again as I have said, treats the unseen in the seen and accepts that all seeing is seeing *as* – where 'seeing' is a metonymy for all the senses and a metaphor for knowledge. Knowledge is always and only metaphor, as Nietzsche recognised. Secondly, there is a persuasion by an embracing and a confession of an unseen above and beyond the unseen that pertains to the practices of everyday life.

To give any account of the experience of such piety requires the use of a complex weave of paradoxes. We can see this in phrases like '[f]aith is the substance of things hoped for, the evidence of things not seen' (*Letter to the Hebrews* 11: 1). In Greek this sentence reads:

Ἔστιν δὲ πίστις ἐλπιζομένων ὑπόστασις, πραγμάτων ἔλεγχος οὐ βλεπομένων

I give the Greek not to show off, but to clarify and point out what is going on in the articulation of these complex and balanced antitheses for the Christian faith. The sentence begins with the verb in the present tense, the third person singular of 'to be'. In grammatical terminology: before we have the subject of the sentence (faith), we have the ontological conditions within which the subject is located. Then we have the subject, transliterated as *pistis*. I will have more to say about *pistis* in what follows, but we can translate it either as 'faith' or 'belief'. There is no object, only a second subject which, transliterated, is *hypostasis*. This is a word with a long and complex history in Christian Patristic debates, but all that is in the future for St Paul. 'Substance' is the right translation, but also carries with it a long semantic history of philosophical and theological debate we don't need at this point. 'Essence' might be slightly better, because the word has ontological weight and relates back directly to the verb 'to be', which opens the sentence. Poised exactly between these two subjects in the nominative (which, grammatically, means they can be converted into or stand in for one another because they name the same thing) is the present passive participle of the verb 'to hope', and it is in the genitive: hope is what belongs to and is a property of both 'belief' and 'essence'. In part, we saw this in the chapter on poetics (VI).

Having defined belief as fundamental to being itself and as possessing the future-orientated disposition to hope, then we come to the subclause 'the evidence of things not seen'. The subclause begins with the subject, *pragma* (from which we get the word 'pragmatic'). It's translated here vaguely as 'things' because it is in the plural, but it could be translated with greater specificity: acts, deeds, facts, affairs, enterprises or issues. It's not vague or abstract in any way; rather it is active and highly concrete. It is also in the genitive, like the participle for hoping (though that is singular and refers to belief). It is the object of the present passive participle, which is in the negative at the end of the sentence, transliterated as *ou' blepomenōn* – 'not being seen'. These activities, then, of what is unseen, belong to something, and that is 'evidence'. They are the very properties of this 'evidence'. Here the nominative subject of the subclause is sandwiched emphatically between the two characteristics it possesses (like belief and essence in the main clause). The word is, transliterated, *elegchos*, and it does bear the sense of 'evidence' if we understand that term not scientifically but legally. It is related to and can be translated as trial, conviction, judgement, examination or proof.

I realise this is all very technical, but attention to the technical is important if we are to understand something about the nature of religious belief expressed here. Believing cannot be disassociated from hoping; and those facts and actions that are not seen are still evident in the very examination and trial of the facts and actions themselves. The invisible therefore is not divorced from the visible. It does not demand a leap beyond what is real and actual (both translations of *pragma*). The invisible is a property of the visible, and religious believing is an act of response to that invisible in the visible; a response that cannot be separated from the affect hope.

THE MYSTERY OF ALL FLESH

Now I could just jump to another passage from the writings of St Paul here, because, in the continuation of the verses I quoted at the beginning of this chapter, he concludes with the statement: 'For the invisible things of [God] from the creation of the world are clearly seen, being understood by the things that are made, even his eternal power and Godhead' (Rom. 1: 20). But I will resist the temptation, because what is interesting in this account of the invisible as it pertains ontologically to the visible is the way it relates to a number of studies of a similar phenomenon in quite different fields of enquiry. In Chapter VI I drew attention to the invisible that is inevitably associated with the visible, and the considerable social and cultural impact of that invisibility. I wish to develop that with a religious proviso: the divine invisibility may have certain analogues with the invisibilities I pursue now, but it would be a mistake to conflate the two.

Analogy is a useful but frequently misleading tool. The analogy between the human and the animal whereby we are put directly in the same chain of development as birds and primates, for example, often overemphasises similarity and underplays difference. Analogy becomes a means of calculating proportionality. But I want us to keep in mind that analogy, at least within the monotheistic philosophical traditions, emphasises divine difference and therefore the remoteness of similarities that nevertheless still pertain. We will return to this towards the end of this chapter. For the moment, what is important is to recognise that the more proportionality is overemphasised in the use of analogy, the greater the danger of conflation between the two subjects being compared.

And so to the invisible that adheres to visibility itself. Schematically, I will refer to four modes of this. But since all four of these modes rest on perception, we need to begin by recognising that all our physiological accounts of perception are themselves incomplete. This, in part, explains why seeing is always seeing *as*. Take our accounts of vision. As the clinical neuroscientist Raymond Tallis reminds us:

> There is a kind of physical explanation of how light gets into the brain and tickles up my neurons but there is no physical explanation as to how my gaze looks out at a brightly lit world of illuminated objects. Tickled up neurons don't explain how I see something outside those neurons, outside my brain, outside my head, *as* something outside myself.

The relationship between the '[t]ickled up neurons' and seeing something *as* is not a matter of cause and effect. The first event may be a necessary condition for there being a second event (seeing *as*), but any number of other factors (present circumstances, past experiences and future anticipations, to give just a few examples) impact upon that seeing *as*.

THE INVISIBILITY WITHIN PERCEPTION

The incompleteness of accounts of perception at the physiological level becomes the basis for all the four modes of invisibility as it adheres to the visible. The first of these is perspectival invisibility; that is, an invisibility that issues from our inability to view the visible from a multidirectional or omniscient perspective. There is no view from nowhere, which means there is always an invisibility that pertains to the visible and partial that we do see. The American philosopher Stanley Cavell discusses perspectival invisibility in his famous embracing of the sceptical in *The Claim of Reason*. A philosopher holds up an envelope and asks the class what it is they see. An envelope, they claim. But how do you know it's an envelope when all you see is one side of it? The back side, which may indeed be the side with the flap that lifts so you can insert your letter, is not visible, and you make it visible in your identification of it *as* an envelope. On the basis of familiarity with an envelope you complete the perspective that is not offered. But Cavell goes on to suggest a trickster might well have cut away the back part, and you would have been deceived and your identification of the existence of an envelope wrong.

In a sense this scepticism is nothing more than another aspect of seeing *as*: all perception is interpretation. The interpretation can be corrected or corroborated if the class can take hold of the 3D object in question. But the question remains: what are you seeing when you see? Or, what are you reading when you read (the world)? But this invisibility and the way it is completed by the observer raise questions about intentionality. I do not just passively receive the sensations or *qualia* of an object I look at; I look at it in a certain way that gives it meaning or identifies it as meaningful. My perception is active. It is engaged. It is directed towards seeing what something is about. In a move beyond philosophical scepticism, phenomenology seeks to enquire into the nature and structures of such intentional looking.

There is another mode of invisibility that we can never see, however much we aspire to a three-dimensional perspective – though its impact is profound upon what we do see, how we see it, and how we respond. There is that which is hidden from our eyes. As I mentioned earlier in this book, thought is invisible. Ideas are invisible. Okay, they can don the mantles of materiality in language, whether that language is gestured, danced, painted, sculptured, built, spoken, written or any combination of these symbolic practices. Our cultures are and can only be material, even when they are intellectual. And thinking cannot be unhinged from the languages in and through which we think. But, as St Augustine discovered to his astonishment when observing St Ambrose in his study one day, we can read in our heads. The language may not have any material expression.

We have and experience a mental life that no one else has direct access to – even through magnetic resonance imaging (MRI) or its less precise (for localising activity) sibling, electroencephalography. And this is important for how we assess the contribution of neuroscience or cognitive psychology to an investigation into believing, since beliefs also have a hiddenness. MRI scans various chemical operations along the fibre tracts that compose the neural networks of the brain. 'Diffusion' MRI works with water molecules and the ways a neuron constricts their movement. This activity has consequences for blood flow and oxygen levels in that flow. 'Functional' MRI tracks these blood-oxygen shifts. The results are fed through a computer. In other words, brain scans and the pictures that emerge from them are not a direct means of seeing into the brain. Furthermore, there is a significant time gap between the milliseconds clocked by neural activity and the detected changes in blood flow – which take anything between two and ten seconds and can be providing oxygen to any number of other neural processes. Neuroscientists like Antonio Damasio necessarily appeal for their investigations to brain maps and body maps, but we have to heed the few occasions when they realise they are speaking in metaphors. Yes, we can arrive at a brain scan and we can read it, but these scans are highly sophisticated mediations, designed and programmed by human beings according to certain agreed specifications. Summing up the problems of over-reliance on such scans for correlating activity to human behaviour, the clinical neuroscientist Raymond Tallis observes: 'In short, pretty well everything relevant to a given response at a given time might be invisible on an fMRI scan.'

In reading, the signifying and mediating signs can melt into consciousness unless we attend to them. But we cannot attend to them overmuch without being unable to read at all. We noted Sartre on this point in Chapter VI. Reading is a conscious (though not entirely conscious) process, and consciousness has outward and physiological manifestations that are symptoms and signs of that which remains, fundamentally, hidden. Diehard materialists, as I have said, have argued long and strong that consciousness is only an epiphenomenological effect of electrochemical, cardiovascular, autonomic exchanges processed mainly in the spinal cord, brainstem and brain. Consciousness does not exist apart from these processes. We have treated some of this science earlier, and we will look more closely at aspects of it in this chapter. But even epiphenomenologically, consciousness is not visible as such. And besides, there is something incoherent about the Greek prefix *epi* in this context. It means 'on' or 'upon', and means here that consciousness follows upon, that is, *from* neural activity – as an effect from a cause. In this way the product (consciousness) is distinguished while remaining bound to that which produces it (neural excitation). But to move from effect (consciousness) to cause (neural activity) is an inference, and there can be no inference drawn without consciousness; that is, without a conscious observer making the inference. In other words, consciousness as epiphenomenal is both that which is produced and that which enables there to be a production. So materialists who assign consciousness as an epiphenomenon are making consciousness both cause and effect. Hence the incoherence of their position; for nothing can cause itself. Or (and other critics of biologicalism have pointed this out) the consciousness of an observer is being smuggled in while also being denied. This incoherence is why the disagreements between materialists and idealists, and every shade of critical realist in between, still rage. But the debate is an old, old one: philosophy has perennially discussed the relation between thought and word, the nature of representation, and the association between mind and world.

In his book *In Defence of Wonder*, Tallis writes:

> Naturalist, which are ultimately materialistic, explanations are currently in the ascendant in secular circles. But they leave consciousness, self-consciousness, the self, free will, the community of minds and most features of the human world unexplained. Supernatural explanations just parcel up our uncertainties in the notion of an entity – God – that is not only unexplained, but usually contradictory. The foundations of knowledge elude us.

You will gather from what follows in this chapter that I do not accept that religion simply 'parcels up our uncertainties'. Such a statement is an example of reductions in complexity that Tallis himself is prey to as he writes his polemic against materialists. Religious belief need not be uncritical, nor rule out the ability to make reasoned judgements upon what is experienced. Religious belief can give a reasoned account for itself. Indeed, I am providing one such account in what follows in this chapter. But Tallis' fundamental point, that we live with 'half knowledge' (recall Keats on 'negative capability') or beliefs, I accept. '[W]e are negligibly small things in a vast universe that outsizes and outlasts us a trillion-fold' (Tallis). In the end there is no final account that can be given for what we believe.

INVISIBILITY AND INTENTIONAL CONSCIOUSNESS

This second mode of the invisible that adheres to the visible has been the distinct province of phenomenology's examinations. Such examinations take us to an altogether different level of concealment. In his last published essay, 'The Visible and the Invisible', the French phenomenologist Merleau-Ponty insists he is not treating 'an absolute invisible' such as God, 'but the invisible of *this* world'. His examination is not into transcendence per se, but rather intentional transcendence. To understand the difference we can take an example that the German phenomenologist Edmund Husserl used in his *Cartesian Meditation*s: a cube. In ways that are not too dissimilar from Cavell and perspectival invisibility, Husserl writes that when we see a cube we do not and cannot perceive its six sides. We can only see two or three. And yet we know that a cube, to be a cube, has to have six equal sides. In seeing the cube, then, we 'project' the missing sides in making sense of what we see. We see *as*. In Husserl's technical vocabulary this is 'apperceptive transcendentalism'. It is 'apperception' because it is a perception that makes possible a further, correlated but unpresented perception. It is transcendental because it affirms what is beyond and external to the perceiver and what is perceived. Apperceptive transcendentalism provides the conditions for the possibility that what is perceived is meaningfully recognised as a cube. The three or four invisible sides of the cube are actually present along with the other sides that we can see, but they are concealed *in* the visibility of what is seen. This 'projection' or 'expectation' (earlier I spoke about 'anticipation') that posits as co-present in an object that which is invisible *in* its visibility is intentional transcendence – because the meaning of the object goes beyond what is perceived of the object in itself (if indeed we can even see any object at all in itself).

Merleau-Ponty develops this recognition of intentional transcendence into what he calls 'perceptual faith' (*la foi perceptive*):

> Meaning is *invisible*, but the invisible is not the contradictory of the visible: the visible itself has an invisible inner framework (*membrure*), and the in-visible is the secret counterpart of the visible, it appears only within it, it is the *Nichturpräsentierbar* [unpresentable] which is presented to me as such within the world.

'Perceptual faith' is the seeing of meaningful form through intentional expectation and projection. If it is 'faith' in an invisible *logos* that opens horizons of meaning within *phusis* or belonging to natural phenomena, it is not then some intellectual assent to the unknown that denies material reality. It is a 'faith' that is co-posited with perception itself. The use of the German term *Nichturpräsentierbar* is a curious use of a negative *Nicht* prefixed to the noun 'presentable' (*präsentierbar*) in a manner that is affirmative, since it is this 'unpresentable' which makes possible what is presented (and vice versa). 'Unpresentable' is my rather poor translation, which, for the time being, I cannot better. What the word points to is far deeper than the 'unpresentable'. The German prefix *ur* in *urpräsentierbar* indicates an origin, a more primordial source which subtends what is unpresentable. This draws Merleau-Ponty's 'unpresentable' into the proximity of what in the monotheistic faiths is termed 'negative theology'. But this is exactly the point where we have to recall the dangers of analogy: proximity is not identity. And who is there that can measure the proportions of sameness and difference with respect to that proximity?

Nevertheless, in an important lecture to the *Société française de philosophie* in 1946, having outlined his thesis on the relationship between the visible and the invisible, transcendent horizons within the immanent, Merleau-Ponty draws a direct comparison between phenomenology and the Christian world view:

My viewpoint differs from the Christian viewpoint to the extent that the Christian believes in another side of things where the '*renversement du pour au contre*' takes place. In my view this 'reversal' takes place before our eyes. And perhaps some Christians would agree that the other side of things must already be visible in the environment in which we live.

Indeed, some Christian theologians would agree – to name Marie-Dominique Chenu and Henri de Lubac as just two of them – and any number of Christian phenomenologists influenced by Merleau-Ponty (most of them French). For these philosophical theologians there is no *renversement* as such, for there is nothing *contre* in the transcendent to the world as it is. Nevertheless, this is a remarkable statement by Merleau-Ponty – a statement that begins by distinguishing phenomenology from Christianity but ends by reframing both intellectual projects.

The statement was picked up in the discussion that followed the lecture, leading Merleau-Ponty to spell out one of the implications of his analysis. 'As to mystical experience, I do not do away with that either,' he told his audience. If we accept the 'mystical experience' as the experience of what is invisible and *Nichturpräsentierbar*, the enigma within and inseparable from the material, then, on Merleau-Ponty's phenomenological terms, who a priori can decide whether with such an experience we are treating not 'an absolute invisible' such as God, 'but the invisible of *this* world'?

This question is particularly prominent, since Merleau-Ponty himself recognised that the phenomenological enquiry is and will always be incomplete: 'the most important lesson which the reduction teaches us is the impossibility of a complete reduction.' So while judgements always concern the visible, the invisible itself cannot be circumscribed. And if the visible is endlessly open to the invisible and can never be grasped as such without 'a complete reduction'; if the visible is not contained but is saturated with an invisibility that continually leaks from it, then towards what does it tend? Quite simply, it cannot be divorced from and pitted against a construal of an absolute transcendent.

In that late essay 'The Visible and the Invisible', Merleau-Ponty described the flesh of the world as 'a pregnancy of possibles, *Weltmöglichkeit*'. One can admit, as Edmund Husserl does explicitly in #58 of his *Ideas*, that absolute transcendence or the transcendence of God must be excluded from the study of phenomenology, which treats only 'a field of pure consciousness'. But even monotheistic theologians would admit that God is not an object in this world; or a proper name, for that matter. From the position of the fourth-century Patristic Christian theologian Gregory of Nyssa, the 'term "Godhead" is significant of operation, and not of nature'. So, again, who can draw the line between absolute and intentional transcendence and claim the invisible begins here and ends there? Who can strictly announce that the invisible is *only* the invisible of this world? Consider the observation of a more recent French phenomenologist, Jean-Louis Chrétien, who, while respecting that the business of phenomenology is not to prove the existence of God, nevertheless wishes to examine, as early Heidegger did, religious phenomena phenomenologically: 'The invisible, before which the nature of being human is revealed, can range from the radical invisibility of the Spirit to the inward sacredness or power of the visible itself, like a mountain, a star, or a statue.' Of course, the corollary in this line of thought is that what moves us beyond phenomenology and towards a theology of phenomena (which is nothing more or less than a doctrine of creation) is the corporeal itself, the mystery of embodiment, the mystery of both flesh and its ability to perceive.

INVISIBILITY AND THE IMAGINATION

From the invisibility that adheres to visibility in perspective, and the invisibility that adheres to intentional consciousness, we come to a third mode of the invisible: the work of the imagination. The imagination is not just a matter of having thoughts. It is not just a matter of the meaningful and how we come to project it, or the intentional operations of consciousness. Imagination, as we saw when looking at Tolkien in Chapter VI, creates worlds that never existed and engages our belief in them. If, returning to Merleau-Ponty, the flesh of the world is 'a pregnancy of possibles, *Weltmöglichkeit*', then imagination creatively plays with, extends and inhabits those 'possibles'. This capacity could be viewed as an aspect of the 'projection' and 'anticipation' we discussed earlier, except with time and memory it operates backwards as well as forwards. Neither the past nor the future is visible as such, while we continually live with the implications and consequences of their invisibility.

In preparation for a meeting with a colleague or an interview I may generate any number of scenarios, none of which will coincide with the facts of the situation when I engage in it. It does not stop me anticipating and engaging with those 'possibles'. There is a sense, as Heidegger observed, that because we see *as* we create the worlds which we inhabit, singly and collectively. But we also create imaginary worlds within those worlds.

To phenomenology's 'intentional transcendentalism', then, and its mode of invisible visibility, we have to add what I want to call 'transcendental freedom'. This is the ability to transcend our perspectives and intentional perception through the imagination. Of course, the two other modes of invisible visibility are the conditions for the possibility of imagination's 'transcendental freedom', but with this freedom we engage with what Sartre called the 'irreal'. Recall that the 'irreal' cannot be seen, touched, or smelled except irreally. Sartre himself relates belief to this freedom to imagine:

> [O]ne of the essential factors of the imaging consciousness is belief. This belief aims at the object of the image. All imaging consciousness has a certain positional quality in relation to its object. An imaging consciousness is, indeed, consciousness of an *object as imaged* and not consciousness *of an image*. But if we form on the basis of this imaging consciousness a second consciousness or reflective consciousness, a second species of belief appears: the belief in the existence of the image.

We are back in the caves of Altamira, Chauvet and Lascaux, and ice-age art, where the image is not an *image of* but an *object imaged*. Sartre is explicitly referring to an art form he was fully acquainted with, the novel. In the space of possibles opened by the imagination we encounter the transcending invisibility of our freedom (in which lies our hope, as we saw). It is not an unbounded freedom. It is not a freedom without determination of some sort, to some extent, though none of us can articulate to what extent – and this itself is freeing.

INVISIBILITY AND THE DIVINE

And the final mode of invisibility is the divine one St Paul spoke about, and which I quoted earlier: 'For the invisible things of [God] from the creation of the world are clearly seen, being understood by the things that are made, even his eternal power and Godhead' (Rom. 1: 20). If I say less about this invisibility than the others, it is because this is not a theological book. Here I am merely raising the questions as they relate to an examination of belief and its relation to religious faith. Given the paradox articulated by St Paul here, and not necessarily a contradiction, what then can we say? There are two prominent possibilities. Either religious faith, in pursuing the invisible that is *beyond* the invisibilities that adhere to the visibilities we have been outlining, is a self-conscious acceptance of believing: a belief in the fundamental disposition to believe, which in hoping and desiring orientates itself towards an ultimate and absolute *teleos* – the divine. Or faith is a response to an invisible that operates always *within* the visible, always calls forth believing as seeing *as* and moves us then *beyond*. For a theologian, I confess, no choice is necessary, for – and here comes St Paul again – 'in God we live and move and have our being'.

The belief in a divine invisibility (Merleau-Ponty would say an 'absolute transcendence') is founded upon an intuition of being created. Of course, we could have been created by aliens from a distant galaxy. But religious intuition is founded upon our having been created by the loving and therefore personal God. And it has to be accepted that such an account of creation does fly in the face of tooth-and-claw Darwinian evolution, which is random – if not downright cruel, highly inefficient and indeed wasteful – in its selective process. Even the teleology of so-called 'teleosemantics' and 'natural teleology' (Millikan), where meaning is rooted in the biological, recognises that any designs that emerge in which there is a resemblance between dispositional properties of cells, digestive systems, adrenalin flows and human beliefs 'are the upshot of prior processes of selection. A trait has a function if it has been designed by some process to produce some effect [...] the selection process will be non-intentional natural selection' (MacDonald and Papineau).

Many are the theological minds that have been exercised in attempting a reconciliation here, because the stakes are high. As the poet William Carlos Williams opens one of his most famous poems: 'So much depends…' Without a reconciliation, a dualism opens up between the material and the spiritual, which some religious traditions (Judaism? Islam?) might be happy to embrace but, because of the doctrine of the incarnation, not St Paul and not Christianity.

For the moment let us pursue our examination of religious faith by stepping back to that third mode of invisibility adhering to the visible: 'transcendental freedom' as it relates imagination to believing. We will take Sartre's example of a novel – indeed, a series of novels by a single author – to explore this creativity that bends poetic faith quite explicitly into religious faith. In making this step, we will explore the freedom in the space of possibles opened by imagining in order to approach that fourth mode of invisibility, the divine.

BELIEVING, FAITH AND IMAGINATION

In the Gospel of St John, Chapter 12, we find the following account of Jesus praying publicly after his baptism:

> 'Father, glorify thy name.' Then came a voice from heaven saying, 'I have both glorified it, and will glorify it again.' The people therefore that stood by, and heard it, said that it thundered; others said, 'An angel spoke to him.' Jesus answered and said, 'This voice came not for me, but for your sakes.'

It is well known that one of the major themes in John's Gospel concerns believing and its relationship to seeing and hearing the gospel preached. The theme culminates in the penultimate chapter of the Gospel with the scene between Christ and doubting Thomas and the statement: 'blessed are they that have not seen and have believed.' What is interesting in this passage is the way the same occurrence can constitute different forms of believing and seeing with respect to the invisible and the visible.

One group perceives thunder and believes the phenomenon to be a natural one. Another group perceives something (perhaps the same thunder), but believes it is an angel speaking to Jesus alone (for presumably they themselves hear only a noise). And finally, Jesus and the Johannine narrator hear the voice of God – a voice which, on Jesus' statement, was available for all to hear, since it was a voice for others, not himself. The situation is reminiscent of those different readings of the happenings at Peterhouse on that late autumnal evening. Was it the plumbing? Was it a ghost? Was it the Devil? Certainly I had at least one white witch offering to exorcise the College's Combination Room. In the Gospel account it is not a difference in interpretation which separates the three understandings of what had occurred; rather, it is a difference in perception: a difference in the quality of perception and belief-informed intentionality. There is an alleged hierarchy in this quality, with Jesus and whoever heard the voice of God perceiving more truly than those who believed an angel had spoken, or that it had thundered. And this quality of perception I would relate to the imagination; for it is how something is imaged for us, imagined, that governs what is perceived and understood.

Of course, the imagination can play false, as Shakespeare reminds us in *A Midsummer Night's Dream*: at night how often does a bush become a bear? We might say, after Kant, that imagination is an operation between perception and understanding. But perception and understanding are not isolated and sequential events (as Kant thought); they are woven into a narrative of believing and into exercises of the imagination that have a history. On the one hand, a group have heard a rumbling in the sky before and this has signified thunder; on the other, a group believe in angels speaking (have even, perhaps, experienced angels speaking), and their perception of this event calls forth an imagined reconstruction: 'an angel spoke to him.' A third group believe God speaks (even, perhaps, have heard God speak) and so are able to perceive and imagine the invisible become visible, the eternal temporal, and the ineffable one condescend to use a human tongue. Each response to what has been received is an act of belief and imagination – though only one is theologically sound, because it perceives aright; it discerns the operations of God in the world.

Much of my academic work has been engaged in the borderlands of literature, philosophy and theology. Certain key ideas hold the three disciplines together, few more so than the act of believing and the exercise of the imagination. You cannot be a theologian, just as you cannot be a contemporary cosmologist, without imagination. For the work involves searching out and wrestling to understand that which both transcends and enfolds this world. It involves alternative ways of seeing that which imagination makes possible and metaphors translate. It involves possibilities not only for new ways of believing, but also new modes of entrustment to what is believed. In that way, exploring the divine is always an exploration of the imagination or that store of images which the imagination stirs into patterns and narratives (what Augustine termed the 'memory'). But, without venturing into the explicitly theological, let us examine this interconnection between believing, imagination and religious faith as it manifests itself in the novels of Graham Greene.

There are two reasons why I have chosen a novelist to work with, and there is a further reason I have chosen Graham Greene. My first reason for taking the novel as the object of my analysis is that reading is a disciplined practice. Cultural engagement is composed of a series of complex practices and relations: theatre-going, movie-watching, gallery visits, poetry-reading, concert attendance, etc. I view these practices and the relations they establish as what Michel Foucault termed 'technologies'. It's a gross, instrumental word, but it describes practices whereby a sense of being a subject is formed and governed. Famously, Foucault examined these 'technologies', their history and operation (like the practice of confession in the church), as informing the soul and writing upon the body. They were instruments of power and purveyors of ideology. We touched upon this in the last chapter. Certain understandings of the self and its relation to the world are produced through the habit of engaging in such practices.

What I am suggesting is that various cultural practices can also be examined as 'technologies' that fashion human beings, by acting upon them both psychologically and somatically. As we have noted, much contemporary neuroscience, and the turn to affectivity, have confirmed the profound interrelation between the mind (individual and collective) and the body. But while it is certainly possible to examine these cultural technologies – through phenomenologies of listening to music or viewing a painting – the reading of a novel provides us with a certain set of focused conditions. We do not have to handle what we might see as the 'incidentals' or 'externalities' of visiting a gallery or watching a performance – the lighting, the heating, the price of the entry ticket, interactions with other people around us, etc.

The novel is a long and sustained operation upon the imagination and the generation of what Sartre called 'second consciousness'. Furthermore, it is easier to submit the novel's performance upon and within the reader to an analysis because certain conditions for its working are controlled by the text itself. Good reading performances can be held accountable to the details of the language.

As to the second reason, the novelist, like God, creates worlds full of people and objects, creatures and landscapes. Unlike God's creation, these novelistic worlds are fashioned out of the worlds we know. Greene made a number of trips to Brighton, walking its streets, mapping the location of various buildings, surveying the insides of hotels, visiting the racecourse and the Downs, before and while he was working on *Brighton Rock*. Novelists do not create *ex nihilo*. These worlds are exercises of imaginative transformation, and if they are to be successful exercises of imaginative transformation, they have to be believable – they have to persuade, even seduce, the receptive reader. We saw this in Chapter VI.

The art of good novel-writing is to arouse belief by awakening the imagination of whoever reads it. Sometimes the suspension of disbelief in Greene's narratives collapses: as when, in *Stamboul Train*, the lesbian newspaper reporter, Mabel Warren, last seen missing the Istanbul express in Vienna, suddenly turns up in Subotica just in time to save the not-so-naive chorus girl, Coral. But *Stamboul Train* is an early work, and Greene was still learning his craft. Believing (and disbelieving), then, is only made possible in the presence (or absence) of a number of other mental and emotional judgements – about what is plausible, for example. The novel creates an imaginary world that has to be believable and which continually calls upon further acts of belief if it is to accomplish its ends. The author has a plot, a direction in which the action is heading, and the characters are caught up in the webs spun by his or her providential pen. Again, there are analogues here with the operation of divine providence in a history orientated towards a final end.

All this, of course, has been explored by literary theorists like Frank Kermode and George Steiner, and I am not wishing to rehearse their examination of the relationship between the literary and the theological. Although, if I get theological for a moment, I do wish to affirm an analogy between creation as God's own writing (through the Logos) and the author's act of creation (through *logoi*: words and reason). And with certain writers who are conscious themselves of this analogy – Greene would be one of them – the literary can open on to questions that are theological. For example, in *The Honorary Consul*, having kidnapped the said consul – a friend of the narrator, Doctor Eduardo Plarr – the compromised priest Father Rivas states:

> He is not in our hands, Eduardo. He is in the hands of the govern-ments. In the hands of God too, of course. I do not forget my old claptrap, you notice, but I have never yet seen any sign that He interferes with our wars and our politics.

But the novel's plot raises quite explicitly whether God does in fact shape human ends beyond human willing. Both the composition of the world by God and the composition of a world by the novelist are acts of persuasion.

A structure of belief governs the crafting of a novel and the reader's ability to imagine. If we cannot imagine the world we are being offered as readers, then we cannot enter into that structure of believing. This is what I, personally, find with most science fiction – I cannot imagine the worlds some of these authors are generating and so disbelief cannot attain that necessary suspension.

Graham Greene, I submit, consciously works with the question 'what makes a belief believable?' He shows the operation of believing in a number of different contexts that not only distinguish different types of believing but also different structures in which belief operates (including religious belief). Furthermore, he points to how belief is inseparable from being able to imagine, and how both imagination and belief are governed by desire. Put another way, I would argue that the Catholic novel (by Greene), the Jewish novel (by Roth, for example) or the Protestant novel (by Updike, and, more recently, McCarthy) are imaginary investigations into believing that explore the terrain of that third mode of invisibility in the visible. They demonstrate that the novel, often seen as associated with the rise of secularism and the decline of religious belief, refigures the act of believing and therefore is a mode of art concerned with the transposition of belief or the changing structures of believing.

Out of the plethora of perceptions that arise from being immersed in the world, consciousness both images and imagines. This creativity – which is not fully accessible to consciousness – hooks up both to past memories of cognate or associated images, and future anticipations of what will follow. In this way, the faculty of the imagination weaves past to present and future, and so the worlds we occupy and that preoccupy us, individually and collectively, are constructed. (I do not imply by the use of 'construct' here that there is no real world out there or that human beings continually live out illusions.) Perceptions arise because there is a real world of objects out there, and the scenarios we construct are not mere fantasies. We are social animals, so the worlds we construct are shared worlds. We continually modify the world-patterns we make in association with other human beings engaged in the same activity. Our world-making is always in negotiation with other world-making; we are continually undergoing a form of persuasion that this is the true, the real, the way things are. If we remain unpersuaded, then we experience anxiety and become hesitant and undecided. The mental patterns do not form, or form only incoherently.

Take Maurice's experience following the bomb blast that Sarah believes has killed him, in Greene's *The End of the Affair*. Their love affair has been intense and reciprocal, but following the bomb incident Sarah leaves his flat and has no more contact with him until a chance meeting two years later. The pattern of Maurice's world view falls apart, and his hopes that Sarah will ring or write turn to despair. He cannot make sense of her behaviour, especially because the last thing she says to him, as she leaves his bomb-torn home, is 'love doesn't end…' The agitations of reason propose various solutions, such as Sarah having abandoned him for another lover. And so Maurice eventually engages Parkis, the private detective, who reports on Sarah's movements. These reports then trigger another set of imaginative recreations that attempt to explain Sarah's behaviour. All the fermentation of these surmises evaporates when Maurice steals Sarah's diary. It is exactly at the point where the mental patterns cannot cohere, when the plotting of images dissolves into the random and chaotic, that the activities of the imagination are most intense: conjuring scenarios of meaning from the pieces left in what one famous song describes as 'the windmills of [the] mind'. We are back in the Combination Room of Peterhouse in the days that followed the 'sighting' of the 'ghost'. The reason for Maurice's existential despair is in fact his inability to believe the truth of Sarah's words to him. Believing what she had said about love never ending would not have minimised the pain of their separation – the end of the affair – but it would have brought him the realisation of how profoundly Sarah loved him, and how shallow, until the break-up, his own love was in comparison.

What this imaginative activity of mapping and plotting reveals, and many of Greene's novels narrate, is at least a fourfold set of interrelated observations. First, a profound operation of *poiesis* associated with all consciousness. Even in sleep this poetic activity continues to spin chains of images into weirdly evolving plots. Imagination is rooted into our need to 'make sense', to produce coherent patterns that are either faithful to or modify the past, and which anticipate future trajectories. Literature is a self-conscious appropriation of that ongoing activity. It is an intensification of the fabricating processes of the mind, both conscious and unconscious. Of course, when we are treating 'mind' we are concerned with human cognitive capacities and activities explored by neuroscience.

The concept of mind employed in neuroscience is a very modern conception of individual consciousness, with its philosophical roots in Descartes and Kant. There are more imaginative accounts of mind in, say, Augustine and the Cappadocian Fathers, where mind is related to soul – that which animates and is animated by the body; that which communes or has the capacity to commune with God. The soul is the source of intellection, but is profoundly related to a theological anthropology that focuses on human beings created in the image of God. We are makers of images because we are in the image *of*. And in being actively engaged in a world created by God, the imagination as that capacity for image-making works analogically: ferreting out and fabricating relations between things – the mental patterns that 'make' sense of our experience of the world and respond to the Logos through whom all things were made; the Logos who in and as Christ 'is a persuasion, a form' (David Bentley Hart). Theologically, we might even say that the imagination is that receptive capacity of the soul that responds both to a world so created and also to creation as a divine gift. In fact, Hart goes on to speak of 'God's life [a]s [...] rhetoric.' The work of the imagination expands the soul in a movement that participates in what a number of the Greek Fathers called *theopoiesis*, a divine metapoetic activity of the Spirit, in which its own *poiesis* participates. Of course, Coleridge reminds us of this when he writes of the imagination being an echo in the finite of the infinite 'I am'.

This does not mean that the imagination cannot conceive of evil entities – the planned deceptions and self-delusions that the Bible sometimes calls 'the imaginations of their hearts'. But Greene is interesting here for the way he understands evil as imaginative privation. Pinkie, in *Brighton Rock*, the evil Peter Pan who accepts his own damnation and tries to force the wife he detests so much to join him in that condition, is a man without imagination. 'The imagination hadn't awoken,' Greene writes. 'That was his strength. He couldn't see through other people's eyes, or feel with their nerves.' And it is that inability to see that locks Pinkie in a delusion about his own abilities to be the leader of the gang and leads to his own destruction. Of course, Pinkie fantasises: about staying at the five-star Cosmopolitan Hotel in Brighton like the London gang leader Mr Colleoni. But for Greene such fantasies, which we as readers recognise from the beginning, are cliché; they are without real persuasive force and have no purchase on reality. They are as impotent as Pinkie himself – insubstantial daydreams. Such fantasies only feed despair; and despair for Greene is the greatest sin (the rejection of faith, hope and, ultimately, love; and the elevation of pride). In *The Power and the Glory*, when the whisky priest encounters a devout woman in prison who is bitterly disappointed in him, Greene has the priest observe, 'Hate was just failure of imagination.' Perhaps, again like Coleridge, we need to distinguish between fantasy (or fancy, as he called it), which is a much lower mental capacity, and the operation, even discipline, of imagination. Fantasy is not self-transcending. It is a form of self-idolatry, for it begins and ends with projection: the screening of a narrative in which the ego is always at the centre of the plot. Such fantasies, like evil and sin, have no ontological weight – they are acts of decreation or non-being.

If sense is made in our imaginations, as the patterns and maps are fabricated, then religious belief is a mode of perception. The narrative of Jesus' baptism in the Gospel of St John has an analogue in *Brighton Rock*. Pinkie, terrified he is going to be betrayed by one of his inner circle, Spicer, is in conversation with his faithful friend, Dallow:

He said to Dallow. 'You got to watch the place [Spicer's in hiding]. I don't trust him a yard. I can see him looking out there, waiting for something, and seeing *her* [Ida, the blowsy blonde who believes (correctly) that Pinkie has murdered Hale].' Dallow replies:

'He would not be such a fool.'

'He's drunk. He says he's in Hell.'

Dallow laughed. 'Hell. That's good.'

'You're a fool, Dallow.'

'I don't believe in what my eyes don't see.'

'They don't see much then,' the Boy said.

Observe that interplay between 'trust', 'fool', 'Hell', 'good' and seeing. It is because of the relationship between knowledge and seeing *as* that imagination is always linked to 'belief'.

In many of Greene's novels the governing question is not what is known but what is believed, though frequently the truth is out to a certain extent by the end of the novel: for example, we know Sarah loved Maurice; we know Harry Lime (in *The Third Man*) has faked his own death and is the villain, not the hero. Greene frequently treats the antitheses between states of deception and acts of faith, seeing and seeing *as*, trust and suspicion, betrayal and faithfulness, confidence and incredulity, and the calculus of probability–improbability that accords with witnessing and evidence. These antitheses and this calculus establish a structure of believing. It is not simply that his characters enact scenarios in which these states and this calculus are exemplified; the very act of writing literature itself, the implicit contract between the novelist and his readers, creates a space for the performance and reflection upon the performance of such themes. The world, for Greene, and the fictional world for Greene's characters and Greene's readers, is a laboratory where belief is created and tested.

One of the technical devices he employs to examine this testing is the story within a story. In *The Confidential Agent*, a novel written after *Brighton Rock* and before *The Power and the Glory*, the protagonist, D, a man who 'carried what were called credentials, but credence no longer meant belief', lands in Dover with the mission to secure coal from the wealthy colliery owner Benditch to help with the civil war in his own country. But an agent from the opposition has also been sent for the same reason, and to hunt D down. Caught in the middle is a young woman, Rose, daughter of Benditch, who befriends D. On the way to meeting Rose, D is intercepted, shot at and pursued by one Currie, who is well known to Rose. On meeting, D gives Rose an account of the chase. Rose enters a space where her believing has to be reconfigured.

> 'How could they shoot at you in the street – here? What about the police, the noise, the neighbours? [...] I don't believe it. I won't believe it. Don't you see that if things like that happened life would be quite different? One would have to begin over again [...] Prove it. Prove it,' she said fiercely. [D manages to dig the bullet out of the wall.] 'Oh, God,' she said suddenly, 'it's true.'

The 'Oh God' may seem like a throwaway expletive – Rose professes no religious conviction, and when D in a moment reflects upon the misery in the world and how if 'you believed in God, you could also believe that it [the world] had been saved from much misery', he concludes that 'he hadn't that particular faith'. But the 'Oh God' is employed both colloquially and expressively. It correlates with Rose's recognition that certain forms of seeing *as* demand radical transformation of one's understanding of life. Certain forms of seeing *as* can take on the quality and power of epiphanies.

This small story within a story, like the reflective mirror in the background of Renaissance paintings of Dutch interiors, is a parable of the operative technology of the novel itself with respect to the reader. There is something almost pathological about Greene's need to put himself, his readers and his characters out on an imaginative ledge and persuade them to jump, believing. He chose, for example, to set stories in countries he had never visited (like the Balkan states for *Stamboul Train*), or visited very briefly for research purposes (like Trier, the setting for *The Name of Action*, Sweden, the setting for *England Made Me*, or Mexico for *The Power and the Glory*). There is an imaginative recklessness here, as if approaching an aesthetic suicide; daring himself to make something believable when the odds for doing so are very remote. He forces his imagination to work with very little material, pushing it wilfully into the incredible, problematic and the improbable; into worlds that are dark, grotesque, warped with irony and often religious. In this way each novel can be viewed as an act of faith. Like the Russian roulette he used to play whilst a student at Oxford, he risks everything and asks his readers to risk everything, testing the possibilities for redemption.

Particularly in the Catholic novels, this act of imaginative daring – poetic faith, if you like – correlates with the acts of faithlessness that are transformed into acts of religious faith; transformations that the reader is being persuaded are possible. Brought to the point where she will be persuaded by Pinkie to commit suicide and join him in hell, as a Catholic the slum child Rose is transfigured in the closing pages into an English Thérèse of Lisieux. The priest in the confessional Rose enters finally asks her to 'Pray for me, my child', to which she answers, 'Yes, oh yes.' Sarah's harrowing and adulterous love in *The End of the Affair* works the miracles of healing a sick child, removing the ugly facial blemish on the face of the evangelical atheist Mr Smyth, and bringing Maurice and her husband Henry together in a new awakening of mutual dependence.

Greene composes his novels on the edge of the incredulous, seeking out new terrain where what is visible, reasonable and familiar meets what is invisible, miraculous and *Unheimlich*. The literary act of persuading, of taking the reader on an imaginative journey that requires the suspension of disbelief, ends in the tense possibility of welcoming what is strange and highly dangerous: an act of religious believing. The narratives deliver the reader to the portal of a potential conversion.

This journey is captured brilliantly in the ending of *The Power and the Glory*, where a fugitive priest knocks at the door of a Catholic family in a southern Mexican city. A boy opens the door, a boy who until the point of the whisky-priest's death had been a religious sceptic.

'[L]et me come in,' the man said with an odd frightened smile, and suddenly lowering his voice he said to the boy, 'I am a priest.'

'You?' the boy exclaimed.

'Yes,' he said gently. 'My name is Father –' But the boy had already swung the door open and put his lips to his hand before the other could give himself a name.

A fierce, turbulent and exhausting eros frequently drives these imaginative ventures. 'The sexual instinct and the creative instinct live and die together,' the novelist Doctor Saavedra observes in *The Honorary Consul*; and the impotent Pinkie, who can only destroy, has no imagination. Desire shakes the imagination from its lazy slumbering in fantasy; the worlds of the self-evident and certain flake and splinter, and doubt, conjecture and surmise overpower knowledge. Bunyan's Giant Despair prepares to pounce. It is in this way that the question 'What makes a belief believable?' becomes urgent and existential: to characters, to Greene himself and to his readers. If, at the start, the object of this eros (which can have the hues of love or hate) is a man or a woman, we are quickly plunged into much darker depths that leave the human being far behind. It is at this point that another category enters the structure of believing that imagination and desire composes (and which we encountered in the last chapter): the mythological.

Critics of Greene have frequently pointed to the Manichean cosmology that frames his imaginative worlds. Again a set of binaries gives this cosmology shape: hell and heaven, good and evil, the Dionysian and the Apollonian, peace and war, destruction and creation, the saint, the martyr and the sinner. But the cosmology is rooted in a distinctly Catholic imaginary prior to its sanitisation by Vatican II, and it is not nearly as Gnostic as the critics believe. Gnosticism is without humour; and there is always a redemptive rictus that appears on the face of death for Greene. The God of the ironic has a very biblical heritage. Greene's mythology is riddled with ironic inversions. In *Metaphysics* Aristotle observes that 'myth is composed of wonder', and wonder, as I have suggested, is always looking, wide-eyed, towards a transcendent horizon. We saw in the last chapter that myth's persuasive power lies in its credibility, and Greene plays with the credo and the credible such that his mythic world is glimpsed and then fades out. One observes that what is at stake in the novels, as with the story of Jesus' baptism in the Gospel of St John, is a question of ultimate, theological concern.

BELIEF, TRANSCENDENCE AND RELIGION

So, following this exploration of those third and fourth modes of invisibility adhering to the visible, what can we observe about religious believing? We can observe that with religious believing we encounter belief in belief itself; that is, not only a recognition and acceptance of the fact of invisibility as it pertains to our everyday existence, but an investment (of trust and emotion) in the meaningfulness, value and significance of that invisibility.

And other animals are not capable of doing this, as I have pointed out. Well, not according to one of the most important studies on the way the world is experienced by our nearest mammal kin, the chimpanzee (by Daniel Povinelli). This is not to deny both consciousness and a limited self-consciousness to chimpanzees (Gordon G. Gallup). But the extent of that self-awareness is still a matter of much debate, because it is we, the human observers, who identify, measure and interpret that awareness. It is the observer who has to discern the difference between conditioned, reflexive and willed behaviour. As a primatologist, Daniel Povinelli emphasises that this assessment and evaluation of awareness in other animals, including chimpanzees, is by analogy. And the problem is that by drawing analogies and emphasising the proportions of similarity over difference when it comes to our experience of the world versus the way the world is experienced for a chimpanzee, we are treating again what is fundamentally invisible. We cannot see the world in the way a chimpanzee sees it because we are not chimpanzees. We can only observe, in close detail, aspects of their behaviour *we* conclude and see *as* significant. So we project and anticipate levels of intentionality with respect to these observations; intentions that may or may not be there. The limited self-consciousness in these animals is episodic, whereas in human beings it is continually available. Without that capacity to transcend their own consciousness, then Sartre's 'second consciousness' is not possible. 'Second consciousness' plays with and extends the immediate environment by transcending it. So all the inventiveness and creativity of imagination working on intentional perception is not available to them. Reflective consciousness is not available either; and this is fundamental both to inferring causation (from effect) and employing this inference more generally in tool-making, technology (Wolpert) and developments of the concept of 'tool'. They have limited access to symbolic activity and no recognition that this activity is symbolic. Chimpanzees and other animals will have both emotions and dispositions because these are biologically intrinsic to being embodied, possibly even down to the cellular. But they have not the capacity to evaluate emotions as feeling. And so our nearest animal cousins may have dispositional beliefs, but they cannot have religion – self-conscious belief in believing – because they cannot transcend and reflect upon those beliefs.

But, there is no advantage for religious studies in positing a divinity in the 'gaps' not yet explained by the various sciences, including primatology.

And the fact that we cannot fully account for belief, unconsciousness, consciousness or even perception (because of the invisible adhering to the visible) is not in itself an index of a grounding religious world view. It is of no advantage either for religious studies to surrender to a dualism between the invisible and inexplicable powers of mind (our mind or the divine mind) and the material properties of objects and processes in the natural world. Nevertheless, what is yet to be explained or understood does return us to certain aspects of the examinations we have undertaken that raise once more the question of some intrinsic relationship between belief, as a primordial disposition inextricably bound to our embodied experience of being in the world, and the religious commitment to transcendence.

In Chapter II I pointed to a certain transcendence involved in self-consciousness and recognitions of the meaningful outside oneself (even if, at first, this 'outside' is the perspective of perceiving oneself as an object in the world). Raymond Tallis would concur, at least up to this point. It is the fulcrum upon which he wishes to refute the reductiveness of biological materialism: 'the mind transcends, and so is not identical with, activity in the brain.' In the same chapter I also made the point that the first signs of belief among hominids were religious signs (burial of the dead) and intentional, purposeful behaviour (the domestication of fire). We need to examine the implicit relationship between belief and transcendence further with respect to the notion of the bounded 'self', the understanding of a meaningfulness external to it, and intentionality.

TRANSCENDENCE

So what are the requirements for transcendence that have emerged from our enquiry into the invisibility intrinsic to visibility? Here are four.

Firstly, as we have already noted, there needs to be a recognition of an exteriority – that I am not a tree, a chair, etc. This is not a pure exteriority, an objective exteriority. There is no objectivity in so far as not one of us can get outside our selves to know what Kant called 'things in themselves'. We see *as*, which means that the external world is always mediated to us through our body's perception of it – a perception coloured by a thousand variables, from memory and anticipation to the way the light falls on it.

That 'recognition of an exteriority' is not a passive registration by our ears and eyes, our fingers and our taste buds (the most direct appropriation by the senses is thought to be smell). An object scanned by my retina, triggering sensations processed through the visual cortex in terms of cause and effect becomes, at some unidentifiable point, a 'recognition' by me of that object. As we have already examined, in that recognition there is a level of both anticipation and intentionality: the object is meaningful to me. My perception itself is intentional. We noted this above in the phenomenological work of Merleau-Ponty.

Secondly, transcendence both constitutes and requires a subject who perceives. This subject is a necessary condition for the 'recognition'. Materialistic accounts that conflate mind with brain view this 'subject' as illusory. Like 'consciousness' it is epiphenomenal. But this evades, because it cannot explain the mechanisms whereby a notion of the 'self' is co-present with all perception. Dennett's idea that the necessary 'intentional stance' has evolved because it is the brain's efficient way of simplifying endless possibilities that arise from neural processing is, at best, a hypothesis. And it is a hypothesis that does recognise intentionality exists, even if its inconvenience to a materialist account of nature demands going to extraordinary lengths to explain it away. But its illusory nature is a hypothesis; he cannot demonstrate that that is the case. Furthermore, in many of the accounts of the 'self' as an epiphenomenon, intentionality is smuggled in, as we have seen. It is there in the very fact Dennett is able to author his sentences, his books, and have a hypothesis that is and is not shared by other people. And he is aware that other people do not share it, as much of his work is a polemic against the reasoning of these other people. In wishing to exorcise the ghost in the machine, the machine stills needs to be programmed to operate in the way it does. Dennett turns the single ghost into a legion of demons working chaotically in the synaptic gaps, armed with neurotransmitters. Intentionality is denied by the materialists and then smuggled in in order to facilitate the accounts they wish to argue for.

Thirdly, this subject is not just conscious. Other animals possess consciousness, but transcendence requires a consciousness of the contents of one's conscious in order to affirm what I am not – the very distance and difference that characterises transcendence. The degree of self-awareness makes possible the recognition that other people too have mental states.

This is the basis for symbolic activity between people that is the foundation for communication. Return to the final sequence in *Quest for Fire*: the otherness of the other person is not an incommensurate otherness, a pure otherness. If that were the case there could be no shared understanding. The other would be incomprehensible to me. But the 'mutuality' recognised and created in and through the recognition enables there to be a community of embodied minds – and there is no culture, politics, city-building or civilisation without such a community issuing from that recognition.

Fourthly, finally, as a requirement, a characteristic and a consequence of transcendence, the subject must be free. Transcendence constitutes the subject in his or her freedom (and hope) because it expands consciousness by opening up the world before us. When we move from a closed room in which we recognise 'I am not this chair', and the chair is perceived as distant and different, we might not gain from this experience a sense of our freedom. But consider moving out of that room and standing at the top of Goat Fell, the highest peak on the Isle of Arran in Scotland. A vast stretch of water opens between the island and the mainland, an even greater stretch opens between the island and the Atlantic Ocean, and other islands in the vicinity mark out distance and distinction. Now we experience the freedom that is a concomitant of transcendence. In so far as we transcend our environment, this is a freedom bestowed and discovered. If the immensity solicits our wonder – what philosophers like Kant recognised as the sublime – then we also must understand wonder as the foundational affect in worship. But, as we saw, such an experience can also become creative freedom, an exercise of freedom in which freedom is not limited to questions of choice but an invitation to play; an invitation for imaginative acts in which believing is both engaged and expressive.

These four requirements for transcendence point to how it is written into the way human beings perceive *as*. That does not mean that the human capacity to perceive in this way is not a product of our evolution, from hominid to *Homo sapiens*, but something changed radically when one animal form evolved such a capacity. And things have not been the same since. Such an account of transcendence does not demonstrate or even require the existence of God; a divine mind. But such a notion cannot be ruled out a priori. The following question arises: in our exploration of the meaningful in and through our ability to transcend ourselves, why stop at just the human level, or what we take to be the human level? Because the diachronic structures of believing operate always with cultural and historical construals of what it is to be human. And with materialist and frequently non-reductive materialist accounts (Tallis', for example) we are working within a secular understanding of what it is to be human. Another way of putting this is, if the meaningful is not simply a human construct but an aspect of the world in which human beings both create and discover the meaningful, from where does the meaningful come? Nagel:

> [T]o explain not merely the possibility but the actuality of rational beings, the world must have properties that make their appearance not a complete accident: in some way the likelihood must have been latent in the nature of things. So we stand in need of both a constitutive explanation of what rationality might consist in, and an historical explanation of how it arose [...] Such an explanation would complete the pursuit of intelligibility by showing how the natural order is disposed to generate being capable of comprehending it.

As he also points out, even an evolutionary account of the place of reason presupposes reason's validity and 'cannot confirm it without circularity'. If this is the case – and we would have to square this with the blind, cruel wastefulness of the evolutionary process (not at all easy) – why should human self-transcendence lead to a cul-de-sac with a purely secular understanding of what it is to be human? Religious believing points beyond that cul-de-sac. Why a priori should it be viewed as having transgressed some limit? Whose limit is it anyway? Given that transcendence as we experience it is profoundly related to the adherence of the invisible to the visible, who can circumscribe the invisible?

BEYOND SECULAR MEANING

One could, for example – in locating the human production of the meaningful within a more universal account of the meaningful, and in developing an account of transcendence – refer to what has been called in astrophysics and cosmology the anthropic principle. We came across this principle earlier in relation to panpsychism and the protomental: that the universe and its physical constraints are compatible or suitable for sustaining conscious life and our ability to behold such a universe. There is a spectrum of strong to weak acceptance of the anthropic principle, depending upon the levels of acceptance of what are termed anthropic coincidences: recognised constraints and constants of properties within the physical universe. Materialists cannot accept such a principle: life (for them, consciousness is a function and by-product of life) is an infinitely random event, a possibility that is just about as (in)credible as the creationist's acceptance of a divine miracle.

The anthropic principle is much debated. It commits cosmologists to a *uni*verse, and string theorists, for example, embrace the possibility of *multi*verses. For this chapter on the possibility of an intrinsic relationship between belief and transcendence, the issue does not need resolving. It can remain as simply a 'possibility' which arguments can be made for or against.

Let's return to the neuroscience and philosophies of mind sketched in Chapter III: if life is adaptive, and adaptive because sentient organisms process their perceptions in ways that are purposeful for them biologically, and develop a fittingness between them and the environments in which they live, then 'communication' plays a fundamental role in all development. I say 'communication' rather than 'information' because we need to understand that, though used univocally by many of the philosophers of mind and neuroscientists whose work I have cited, it is by no means clear what is defined as 'information'. Nevertheless, if we live in and through the myriad networks of communication between body, brain and the worlds in which they are situated, and encrypted within our DNA, then the question arises whence this global communicative activity comes. Evolutionary biology would say it arises from non-intentional selectivity. Okay. But another explanation, based upon a recognition of a meaningfulness exterior to oneself, is that the world was made to be meaningful and to be understood as meaningful. This explanation would then raise a teleological question concerning a cosmic intentionality that is not reducible to the logics of immanent self-evolving processes (which as Dawkins insists are 'blind' and have no aim or purpose as such). The teleological question would further raise the question about a creator who is in some way either involved in the communication (for some reason) or at least established creation as communicative. Who is speaking to us? And what are they saying?

Let me be clear: I am not arguing that there is any necessary relation between the production of meaning and divine communication. In fact, earlier, I exposed some of the difficulties with the panpsychic hypothesis. I am making no theological claims here. Instead, I am arguing for why the relationship between three elements – the disposition to believe (that arises in and through the production of meaning and which greatly impacts upon it in terms of the contents of our consciousness), the recognition in self-consciousness of a meaning transcending and external to oneself, and religion – is so close as to be understood by some as a necessary relation, and was so from the dawn of early hominid consciousness (which might go back 2 million years) until fairly recently. In fact, to take this further, religion through the logic of these relationships has, again until fairly recently, been the primary means whereby belief becomes believable. As both St Augustine and St Anselm enjoined: believe that you may understand. This is a reversal, evidently, of the modern order.

CONCLUSION

We can sum up the preceding discussion by making three observations about the relationship between belief and religious faith.

First, religious faith is a specific commitment to belief, to the invisible that pertains to and subtends the visible. It values believing; in fact, in the reversal of the modern order in which knowledge and understanding take priority over belief. I believe in order that I may know. But, as I have been arguing throughout, this is the way things are: any knowing is always knowing *as*. It is always partial. It is always a dwelling 'in uncertainties, mysteries, doubts' (Keats). It is a knowing shot through with and issuing from deeper primordial dispositions *to* believe.

Secondly, religious faith is therefore a specific orientation of the more primordial disposition to believe. It is not a different type of believing. It is the same disposition framed by and exercised within specific religious practices. This does not mean that the culturally and historically informed practices are interchangeable between religious faiths. Neither does this mean that these practices are only the symbolic clothing for a deeper ontological reality (as in the liberal theologian Paul Tillich's discussion of 'ultimate concern'). As we saw with the archaeology, biology and the synchronic and diachronic structures of believing, belief is rooted in and always orientated towards the material. To use a Christian metaphor: belief incarnates and is always incarnational. The symbolic activity is not divorced from the physiological and emotional activity of believing. They are continually informing and modifying each other. The experience of religious faith – by a Muslim, a Jew, a Christian, or a Hindu – is not identical, although each faith and experience is an orientation of the primordial disposition, and that disposition is a response to what is transcendent. How they experience the modes of that transcendence cannot be the same, because what is meaningful and what becomes meaningful in the experience cannot be separated from the synchronic and diachronic structures that have shaped and given expression to that experience within a specific (and never culturally isolated, never homogeneous) religious tradition.

Theologians from and of these various traditions might wish to develop theologies of experience, but there is never something generic that might be called just 'religious experience'. For the theologians reading this, then: Tillich (and liberal Christian theologians of his ilk) is wrong because his account of human experience is wrong. Can we say then that each of these different theologies reveal aspects of the one God? That sounds like another, albeit more complex, take on liberal theology. And, as a statement, it too would be wrong, because all we know about 'aspects' relates to objects. I visit a cathedral and see one aspect of it from outside, and there is another aspect of it from inside. But whatever 'God' is or names, God is not an object. So we cannot speak of these theologies as different aspects of the one God. Therefore, what can we say? Only that the mystery pertaining to the invisible in the visible, the mystery of consciousness itself that cannot either understand the relationship between mind and brain or dissolve one into the other – a mystery then that constitutes the mystery of being human itself – is considerably deepened when it comes to the nature of transcendence and any notion of a transcendent intentionality written into our being created at all.

Thirdly, if believing is constitutive of seeing *as*, then religious believing is a mode of perception. This takes us back to that account of Jesus' baptism in the Gospel of John. Religious believing is a way of responding to the world that recognises and valorises the invisible operative *within* what is materially visible of that world. All seeing *as* is interpretative. We don't just see. So in religious believing there is an interpretative process, as there is in every other seeing *as*. This might explain why in several languages (German and Greek, for example) the word for 'belief' and the word for 'faith' are the same (*Glauben* and *pistis* in the two languages cited). We have come to understand from our examinations of the very different projects of Stanley Cavell and Maurice Merleau-Ponty that perception is always incomplete. In fact, the incompleteness is built into perception such that we are continually 'haunted by a sense of what we do not know' (Tallis). So, if transcendence begins in the recognition that I am not *this* chair here or *that* person over there, *this* dog or *that* tree, if transcendence begins with the perception of what is other and external, then transcendence itself begins and ends in what is hidden, concealed – the original Greek meaning of the word *mysterion*.

We would expect, then – in the practice of faith seeking understanding, of believing in order to know – multiple forms of belief cooperating with and diverging from different modes of perception. And this is what we find attested in third-person narratives of the relationship between perception and belief in the novels of Graham Greene, for example.

BUT – and this returns us to the analogical – a 'gap' remains between the human and the divine, human *scientia* and divine knowledge. This is not a theological book, and so not a theological investigation. We can go no further with our examination of belief. We are led, though, to that gap, that visible invisibility, between Adam's finger and God's in Michelangelo's painting in the Sistine Chapel. The gap is unbridgeable *for us*, but it opens up the greatest of all space of possibles. The space demands we point ahead of ourselves, into what is hidden in the invisibility, into the heart of believing itself – for something being given and for something for which we are groping. In Christian theology this space of possibles is depicted in the story of a father who comes to Jesus with a child who is possessed. The case is a bad one, and Jesus tells the man that a miracle is possible, for 'All things are possible for the one who believes.' The father responds: 'I believe; help my unbelief!' (Mark 9: 23–4).

CONCLUSION

Lost in Paradise

We are not what we were. We are not stardust blown around by solar winds following a Big Bang. We are not single-cell organisms learning to swim in a primordial soup. We are not creatures who have crawled from the swamp, climbed trees and then begun to swing among the branches. Around 2 million years ago, early forms of human being developed the capacity to symbolise. They became a symbolic species, and this enables us to give expression to the primordial disposition to believe and its attendant dispositions: to desire, to anticipate, to project, to imagine and to hope. We became not just conscious beings but the most intellectually advanced thinking and self-conscious beings. The entry into the symbolic enabled the storage and transmission of our beliefs, enabled the teaching and learning of beliefs, the generation of world views, rationality, explanations and narrations. These cognitive and affect-laden, mental and somatic productions were shared from the beginning. That sharing was the basis for communication and its advanced development. In being shared, they organised collectives of peoples and the first communities.

And so began the story of how we came to live more and more in our heads, in and through our symbolic capacities, detaching ourselves from, denying, and controlling the physiological and emotional substrate of our existence. We began to live within the scripting, editing, deleting, and cutting-and-pasting of lives that were composed from the tissue and texting of our minds. Some live in their heads more than others, in various ways: from daydreaming, to reading, to problem-solving, and watching television. The trend will continue. Academics have always been ahead of the game here.

We evolved, physically and culturally, in that ongoing pursuit of stable flourishing, that drive for the maximally conducive conditions for our reproductive well-being. From around 10,000 years ago we founded settlements, built environments and cities, and dramatically improved the storage and dissemination of our symbolising through various forms of inscription – from incisions on pieces of ochre to cave painting, carvings, sculpture and alphabetic script. From being a speaking species we became a textual species; a species that could establish empires of hierarchised belonging and civilisations of hierarchised value (moral, religious, political and aesthetic). That entry into the symbolic could never be dissociated from – because it was profoundly indebted to – our technological advance. And that advancement deepened our dependence upon the symbolic in ways that increasingly distinguished us from all other animals. As human beings we increasingly became defined by our symbolic capacity and our concomitant ability to carve something from what was unseen, to bring the visible from the invisibility of our disposition to believe and its attendant dispositions.

Our development as *Homo sapiens* lay in our ability to generate actualities from virtualities. As a symbolic species we were already committed to virtual realities that were so closely allied to aspirations, ambitions, hopes and dreams. We dwelt within the myths we composed, the utopias we fantasied, the dystopias we feared. We believed in better (Sky TV), and our pursuit of the better went hand in hand with our technological innovation, so that now – and this now is always and already diachronically moving forward – we become self-conscious of our make.believe (Sony), our simulations, our simulacra. We leave reality at home (Odeon Cinemas) in the 3D special effects of action movies, in the golf, tennis and bowling of interactive boxes, among the digital dungeons and armament supplies of cyber games, and through being plugged into our MP3 players, tablets and iPhones. We are immersed in the symbolic. It's like surround-sound home theatres. And the bandwidths get broader and broader, faster and faster. We are losing ourselves in our virtual realities, our second lives, our avatars; we are losing our capacity to symbolise.

When I began this book I downloaded video clips of the UN intervention in the Libyan crisis. I listened to talk from the US, France and Britain about the possible deployment of troops, the bombing of Gaddafi's armed tanks, the maintenance of a no-fly zone, and the reassurances that this was not another Iraq or Afghanistan. History repeats itself today with respect to Syria as this book is coming to an end. Back then I read of the rebels in Benghazi dancing on their cars in jubilation at the UN resolution, fireworks and music inflaming their resistance. I saw photographs taken on mobile phones of children smiling and making victory signs, of women armed with Kalashnikovs, of young men with determined, sweat-streaked faces shouting out their defiance. And what was I to make of all this and so many crises since that followed in the wake of the Arab Spring? What do I know of these situations, of the experiences of these peoples, of their cultures or their histories? In the case of Libya, I know only as someone who has studied Christian theology that Augustine was born somewhere in the deserts and that his life, for the most part, was mapped on to its shoreline in cities like Hippo Regius and Carthage; cities that are no longer there or are only white ruins, sand-blown and moon-washed. I see, I hear, I read, I think – and so I experienced the unfolding of this violent and uncertain event, and so many others. There will be pain and blood and hunger and despair. There will be grief and joy, outrage and consolation, greed and sacrifice, friendships and enmities – experiences that will shape and scar the soul for generations. But what do I know of this?

I don't know. I believe.

I believe history was unfolding there where the shelling started while I began tapping the keyboard here, overlooking a garden almost ready to burst from bud to blossom as spring arrived. I believed the reports of news reporters and camera crews, television and radio stations and the clips on YouTube and Facebook. I believe in the sense that I am convinced the situation being transmitted and recorded was occurring. It was not a Hollywood production set somewhere in the Sierra Nevada with an epic cast of hirelings. It took place. But what I don't know is how to evaluate what happened. Who was/is right and who was/is wrong? Who's to say, and on what basis, and with what authority? Whose interests were being served in the presentation of the situation and in the action (either by Gaddafi's forces or the UN forces) that proceeded? Who desired what – and why – in these events? And where does religion figure (the Muslim Middle East and the Christian West with its Jewish allies); and politics (the spread of democracy and the rule of dictatorship) and economics (the oilfields, the lakes of black gold)? Believing gives way to a hazy realm of half-hatched opinion, snuffling surmise, and molten images that will not bond.

I use only an example to hand. Having come to finish this book, the world is elsewhere and Libya facing a different set of questions. We are all facing a different set of questions. That is not the point. The point is that the investigation into believing that I have conducted is not some abstract, anthropological, physiological or philosophical analysis. Of course in places it is abstract, anthropological, physiological and philosophical. But the point of the investigation is the human condition itself, human experience itself: the lives we all lead. The aim of the investigation is to change the way we see believing and, therefore – for those with or without religious convictions – how we might appreciate faith. In the phantasmagorias of our virtual realities, the task, it seems to me, is vital (as in life-giving). For we are increasingly living on placebos, and there's no going back.

Plato's cave has never seemed so vast.

We began this exploration with a story of what many thought was unbelievable, the encounter of two College staff at Peterhouse with a 'ghost'. We will never resolve that mystery in a way all parties would accept. But I can't resist ending on a similar story. This also took place in late November, though not in the same year, and it too began in Cambridge. A visiting lecturer from Moscow, a friend, was staying for the weekend. I'll call her Natasha, after one of my favourite heroines of Russian literature. Natasha was in her early fifties, and if in certain lights she looked much older, that was because life had not been easy for her. She was an extremely able academic, teaching English literature (which was very badly paid). Her husband, a long-term alcoholic, was no longer on the scene. She struggled to bring up their daughter and educate her well. At the time Natasha was putting her daughter through medical school. And the only way to pay for that was to give private English lessons – a lot of them – to Russia's expanding middle class. She was bone-tired whenever I met her, though perennially cheerful and optimistic. She was a devout Orthodox Christian. In the not-too-distant past she had spent some time in hospital having a serious operation, the details of which I now forget. And on the Saturday of her stay she asked if we could visit Ely Cathedral.

It was a gloomy late afternoon in autumn. No rain, but iron-grey clouds so thick they seemed to isolate the East Anglian fens from everywhere else. We drove the fifteen or so miles, and dusk was falling prematurely. Choral evensong would be over and the Cathedral closing. But I carried my trump card – a clerical ID that would get us entrance for twenty minutes or so at the very end of the day.

When we gained our entrance it was clear the vergers were shutting up shop. The lights were dim, though the candles were still lit. A fenland dark was pressing up close to the great Gothic windows. We walked around the cavernous space, the only visitors there. A handful of people busied themselves closing the Cathedral shop and entrance to the tower. We came to sit quietly beneath Ely's famous lantern tower, a complex wooden octagon high above the chancel, inset with the paintings of angels. Natasha sat quietly at my side for a long time, gazing up through the lantern, and then she lowered her head, turned to me and said, very simply, 'They don't look like that. Angels,' she explained, as I stared at her. 'They don't look like that.'

I said nothing. What could be said? Later, driving back to Cambridge down the foggy A10, she added, 'They were standing in the operating theatre. I saw them before they anaesthetised me.' And neither of us said anything further.

BIBLIOGRAPHY

INTRODUCTION

Bourdieu, Pierre, *The Field of Cultural Production: Essays on Art and Literature*, trans. and ed. Randal Johnston (Cambridge: Polity Press, 1993).

Brown, Wendy, 'The Sacred, the Secular, and the Profane: Charles Taylor and Karl Marx', in Michael Warner, Jonathan Vanantwerpen and Craig Calhoun (eds), *Varieties of Secularism in a Secular Age* (Cambridge, Massachusetts: Harvard University Press, 2010), pp. 83–104.

de Certeau, Michel, *The Possession at Loudun*, trans. Michael B. Smith (Chicago: University of Chicago Press, 2000).

Geertz, Clifford, *The Interpretation of Cultures* (New York: Basic Books, 1973).

Goleman, Daniel, *Emotional Intelligence: Why It Can Matter More than IQ* (New York: Bantam Books, 1996).

Kant, Immanuel, *The Critique of Pure Reason*, trans. J. M. D. Meiklejohn (London: Dent & Sons, 1934).

Kihlstrom, John F., 'The cognitive unconscious', *Science*, vol. 237, pp. 1445–52.

Oppenheimer, Stephen, *Out of Eden: The Peopling of the World* (London: Constable & Robinson, 2003).

Poovey, Mary, *A History of the Modern Fact: Problems of Knowledge in the Sciences of Wealth and Society* (Chicago: University of Chicago Press, 1998).

Ricoeur, Paul, *The Conflict of Interpretations: Essays in Hermeneutics*, trans. Kathleen McLaughlin et al. (London: Continuum, 2004).

Wolpert, Lewis, *Six Impossible Things Before Breakfast: The Evolutionary Origins of Belief* (London: Faber and Faber, 2006).

CHAPTER I

Corballis, Michael, *The Lopsided Ape: Evolution of the Generative Mind* (Oxford: Oxford University Press, 1991).

Deacon, Terrence W., *The Symbolic Species: The Co-evolution of Language and the Brain* (New York: W. W. Norton, 1997).

Donald, Merlin, *Origins of the Modern Mind: Three Stages in the Evolution of Culture and Cognition* (Cambridge, Massachusetts: Harvard University Press, 1991).

Dunbar, Robin, *Grooming, Gossip and the Evolution of Language* (London: Faber and Faber, 1996).

Gould, Stephen Jay, *The Mismeasure of Man* (New York: W. W. Norton, 1981).

Huard, Roger L., *Plato's Political Philosophy: The Cave* (New York: Algora Publishing, 2007).

Irigaray, Luce, *Speculum of the Other Woman*, trans. Gillian C. Gill (Ithaca, NY: Cornell University Press, 1985).

Lakoff, George and Johnson, Mark, *Philosophy in the Flesh: The Embodied Mind and its Challenge to Western Thought* (New York: Basic Books, 1999).

Plato, *The Republic*, trans. Desmond Lee (Harmondsworth: Penguin Books, 1974).

Tallis, Raymond, *Michelangelo's Finger: An Exploration of Everyday Transcendence* (London: Atlantic Books, 2010).

—— *Aping Mankind: Neuromania, Darwinitis and the Misrepresentation of Humanity* (Durham: Acumen Publishing, 2011).

CHAPTER II

Finlayson, Clive, *The Humans Who Went Extinct: Why Neanderthals Died Out and We Survived* (Oxford: Oxford University Press, 2009).

Hegel, G. W. F., *Phenomenology of Spirit*, trans. A. V. Miller (Oxford: Oxford University Press, 1977).

Heidegger, Martin, 'Building, Dwelling, Thinking' and '...Poetically Man Dwells...', in *Poetry, Language, Thought*, trans. Albert Hofstadter (New York: Harper & Row, 1975).

Lieberman, Philip, *The Biology and Evolution of Language* (Cambridge, Massachusetts: Harvard University Press, 1984).

Lovejoy, C. Owen, 'Hominid origins: the role of bipedalism', abstract of a paper to be presented at the 49th annual meeting of the American Association of Physical Anthropologists, *American Journal of Physical Anthropology* 52:2 (1980), p. 250.

Ploog, Detlev, 'Neurobiology of primate audio-vocal behavior', *Brain Research Reviews* 3 (1981), pp. 35–61.

Povinelli, Daniel J., *Folk Physics for Apes: The Chimpanzee's Theory of How the World Works* (Oxford: Oxford University Press, 2000).

—— *World Without Weight: Perspectives on an Alien Mind* (Oxford: Oxford University Press, 2012).

Premark, David, *Gavagai!: Or the Future History of the Animal Language Controversy* (Cambridge, Massachusetts: MIT Press, 1987).

Rappaport, Roy A., *Ritual and Religion in the Making of Humanity* (Cambridge: Cambridge University Press, 1999).

Solecki, Ralph, 'The implications of the Shanidar Cave Neanderthal flower burial', paper presented at the 24 May 1976 meeting of the Section of Anthropology, *Annals of the New York Academy of Sciences*.

Sutton, D. and Jurgens, U., 'The neural control of vocalization', in H. D. Steklis and J. Erwin (eds), *Comparative Primatology and Biology*, vol. 4 (New York: A. R. Liss, 1988), pp. 625–47.

Tomasello, Michael, *The Cultural Origins of Human Cognition* (Cambridge, Massachusetts: Harvard University Press, 1999).

Vandermeersch, Bernard, 'The excavation of Qafzeh: Its contribution to the knowledge of Mousterian in the Levant', *Bulletin du Centre de recherche français à Jérusalem*, 10:2 (2002), pp. 65–70.

Walker, Michael, 'Excavations at Cueva Negra del Estrecho del Rio Quipar and Sima de las Palomas del Cabezo Gordo', in S. Milliken and J. Cook (eds), *A Very Remote Period Indeed: Papers on the Palaeolithic presented to Derek Roe* (Oxford: Oxbow Books, 2001).

Wright, Terence C., 'Edith Stein: prayer and interiority', in Bruce Ellis Benson and Norman Wirzba (eds), *The Phenomenology of Prayer* (New York: Fordham University Press, 2005).

CHAPTER III

Dennett, Daniel C., *Consciousness Explained* (Harmondsworth: Penguin Books, 1993).

Durkheim, Émile, *The Elementary Forms of Religious Life*, ed. Mark S. Cladis, trans. Carol Cosman (Oxford: Oxford University Press, 2001).

Freud, Sigmund, 'The Uncanny', trans. James Strachey, in *The Penguin Library of Freud*, vol. 14 (Harmondsworth: Penguin Books, 1985).

—— *Totem and Taboo*, trans. James Strachey (London: Routledge & Kegan Paul, 1950).

Jentsch, Ernst, 'Zur Psychologie des Unheimlichen', *Psychiatrisch-Neurologische Wochenschrift* 8:22 & 8:23 (1906).

Laughlin, Charles D., McManus, John, and d'Aquili, Eugene G., *Brain, Symbol and Experience: Towards a Neurophenomenology of Human Consciousness* (New York: Columbia University Press, 1992).

Lewis-Williams, David, *The Mind in The Cave: Consciousness and the Origins of Art* (London: Thames & Hudson, 2002).

—— *Conceiving God: The Cognitive Origin and Evolution of Religion* (London: Thames & Hudson, 2010).

—— and Pearce, David, *Inside the Neolithic Mind: Consciousness, Cosmos and the Realm of the Gods* (London: Thames & Hudson, 2005).

McGilchrist, Iain, *The Master and His Emissary: The Divided Brain and the Making of the Western World* (New Haven: Yale University Press, 2009).

Martindale, Colin, *Cognition and Consciousness* (Homewood, Illinois: Dorsey Press, 1981).

Mithen, Steven, *The Prehistory of the Mind: A Search for the Origins of Art, Religion and Science* (London: Thames & Hudson, 1996).

Renfrew, Colin, *Prehistory: The Making of the Human Mind* (London: Weidenfeld & Nicolson, 2007).

CHAPTER IV

Carruthers, Peter, 'HOP over FOR, HOT theory', in Rocco J. Gennaro (ed.), *Higher-Order Theories of Consciousness: An Anthology* (Amsterdam: John Benjamins, 2004).

Churchland, Patricia, *Neurophilosophy: Toward a Unified Science of the Mind–Brain* (Cambridge, Massachusetts: MIT Press, 1986).

Churchland, Paul, *The Engine of Reason, the Seat of the Soul: A Philosophical Journey into the Brain* (Cambridge, Massachusetts: MIT Press, 1995).

Damasio, Antonio, *The Feeling of What Happens: Body, Emotion and the Making of Consciousness* (London: Vintage Books, 2000).

—— *Self Comes to Mind: Constructing the Conscious Brain* (London: Vintage Books, 2012).

Deacon, Terrence, *Incomplete Nature: How Mind Emerged from Matter* (New York: W. W. Norton & Company, 2012).

Humphrey, Nicholas, *A History of the Mind: Evolution and the Birth of Consciousness* (New York: Simon & Schuster, 1992).

Lycan, William G., 'The superiority of HOP to HOT', in Rocco J. Gennaro (ed.), *Higher-order Theories of Consciousness: An Anthology* (Amsterdam: John Benjamins, 2004).

Macdonald, Graham and Papineau, David (eds), *Teleosemantics: New Philosophical Essays* (Oxford: Oxford University Press, 2006).

Millikan, Ruth, *Language, Thought, and Other Biological Categories: New Foundations for Realism* (Cambridge, Massachusetts: MIT Press, 1984).

Minsky, Marvin, *The Society of Mind* (New York: Simon & Schuster, 1986).

Nagel, Thomas, *Mind and Cosmos: Why the Materialist Neo-Darwinian Conception of Nature is Almost Certainly False* (Oxford: Oxford University Press, 2012).

Panksepp, Jaak, 'Toward a general psychobiological theory of emotions', *Behavioral and Brain Sciences* 5 (1982), pp. 407–67.

Penrose, Roger, *Shadows on the Mind: A Search for the Missing Science of Consciousness* (London: Vintage Books, 1995).

Rizzolatti, Giacomo and Craighero, Laila, 'The mirror-neuron system', *Annual Review of Neuroscience* 27 (2004), pp. 169–92.

Rosenthal, David M., 'Varieties of higher-order theory', in Rocco J. Gennaro (ed.), *Higher-Order Theories of Consciousness: An Anthology* (Amsterdam: John Benjamins, 2004).

—— *Consciousness and Mind* (Oxford: Oxford University Press, 2005).

Searle, John, 'Minds, brains, and programs', *Behavioral and Brain Sciences* 3:3 (1980), pp. 417–57.

Wittgenstein, Ludwig, *Philosophical Investigations*, trans. G. E. M. Anscombe (Oxford: Blackwell, 1953).

CHAPTER V

Bauerschmidt, Frederick, *Thomas Aquinas: Faith, Reason, and Following Christ* (Oxford: Oxford University Press, 2013).

Brown, Callum G., *The Death of Christian Britain: Understanding Secularisation 1800–2000* (London: Routledge, 2001).

de Certeau, Michel, 'White Ecstasy', in Graham Ward (ed.), *The Postmodern God: A Theological Reader* (Oxford: Blackwell, 1997), pp. 155–8.

Dear, Peter, *Revolutionizing the Sciences: European Knowledge and Its Ambitions, 1500–1700* (Basingstoke: Palgrave Macmillan, 2008).

Foucault, Michel, *The Birth of the Clinic: An Archaeology of Medical Perception*, trans. A. M. Sheridan (London: Routledge, 1989).

Kirk, Robert, *Raw Feeling: A Philosophical Account of the Essence of Consciousness* (Oxford: Oxford University Press, 1994).

Locke, John, *An Essay Concerning Human Understanding* (London: Fontana/Collins, 1960).

Midgley, Mary, *The Myths We Live By* (London: Routledge, 2004).

Plantinga, Alvin, *Where the Conflict Really Lies: Science, Religion, and Naturalism* (New York: Oxford University Press, 2011).

Sidney, Sir Philip, *An Apology for Poetry (or The Defence of Poesy)*, ed. R. W. Maslen (Manchester: Manchester University Press, 2002).

Sorel, Georges, *Reflections on Violence*, ed. Jeremy Jennings (Cambridge: Cambridge University Press, 1999).

Strawson, Galen et al., *Consciousness and Its Place in Nature: Does Physicalism Entail Panpsychism?* (Exeter: Imprint Academic, 2006).

Taylor, Charles, *Sources of the Self: The Making of the Modern Identity* (Cambridge: Cambridge University Press, 1989).

—— *A Secular Age* (Cambridge, Massachusetts: Belknap Press, 2007).

Ward, Graham, *The Politics of Discipleship: Becoming Postmaterial Citizens* (London: SCM Press, 2010).

—— and Hoelzl, Michael, *The New Visibility of Religion: Studies in Religion and Cultural Hermeneutics* (London: Continuum, 2008).

White, Roger, 'Does origins of life research rest on a mistake?' *Noûs* 41:3 (2003), pp. 453–77.

CHAPTER VI

Agamben, Giorgio, 'Poiesis and Praxis', in *The Man Without Content*, trans. Georgia Albert (Stanford: Stanford University Press, 1999), pp. 63–93.

Aristotle, *Poetics*, trans. Malcolm Heath (Harmondsworth: Penguin Books, 1996).

—— *De Anima*, trans. Hugh Lawson-Tancred (Harmondsworth: Penguin Books, 1987).

Bloch, Ernst, *The Principle of Hope*: *Volume One*, trans. Neville Plaice et al. (Oxford: Blackwell, 1986).

Browning, Robert, 'The Pied Piper of Hamelin', in Sir Humphrey Milford (ed.), *Poems of Robert Browning* (Oxford: Oxford University Press, 1952).

Coleridge, Samuel Taylor, *Biographia Literaria* (London: Dent & Sons, 1971).

—— (with Wordsworth, William) *Lyrical Ballads*, ed. Fiona Stafford (Oxford: Oxford University Press, 2013).

Derrida, Jacques, *Specters of Marx: The State of the Debt, the Work of Mourning, and the New International*, trans. Peggy Kamuf (London: Routledge, 1994).

Farias, Miguel, 'The psychology of atheism', in S. Bullivant and M. Ruse (eds), *The Oxford Handbook of Atheism* (Oxford: Oxford University Press, 2013), pp. 468–82.

Joyce, James, *Dubliners* (Harmondsworth: Penguin Books, 1992).

Leavis, F. R., *The Great Tradition: George Eliot, Henry James, Joseph Conrad* (Harmondsworth: Penguin Books, 1972).

de Man, Paul, *Allegories of Reading: Figural Language in Rousseau, Nietzsche, Rilke, and Proust* (New Haven: Yale University Press, 1979).

Marx, Karl, *Das Kapital* (Berlin: Dietz, 1947).

Proust, Marcel, *Remembrance of Things Past: Swann's Way*, trans. Terence Kilmartin (Harmondsworth: Penguin Books, 1983); *Du côté de chez Swann* (Paris: Gallimard, 1987).

Ricoeur, Paul, 'Imagination in discourse and action', in *From Text to Action*, trans. Kathleen Blamey and John B. Thompson (Evanston, Illinois: Northwestern University Press, 1991).

Sartre, Jean-Paul, *The Imaginary: A Phenomenological Psychology of the Imagination*, trans. Jonathan Webber (London: Routledge, 2004).

Tolkien, J. R. R., *Lord of the Rings* (London: HarperCollins, 1993).

CHAPTER VII

Adorno, Theodor, *The Culture Industry: Selected Essays on Mass Culture*, ed. J. M. Bernstein (London: Routledge, 1991).

Althusser, Louis, 'Ideology and ideological state apparatuses', in *Lenin and Philosophy and other essays*, trans. Ben Brewster (New York: Monthly Review Press, 2001), pp. 85–126.

Anderson, Benedict, *Imagined Communities: Reflections on the Origin and Spread of Nationalism* (London: Verso, 1983).

Barthes, Roland, *Mythologies*, trans. Annette Lavers (London: Vintage Books, 2000).

Bell, Daniel, 'Return of the sacred? The argument on the future of religion', *British Journal of Sociology* 28:4 (1977), pp. 419–51.

Berger, Peter (ed.), *The Desecularization of the World: Resurgent Religion and World Politics* (Grand Rapids, Michigan: W. B. Eerdmans, 1999).

Bruce, Steve, *Religion in the Modern World: from Cathedrals to Cults* (Oxford: Oxford University Press, 1996).

—— *God is Dead: Secularization in the West* (Oxford: Blackwell, 2002).

Cassirer, Ernst, *The Myth of the State* (New Haven: Yale University Press, 1946).

Castoriadis, Cornelius, *The Imaginary Institution of Society*, trans. Kathleen Blamey (Cambridge: Polity Press, 1987).

Davie, Grace, *Religion in Britain since 1945: Believing without Belonging* (Oxford: Blackwell, 1994).

—— *The Sociology of Religion: A Critical Agenda* (London: Sage, 2007).

Habermas, Jürgen and Ratzinger, Joseph, *The Dialectics of Secularization: On Reason and Religion* (San Francisco: Ignatius Press, 2007).

—— et al., *Awareness of what is Missing: Faith and Reason in a Post-Secular Age* (Cambridge: Polity Press, 2010).

Hugo, Victor, *Les Misérables*, trans. Norman Denny (Harmondsworth: Penguin Books, 1982).

Jansen, Yolande, *Secularism, Assimilation and the Crisis of Multiculturalism: French Modernist Legacies* (Amsterdam: Amsterdam University Press, 2013).

Liogier, Raphaël, '*Laïcité* on the edge in France: between the theory of Church–State separation and the praxis of State–Church confusion', *Macquarie Law Journal* 9 (2009), pp. 25–45.

McLeod, Hugh, *The Religious Crisis of the 1960s* (Oxford: Oxford University Press, 2007).

Putnam, Robert, *Bowling Alone: The Collapse and Revival of American Community* (New York: Simon & Schuster, 2001).

Sorel, Georges, *Reflections on Violence*, ed. Jeremy Jennings (Cambridge: Cambridge University Press, 1999).

Taylor, Charles, *Modern Social Imaginaries* (Durham, North Carolina: Duke University Press, 2004).

Ward, Graham, *Cultural Transformation and Religious Practice* (Cambridge: Cambridge University Press, 2004).

CHAPTER VIII

Cavell, Stanley, *The Claim of Reason: Wittgenstein, Skepticism, Morality, and Tragedy* (Oxford: Oxford University Press, 1979).

Chrétien, Jean-Louis, *Le regard de l'amour* (Paris, Desclée de Brouwer, 2000).

Gallup, Gordon G., 'Self-awareness and the emergence of mind in primates', *American Journal of Primatology* 2:3 (1982), pp. 237–48.

Greene, Graham, *The Confidential Agent* (Harmondsworth: Penguin Books, 1963).

—— *Brighton Rock* (London: Vintage Books, 2004).

—— *The End of the Affair* (London: Vintage Books, 2004).

—— *The Honorary Consul* (London: Vintage Books, 2004).

—— *The Power and the Glory* (London: Vintage Books, 2004).

—— *Stamboul Train* (London: Vintage Books, 2004).

Gregory of Nyssa, 'On "Not Three Gods"' in William Moore and Henry Austin Wilson (trans. and eds), *Select Writings and Letters of Gregory, Bishop of Nyssa*, vol. 5, in Henry Wace and Philip Schaff (eds), *A Select Library of the Christian Church: Nicene and Post-Nicene Fathers* (Oxford: Parker and Company, 1893).

Hart, David Bentley, *The Beauty of the Infinite: The Aesthetics of Christian Truth* (Grand Rapids, Michigan: William B. Eerdmans, 2003).

Husserl, Edmund, *Ideas: General Introduction to Pure Phenomenology*, trans. W. R. Boyce Gibson (London: Routledge, 2002).

Kermode, Frank, *The Sense of an Ending: Studies in the Theory of Fiction* (Oxford: Oxford University Press, 1966).

Merleau-Ponty, Maurice, *The Visible and the Invisible*, trans. Alphonso Lingis (Evanston, Illinois: Northwestern University Press, 1968).

Steiner, George, *Real Presences* (London: Faber and Faber, 1989).

Tallis, Raymond, *In Defence of Wonder, and Other Philosophical Reflections* (Durham: Acumen, 2012).

Tillich, Paul, *Ultimate Concern: Tillich in Dialogue* (London: SCM Press, 1965).

INDEX